Almost

Almost Perfect Pets

A Proactive Guide to
Selection, Health Care
and Pet Parenting

LOWELL ACKERMAN *and*
REBECCA ACKERMAN

McFarland & Company, Inc., Publishers
Jefferson, North Carolina

ISBN (print) 978-1-4766-8607-3
ISBN (ebook) 978-1-4766-4508-7

LIBRARY OF CONGRESS AND BRITISH LIBRARY
CATALOGUING DATA ARE AVAILABLE

Library of Congress Control Number 2021056752

Front cover image © 2022 Rocket400 Studio/
Igor Zakowski/ Studio_G/Shutterstock

Printed in the United States of America

McFarland & Company, Inc., Publishers
Box 611, Jefferson, North Carolina 28640
www.mcfarlandpub.com

Authors' Note

The characters, veterinary hospitals, and events portrayed in this book are fictitious. Any similarity to real persons, living or dead, is coincidental and not intended by the authors. The source notes for the photographs are, however, to real people, whom we thank.

The contents of this work are intended to further understanding and discussion only and are not intended and should not be relied upon as recommending or promoting prevention, diagnosis, or treatment for any particular pet or condition. The reader is urged to review their particular situation with their pet's veterinarian. While the publisher and authors have used their best efforts in preparing this book, they make no representations or warranties with respect to the accuracy or completeness of the contents and specifically disclaim all warranties relative to products and services discussed in this work. The fact that an organization, website, or product is referred to in this work is meant only as a potential source of further information and does not mean that the publisher and authors endorse the information or services the organization, website, or product may provide or recommendations it may make.

The advice and strategies contained herein may not be suitable for your particular situation. You should consult with your veterinarian regarding your pet's specific needs. Further, readers should be aware that websites listed in this work may have changed or disappeared between when the work was written and when it is read. Neither the publisher nor authors shall be liable for any loss or damages, including but not limited to special, incidental, consequential or other damages.

On a personal note, we would like to dedicate this book to all the incredible pets who add so much to the human lives they touch every day. On both a personal and a professional note, we would like to recognize the efforts of Susan Ackerman for her editing and for her commitment to the concept of pet parenting.

Table of Contents

Preface

Modern pet owners are savvy and informed. They know that each of their pets is a unique and precious member of their family. They understand that their dogs and their cats are exceptional in their own right and not interchangeable with other dogs and cats. Today's pet owners want to have information that allows them to plan and prepare to protect the health and well-being of their four-legged family member across its lifespan. They demand that we move beyond a cookie-cutter approach to pet care to an individualized model of care that recognizes the uniqueness of their beloved pet.

As social beings, most people approach pet ownership with a focus on a new, loving relationship. They are right! Sharing your home with a pet is a precious, life-changing experience. The best way to protect that loving relationship is through a blend of being informed, planning, and advocating for the individualized care that your pet deserves. Bringing a pet into your home is a joy, but it also presents possible concerns—expenses, health care issues, bad behaviors, and a host of questions and controversies. The modern pet owner faces choices like never before—on pet selection, on choosing a diet, on vaccine schedules, on genetic testing, and on personalizing health care. The world of pet care has changed dramatically from what it once was, with a number of opportunities as well as challenges. Prevention, early detection, and personalized health care are key components of such cutting-edge pet care.

When someone buys a new car, it comes with a maintenance schedule that captures the best evidence available about how to keep that particular vehicle running smoothly. Pets need the same approach. Pet owners readily understand that the care of a Great Dane is inherently different from that of a Labrador Retriever or a Miniature Poodle (or a Siamese or a Himalayan), and yet most of the pet care information available out there tends to be generalized to the species (dog vs. cat) level rather than being pet-specific and relevant for individual pets. Whether it's planning for a pet's "healthspan" or trying to appreciate "risk factors," the public is hungry for dependable information that might not other-wise be readily available. Today, we have the ability to do so much more!

Personalizing pet care acknowledges what pet owners already know—that their pet is unique, that the relationship they have with their pet is inimitable and that they would like more than just cookie-cutter approaches to keeping their pet happy and healthy for the long term. They just need a guide to help them determine the best approach (and *Almost Perfect Pets* is that guide!).

1

Path to an *Almost* Perfect Pet

The concept of *almost* perfect is an attitude ... a philosophy ... a mantra. It is a rewarding but not necessarily simple path, a way that ensures your furry friend has a long life of companionship and happiness by your side. We achieve this vaunted status with our pets when we've done what we can reasonably do to ensure that they have the best chance of living a long, happy and healthy life while sharing a loving, mutually beneficial relationship with us. It may sound like wishful thinking, but it is entirely possible to achieve *almost* perfect pet status. After all, unlike our children, pets don't go through the terrible twos, they don't hate us as teens, and we don't have to worry about breaking the bank to send them to college.

"*Almost* perfect" does not imply that your beloved pet will never have issues, but if you plan accordingly, these concerns won't feel like momentous problems. There's a difference, and it isn't just semantics. Truly, most of the concerns that people experience with their pets are predictable and manageable. Not anticipating that they could happen is what often makes these things problematic. Fortunately, this book can help!

People get pets for a lot of different reasons, but if the goal is to enjoy life with a furry companion—a furever friend, if you will—it's possible to achieve this and more by following the basic tenets of this book. It doesn't mean that you will never have a veterinary bill or an "accident" on the carpet or a discussion about what to do when you travel, but hopefully you will appreciate the journey you have embarked on with your pet and understand that in every relationship there needs to be accommodations.

When it comes to pet care, achieving *almost* perfect status is a reflection of having reasonable expectations and then appropriately managing those expectations. If you work long hours away from home and you want to adopt a puppy, it is unreasonable to expect a positive outcome in leaving that puppy alone in your home all day. If you want to avoid the time and expense of grooming a pet, it is better to adopt a wash-and-wear breed than to resent the pet (with the luxurious coat that you once admired) for an expenditure that can be entirely foreseen. If you don't like spending money on veterinary care to treat diseases, be committed to doing what is necessary to keep your pet healthy in the first place and have a strategy for dealing with the inevitable costs of health care that are bound to arise.

Why Own a Pet in the First Place?

There are lots of reasons why people want to share their life with a pet, but if you are reading this book, you are likely looking for a companion with which to share your life and maintain a positive lifelong relationship. That's a good thing, because owning a pet is not only rewarding in terms of companionship, but it is likely good for your health as well.

Pets provide unconditional love—and who doesn't want that?—but they provide so much more. If you want to know just part of the story of these benefits, do an online search for the term "human-animal bond," the mutually beneficial relationship that confers health and well-being on both parties. The fact is that people are happier and healthier when they allow pets into their lives ... under the appropriate circumstances. Pets can help you lower your blood pressure, reduce anxiety, and enhance feelings of well-being. Unfortunately, when pets are not cared for appropriately or are part of an unhealthy relationship, they can exacerbate problems and cause extra stress as well.

So the first aspect of raising an *almost* perfect pet is to be introspective and question why you want a pet in the first place. If you are hoping that a pet will make you a more responsible human being, that only works if you are committed to being responsible. It's also inappropriate to buy a pet for someone else as a gift unless that person is truly committed to responsible pet ownership and is really ready to take on that responsibility. Unfortunately, animal shelters are filled with pets whose owners decided afterwards that perhaps a pet was not right for them after all. If your lifestyle really isn't conducive to pet ownership, forego trying it out with a live pet and stay pet-less for the time being—not necessarily forever but for now. If you crave exposure to pets but living with one full time isn't the right decision at the moment, there are lots of options, including caring for pets on a temporary basis, traveling the world and staying in homes of other traveling people who need in-home pet care (yes, that exists!) and even renting, fostering, or borrowing pets (yes, that also exists). There are lots of ways to spend time with pets without making a full-time commitment. However, once you do make that commitment, be prepared to plan for a lifetime.

The concept of a lifelong commitment is central to the notion of raising an *almost* perfect pet. If you are not committed from the start, then every time you experience something challenging with your pet, it will be perceived as a problem and you'll be contemplating exit strategies. Once you've committed for the long haul, your perspective changes dramatically. Those challenges will still exist, but with commitment comes the acceptance that managing them is your responsibility and you need to find solutions. You might be relieved (or troubled) to know that new parents of babies go through the same transition. When sleep deprivation sets in or you have the sudden realization that children have a lot of needs, there might be a fleeting thought that perhaps this wasn't a great idea, and you question the reliability of all your friends who told you the experience would be rewarding. However, once you reconcile yourself to the fact that the child is yours forever and requires your lifelong commitment and love, it is easier to assume responsibility and start looking for strategies for success rather than trying to pass on that responsibility to someone else. The same is true with pets.

Do yourself and a potential pet a favor and seriously question your motives for pet ownership. Without a doubt, pets are wonderful and add so much to our lives, but that doesn't mean that everyone needs to own one. Even if you are a lifelong animal lover and enthusiast, sometimes it just isn't the right time in your life for you to have your own pet. Bide your time, look for other opportunities to interact with pets, and consider when the time will be right before you make that big decision.

The Concept of Pet Ownership

In most countries and in most communities, pets are considered possessions. In general, anyone can adopt a pet regardless of their circumstances, and they can transfer ownership at will. In some locales, there is a push to change laws to make people "guardians" rather than "owners" of pets as part of recognizing the unique qualities of the human-animal relationship as well as the legal rights of animals. It is important to realize that this is essentially a legal argument that doesn't really change the underlying reality that people who willingly commit to raising an *almost* perfect pet are most likely to achieve that goal. It's unlikely that any change in legal status will do anything to change that reality even though there is a lot of sensitivity around the concept of "owning" any living, sentient being. It is important to recognize the inherent value of animals, and it is good to explore both sides of the legal status issue, but it remains a complex subject.

The concept of guardianship is an interesting one, and many pet owners may prefer to consider their pet as a "ward" rather than a possession, but you would need to be prepared to deal with the legal ramifications of such a designation. Guardians have a fiduciary responsibility (a duty to prudently take care of money and other assets) for the benefit of another—in this case, the pet. In fact, if the pet becomes a ward, then the interests of the ward prevail over the interests of the guardian. This is where the charming theoretical appeals of a guardian-ward relationship run into the legal consequences associated with changing the status and rights of pets. This could affect the rights of pets to be entitled to medical care that may be beyond the financial means of the guardian; the questionable ability of guardians to make choices regarding euthanasia, neutering and other procedures; the prospect that animals would have legal rights, which might mean that someone could bring civil lawsuits filed by third parties on behalf of the pet; that legal procedures would be needed to transfer guardianship from one person to another;

Millie (courtesy Brandon Magnuson).

and many other legal ramifications that are too numerous to enumerate. The concept of guardianship is enticing, but it dramatically changes the legal status of animals in good ways and in ways that may be difficult to ponder. That doesn't mean that pets should not be protected by law, but by giving them the same rights as people, we would need to ensure they have the same legal protections as our children and elderly, which could be onerous or even impossible for some pet owners.

Another term that is important in this regard is "pet parent." This is another label, albeit a nonlegal one, to indicate that the relationship is considered more than just ownership. One might infer that pet parents consider their pet to be part of the family and that is a very useful perspective to maintain. However, it is still somewhat vague since pet parenthood means different things to different people, and in some surveys, the vast majority of pet owners already consider their pets to be family members. Of course, it is great to consider a pet as part of the family, but it is important to realize that calling oneself a pet parent does not guarantee that caregivers provide the same level of care to their pets that they do to other family members. Again, it is the commitment to providing a lifetime of care and companionship that is at the heart of any real relationship with our pets, and labels don't change that. When we make reference to pet parenting throughout the book, we are embracing a generalization that pets will become lifelong valued members of a family unit (of any size and configuration) but appreciate that the relationship may be somewhat different in each situation. Because pet parenthood does not come with any legal entanglements, it can mean different things to different people and be interpreted on an individual basis.

Pet parenting as a concept is widely embraced by the public, even though some may have difficulty reconciling themselves as being a mother or father figure to furry offspring. The adoption procedure is very different from the one involved with adding a child to your life. You typically don't have nine months to prepare as you would with a pregnancy, and there may not be the same fuss and fanfare from friends and family, but in the end, there is still a relatively helpless dependent who will be entirely reliant on you for the rest of its life. There is a contingent of friends and coworkers who will understand when you have obligations related to your pet, but there will also be a sizable population of those who cannot understand why your having a pet should inconvenience them in any way.

Even though the numbers change slightly from year to year, we remain a population of pet lovers, and often over half of households own a pet, some more than one. Of course, the family situation has dramatically changed along with the perception of pets over the last several decades. There was a time when many families had a stay-at-home adult, often the "mom," and that meant that there was often a responsible adult at home to care for and provide a social outlet for pets when other family members were at school or work. However, that's not generally true anymore. Although the standard family unit of one husband, one wife, and two-plus children has evolved considerably, modern families of all configurations remain pet-friendly. In fact, total pet numbers and numbers of households owning pets have remained fairly steady. Now, though, it is much more common for all adults in all family configurations to be off at work while any children are at school, making it much more likely that nobody will be home during the day to supervise and interact with a pet. This makes it even more important that loving pet parents follow appropriate guidelines to promote a happy and healthy homelife for all concerned.

Today's pet owner is an informed consumer and, more than at any time in the past, has the ability to make decisions about their pets and the care they receive. The Internet provides ready access to virtually limitless amounts of non-curated information (some accurate, some not) as well as product sales. To some, this might seem empowering that there is so much free information available online, but this information overload can actually complicate the process of collecting relevant information because it is often difficult to understand what might be pertinent and be directly applicable for your particular pet. As one might imagine, if there is just a need for generic information (for example, "What causes ringworm?"), the Internet has a lot of information, and most of it will be relevant. However, when trying to determine what a diagnosis is likely to be, or when prescription medication is needed to treat something, that really needs to be customized to the individual pet, so Internet searches tend to be much less satisfying.

Planning for Success

To raise an *almost* perfect pet, it is best to start with a plan. We do this in everyday life, whether it is caring for our children, maintaining a vehicle, or even meeting our daily requirements at work. All tasks are best tackled when you overcome the treacherous clutches of procrastination and focus on what needs to be done. For instance, when you purchase a new vehicle, it typically comes with a "maintenance schedule," a guide of all the service that should be performed to keep the vehicle running at its best and the interval at which those tasks should be accomplished. It doesn't mean that there won't be particular circumstances that will alter the schedule or that things won't happen that aren't in the schedule (like a flat tire or an accident). It's just a preventive maintenance schedule to inform you of what interventions will help you get the best performance from your vehicle with anticipated use. Consider it a checklist of sorts.

Pets also benefit from a preventive maintenance schedule. If you've owned a pet before, you are probably aware that there are many aspects of care that are recommended according to a schedule. These scheduled care events include such things as office visits, vaccination and parasite control. While health care tends to be very protocol driven and will be covered in much more detail in its own chapter, it is important to realize that there are many aspects of pet care that are crucial and will depend largely on your involvement more than even the efforts of your veterinary team. That's because the veterinary team will typically see a healthy pet a few times a year, while your efforts will be reflected on a daily basis. When it comes to things like training and behavioral intervention, feeding an appropriate diet and weight management, and even oral care (even if you can't convince yourself to brush your pet's teeth every day), your commitment tends to have a direct and powerful impact on a pet's

Nubs in the sink (courtesy Katrina O'Gahan).

health status. Similarly in human medicine, visiting the doctor and getting periodic vaccines is important, but that must be viewed in the context of personal responsibility—for eating healthy, weight management, exercise, not smoking and moderation in alcohol consumption—which often has a powerful impact on health outcomes.

To keep pets problem free and to determine their risk factors for encountering problems, it will be important to know what those risks are. In human medicine, this is often achieved with a health risk assessment in which health care teams ask a series of questions to help them determine your risk for certain issues. They might ask if you have a family history of heart disease or cancer or diabetes. They might ask about whether you smoke or how much alcohol you consume. It isn't to be nosy; these questions are important because they help determine risk factors and whether additional screening is warranted. The same is true for pets, although it is unlikely you will be asked about their alcohol consumption or smoking habits (although we do suggest you notify your veterinarian if your pet has taken up vaping or tequila shots). Still, family history is extremely important when considering potential hereditary risks, as are their activities, potential exposure to other animals and environments, and conditions already evident, such as their conformation (body type, shape, leg and body length, facial anatomy, wrinkles, etc.).

So what? Does appreciating risk factors actually make a difference in keeping pets problem free? Absolutely! From a health care perspective there are actually three different but related approaches to keeping pets problem free, and they apply to nonmedical interventions as well. First is a focus on prevention, keeping animals healthy rather than letting them develop problems before we do something. Don't underestimate the importance of health management (wellness) versus disease management. Second is a focus on early detection, which involves screening pets and intervening before issues get out of hand, typically when there are the most options for management. Third, if problems are unavoidable, especially for potentially chronic problems (allergies, diabetes, arthritis, etc.), treat them appropriately from a quality-of-life perspective for long-term control (managing the underlying problem) rather than just treating the clinical signs (symptoms). There is often a Part B to treatment and that is to lean in to facilitated compliance—using reminders to ensure important treatment and care tasks actually get completed on time. This may seem insignificant, but compliance and adherence are major issues in pets, because they rely on owners to remember to give the medications and to do so on schedule. It is not enough to just buy something to treat your pet. Use apps or programs or whatever you need to ensure that any medications get administered according to recommendations, and do not discontinue them prematurely without checking with your veterinary team. Keeping pets problem free does take some effort, but those efforts pay dividends in terms of your pet's long-term health status.

Each Pet-Owner Relationship Is Unique

Pets are no longer just animate objects we care for—in many ways they become extensions of ourselves. While it is sometimes blamed on generational norms, most of us have a strong vision of what we stand for as individuals. We may not all be social influencers with a dedicated following on social media, but most have an appreciation of what it means to be us, from the choice of which pronouns to apply, to causes we believe in, to our views on the environment and our commitments to others and the future of the planet.

No matter which generational cohort you identify with (baby boomers, Generations X, Y, Z or Alpha), all of us have become more comfortable with technology and spend a good part of our existence online. For many, soliciting "likes" is just part of everyday life and helps validate that view of ourselves that we cherish and that we hope is recognized and appreciated by others. It's not that we necessarily view all outcomes as swiping left or swiping right, but in a busy world with lots of distractions, it can be challenging to be recognized for the individuals we are.

When we consider old models of pet ownership, especially in the period immediately following the Second World War (i.e., after 1945), the situation was quite different. Owning a pet was typically done by young families, commercially formulated pet foods were just being introduced, and pets started to migrate from the yard to living full time in the home. Owning a pet was about teaching children responsibility, and litters of puppies and kittens helped instruct about the "miracle of life." In those early days, pets were certainly valued companions, but they rarely took on the mantle of a true family member, there were limits to the extent of health care they typically received, and their role in the household continued to evolve from outdoor to indoor status.

We now live in a very different world. Regardless of generation, most people today acquire a pet for social reasons—they want to share their lives with another living being. There is no expectation that this needs to happen within a family unit. Individuals of all ages are embracing pet ownership on their own terms. Because of this, there is a very real desire that our pets should complement our existence and even become an extension of ourselves. Just as we might hope a significant other fits neatly into our lives, so we also hope that pets fulfill a similar type of role.

It should therefore be no surprise that pet owners tend to celebrate their successful pet relationships, especially on the Internet. We post pictures of our pets in all their spectacular cuteness, and as pet lovers ourselves, we enjoy and repost animal-related content that we find and want to share with others in our orbit. While some may be humbled by the fact that their pet gets more online attention than they do, and some pets may even command their own sites, content, and fan base, we nonetheless accept the praise on behalf of our furry companions.

The important thing to appreciate in this regard is that while lovable pets can enhance our individuality and be regarded as an extension of that individuality, those benefits don't happen by accident. It takes a lot of work and effort to raise a pet that is widely admired. On the other hand, a poorly behaved or mistreated pet can severely hurt our self-image, so raising an *almost* perfect pet is about so much more than just what it means for the pet itself. Do yourself and your pet a favor, and invest the time needed to ensure that the furry extension of yourself speaks volumes about your commitment to others, especially the pet you've chosen to include in your life.

Pet-Specific Care

One of the major developments in human medicine has been the replacement of cookie-cutter approaches with what has become known as personalized medicine. The same evolution has taken place in veterinary medicine, where the practice is often described as "pet-specific care." This is a concept in which recommendations are made based on the specific needs of the pet and owner rather than a generic recipe for all animals in general. This is covered in more detail in its own chapter, but it is worth introducing the concept here since, when it comes to health care, one size definitely does not fit all.

For example, it is commonly appreciated by veterinary teams that conformation extremes (exaggerated body features brought about by intentional breeding strategies), which tend to be inherited in many breeds, can predispose pets to medical concerns. So, pets bred to have squashed or flat faces (e.g., Pug, Bulldog, Persian, Himalayan, etc.) are at higher risk of breathing problems, often referred to as Brachycephalic Obstructive Airway Syndrome. These animals

Minerva (courtesy Joan Tansi).

may require special ongoing care, and sometimes corrective surgery, just to lead normal lives. Other animals may be prone to inherited diseases such as glaucoma, hip dysplasia, or polycystic kidney disease, to name just a few, and if we can identify those with risk factors, we can offer the appropriate level of screening and care to those members of the specific populations that need it while recognizing that this additional care is not needed in animals that are not at risk. It is this ability to customize care to that which is most pertinent that is the hallmark for pet-specific care and personalized medicine.

So, pet-specific care is not necessarily about finding out everything the Internet says could go wrong with a pet but to understand and appreciate what could be relevant for your particular pet and provide the right level of intervention based on your pet's unique needs. To accomplish this, veterinary teams providing such care need to appreciate the concept of "risk factors" and their appropriate management. Not all dog breeds are at high risk for glaucoma. Not all cat breeds are at high risk for polycystic kidney disease. Hyperthyroidism is more common in elderly cats, while umbilical hernias are more commonly seen in puppies. Dogs that go for walks in the woods or drink from streams have different risk factors than those that never leave home. Cats that wander outdoors and might come in contact with other animals have significantly different risk factors than those that are entirely housebound. This affects vaccine recommendations, parasite-control requirements, and possible risk of contagion to family members (zoonotic spread).

We mentioned earlier that the Internet provides a wealth of non-curated information on a variety of topics, and it is an incredible resource, but it takes more than that to put things into perspective. Even though some pet owners may want to attempt more of a do-it-yourself (DIY) approach, it can be difficult to make the right decisions without appropriate resources. For example, genetic testing has become popular in human and veterinary medicine, and many tests are available direct to the public (online or through retailers). However, for many of these test results, it is difficult to do anything meaningful without the right advice. So, if a pet has a positive genetic marker for a form of glaucoma, does that mean it has glaucoma or will develop glaucoma? It actually means that the pet has a risk factor for a specific form of hereditary glaucoma, and while this is a very useful indicator, it really is meant to inform that this risk factor should prompt the veterinary team to periodically measure the pressures within the eye to see if glaucoma does develop and determine if and when treatment should be initiated. That can lead to a problem-free way to manage the issue, but on its own, pet owners cannot manage the situation without help. Not to worry, as this is often the case in human health care as well, and it often takes a village to ensure healthy outcomes in medicine. Potentially of more importance when it comes to interpreting DIY genetic testing is that there are a lot of different genetic variants that can increase the risk of glaucoma in individual pets, and not all have DNA tests associated with them. So, just because a pet tests negative for one or more genetic variants does not mean that they are not prone to glaucoma or will never develop it. Such strategies are covered in more detail in the chapter on early detection, but most require a good working relationship between you and your veterinary team to make sense of very complicated health and risk information. These tools are incredibly valuable, and it can be fun to order these tests online, but they can also be scary if the results are not given an appropriate context.

The most important thing to understand about risk factors is that they do not imply that the disease for which they signal potential risk will ever develop. Finding a genetic marker for a condition does not mean that the condition will ever materialize. A pet with a "breed predisposition" that suggests the risk of a problem being more common in the breed in general does not mean it will ever develop in an individual pet. A pet venturing into an area known to be populated with ticks does not mean that the pet will eventually develop tick-carried diseases. Similarly in human medicine, smoking does not always eventuate in lung cancer. The reason that we pay so much attention to risk factors, in human medicine and in pet medicine, is that they help us identify *potential* problems so that we can be proactive in dealing with them, perhaps even preventing them. It is important not to overstate risk factors, but it would also be a mistake to ignore them.

Putting It All Together

Raising an *almost* perfect pet is all about having reasonable expectations of where challenges will likely exist and being prepared to deal with those challenges. Knowing what to expect as you are raising your pet allows you to be proactive rather than being blindsided by things that are often predictable. If you are doing things correctly, you should be engaged more in health management than in disease management.

It is entirely possible to be proactive with most risk factors and the things you can do to help manage them. If you can acknowledge that pets, like people, can develop issues such as diabetes, heart disease and cancer, and the sooner you can intervene often provides you with the

Ivan (courtesy Tyra Sherry).

most options, you are in good stead to raise an *almost* perfect pet. If you can also appreciate that in such cases you want to provide the best care possible but might not have the needed financial resources, you might want to explore risk management strategies, such as pet health insurance. If you realize that the most common causes for pets being relinquished to a shelter and/or euthanized are actually behavior problems, not medical issues, you can appreciate how important it is to invest time and resources in appropriate training. Once you are aware that overfeeding is the most common nutritional problem there is for pets, not nutritional deficiencies, it is possible to plan accordingly and keep pets lean rather than look for corrective nutrients to supplement or fad diets to introduce. It's just a question of putting the effort where it is likely to do the most good.

With health care, there is a renewed interest in "healthspan" rather than "lifespan." It's nice for your pet to live as long as possible, but this needs to be regarded in context with quality of life, and our goal is to keep our pets healthy and happy for as long as possible (healthspan) rather than just keep them alive longer (lifespan). This requires a close working relationship with your veterinary team, staying ahead of medical problems, preventing problems whenever possible, and making treatment decisions not just based on what is easiest or quickest in the moment but on the basis of better long-term health outcomes.

It can be difficult to focus on long-term health outcomes when so much of what we deal with on a day-to-day basis involves immediate needs, but it's worth keeping things in perspective. When a pet is scratching uncontrollably due to allergies, for example, the temptation may be to give a medicine that is cheap and effective at controlling the clinical signs (symptoms). After all, if that scratching kept you awake most of the night, shouldn't stopping the scratching be the top priority? In reality, if the scratching was due to allergies, and allergies are a long-term (often lifelong) problem in pets, then it is important to actually have a strategy that is sustainable and doesn't have long-term side effects. If we want to preserve healthspan in our pets and not just trade a problem now for a bigger problem later, then it is worth considering all the options and not just settle for temporary solutions.

It is easy to be distracted by the seemingly limitless amounts of information available on the Internet, but don't be fooled—more is not necessarily better. There may be a decline of deference in today's consumers, with individuals thinking they can find the information they need and make the best choices themselves, but that doesn't necessarily work for health care. The greatest value comes from having a trustworthy resource to separate the wheat from the chaff, so you can concentrate on the interactions most relevant to keeping your pet problem free!

Case Example

Callie is a single mother with two school-aged children who have been pestering her to buy them a pet. Callie had a pet when she was growing up, but if she is being honest with herself, it was her mother who took responsibility for providing most of the pet care (even though Callie promised to do so when she was the child making the request). Callie works long hours, and her children have busy social schedules, but as a single parent, she's wondering if a pet might help compensate for what she believes is a somewhat dysfunctional family life after her divorce.

Callie doesn't make any promises, but one time when they are on a shopping trip at the mall, her children convince her that they should visit a pet store ... just to look, not to buy. They do so and promptly fall in love with an adorable Saint Bernard puppy. The price tag is two weeks of salary for Callie, and they live in a small apartment, but the children are smitten with their prospective new best friend, and she would really hate to disappoint them.

Callie considers the purchase and whether (if she puts it on her credit card) she will have saved enough by the time the statement arrives and the payment is due. Other than this large initial expense, she hasn't even had time to consider what other financial surprises will come next, as well as what will happen when she is at work and the children are at school. She had really thought that a smaller dog or even a cat would probably be a better choice for their lifestyle, but her children would be devastated if she backed out now. What might have been a better approach for Callie?

Recommended Reading

American Veterinary Medical Association. 2017–2018. *U.S. Pet Ownership & Demographics Sourcebook.* Schaumburg, IL: American Veterinary Medical Association.

Hemp, P. 2009. "Death by Information Overload." *Harvard Business Review* (87) 9: 83–89.

Human-Animal Bond Research Institute. https://habri.org/.

Lue, Todd W., Debbie P. Pantenburg, and Phillip M. Crawford. 2008. "Impact of the Owner-Pet and Client-Veterinarian Bond on the Care That Pets Receive." *Journal of the American Veterinary Medical Association* 232 (4): 531–40. https://doi.org/10.2460/javma.232.4.531.

"Millennials and Their Fur Babies." n.d. https://s1.q4cdn.com/959385532/files/doc_
downloads/research/2018/Millennials-and-Their-Fur-Babies.pdf.
"Pet Industry Market Size & Ownership Statistics." n.d. American Pet Products Association. http://www.americanpetproducts.org/press_industrytrends.asp.

Appropriate Pet Selection

A Companion for Life

Many would-be pet owners acquire a pet without a good understanding of its long-term needs. This lack of understanding can translate to improper planning for a lifetime of care, disillusionment with the concept of pet ownership, and even relinquishment of the pet to an uncertain future at a shelter. Wanting the best for your furry friend involves thinking ahead.

It may sound premature to develop a strategy before you ever own a pet. After all, what decisions could you possibly need to make before you have even acquired a pet? You might be surprised. In too many instances, pets get adopted on impulse, as though we couldn't predict that we would find any number of animals to be devastatingly cute and in need of homes. It is precisely because of this inevitable allure that we need to develop the discipline to consider as much as possible in advance and to choose with deliberation and clear thought.

Acquiring a Pet: Check First Before Ever Selecting a Pet

Don't simply assume that your living situation allows you to have a pet. Do some checking. Talk with your insurance provider, and then broaden the inquiry, if relevant, to rental units, homeowner associations and other entities which may have policies regarding pets. Prevent a nasty surprise by understanding limitations up front. If you're still living at home or sharing a dwelling with others, it is just good manners to make sure there are no objections before bringing an animal into a space you share with others.

It seems like a no-brainer that a homeowner should be able to go out and select a pet without any limitations, but this may not be true in your particular circumstances. Many homeowner insurance policies have exclusions for certain pets or breeds, and learning this after the fact can be devastating. In some cases, keeping some breeds on your property could invalidate your insurance coverage. It may not be fair, and it may not be right, but if your insurance company has an exclusion for certain breeds in its policy, you should know that before you go shopping for a pet. If you think you can just get past those exclusions by not telling the insurance company about your pet, you may be in for a rude awakening. Your insurance company could cancel your homeowner's policy or deny coverage for a claim, even a claim unrelated to your pet, simply because you have misrepresented your situation. And if your pet causes damage or injury, you might find yourself on the hook for a host of expensive charges.

Be smart. Check with your insurance company and others before you begin your pet search. If you believe your insurance company is unreasonable in their exclusions, this gives you time to shop for a new provider before you adopt such a pet. In any case, never lie to the insurance company, your landlord, or homeowners' association, or you must be prepared to deal with the potential fallout. Remember, raising an *almost* perfect pet is all about reasonable expectations. Getting evicted, facing a lawsuit, or risking your insurance is no way to enhance a new human-animal relationship.

Pet-Proofing Your Living Space

Before you bring a pet home, or even go window shopping for a pet, you'll want to make sure you have done everything you can to create a safe home environment. You would never bring a baby into your home without thinking about safety. Your new pet will need the same planning. In fact, it's actually easier to childproof a home than pet-proof it, because you have some time before babies become mobile enough to get into much trouble. The same is not true for pets. They are active and naturally inquisitive from day one, and they are prepared to chew on and swallow anything that they can. If unsupervised, they can chew electrical cords, damage things in the home, eat trash, and get into whatever is within reach (including medications, poisonous plants, needles and thread, household cleaners, your favorite belongings, etc.).

If you think you might be tempted to impulsively adopt a pet as soon as you see that special critter, it is important to think through

Mariska exploring (courtesy Tyra Sherry).

home safety before you ever start the search-and-visit process. While your long-term plan may involve giving your beloved animal free range in your home even when no human is present, you cannot start this policy as soon as your pet enters your home. It would not be safe for your new family member or your belongings and may quickly lead to disillusionment. Instead, plan ahead, knowing that it will take time, bonding, and training before any pet can be given open access to your living space.

So, when it comes to indoor safety, you'll want to consider what it would take to keep the pet isolated and safe for any period when a human is not available for direct supervision. There might be rooms that can be completely pet-proofed and closed off (e.g., bathroom, laundry room) where your pet could be safe. Crates are also popular options as long as the confinement is for reasonable periods of time. Don't turn a crate into a prison, or pets will resist going in and undesirable behaviors will become evident and ingrained. Confinement training is meant to provide a safe area for pets and limit their access to places where they could do damage or get hurt. In many ways, it is similar to placing a child in a playpen or crib. It is not meant as a punishment, and with proper training, pets can consider the crate as a place of refuge and somewhere where they can feel safe and protected. Once again, the concept of problem free is all about having realistic expectations, and caging a social animal for extended periods or tying it to a post in the yard are not actions that will foster the desired human-animal bond.

Walk through your living space, and try to appreciate where problems could exist. Make sure all medications, cleaners, poisons (insecticides, rodenticides, antifreeze, etc.) and other dangerous items are completely inaccessible. For most cabinets, use childproof latches. Keep trash containers sealed or within a secure cabinet. Remember that pets have a much keener sense of smell than we do and will quickly find anything they consider interesting, but their noses don't tell them which things could be dangerous. So, foods like chocolate, macadamia nuts, sugar substitutes (xylitol), raisins and grapes and several other items can be toxic, but that won't stop pets from gorging on them if found. Remember too that many pets are nimble, and they will think nothing of climbing on one surface to reach another—for instance from a counter to the top of a refrigerator—so it may not be sufficient to simply place items "out of reach" as you would for a baby. It's also important to block access to any nooks and crannies and behind furniture where pets could get themselves trapped, where they could encounter electric cords or otherwise find themselves in trouble with no responsible human nearby. Also take inventory of houseplants and learn which ones might be toxic. Dangers may not always be obvious. For example, members of the true lily and daylily families can be quite toxic for pets, especially cats. There's no need to panic, but a quick Internet search can help you determine if the plants you currently have in your home would be toxic to an incoming pet (see Recommended Reading). Also, keep the toilet lid closed so pets don't drown, don't get exposed to toilet cleaners and sanitizers, and so they don't drink toilet water and then potentially spread toilet germs to household members (such as with kisses when reunited with their loved ones).

Similarly, think about the outdoor situation before you bring home a pet. If the yard isn't fenced, how will you prevent your pet from getting out or other animals from coming in? Will you have your pet on a leash while out, or do you need a fence so your companion can spend time exploring on its own? Do you have a shaded area in your yard so the pet can avoid direct and prolonged sun exposure? If not, can you create some shade, or will you need to limit yard time on hot or sunny days? Think about providing your new loved one with access to fresh water, but not deep water in which it could drown. It's fine if pets spend a short amount of time alone in the yard, but spending extended periods of time outdoors unsupervised can give pets the opportunity to get into trouble, especially young or new pets.

How long can pets be left alone in a home, even if confined? To a certain extent, it depends on the species and age. Puppies are very social, and if expected to remain in confinement for more than a couple of hours, they will likely consider this punishment, which can harm social bonding. With gradual extension and a reward-based system, dogs can eventually be confined for up to eight hours in a crate, and this is much easier to attain if someone can come in midday to check on them, play with them, and give them the opportunity to take care of their toileting needs. As dogs become elderly, it should be expected that they will need more bathroom breaks than they did as young adults. Once again, if you want to keep your pet problem free, support their abilities to maintain appropriate toilet habits.

The situation is often somewhat simpler for cats. Kittens should not be left alone in a pet-proofed home for more than four hours at a time, but adult cats can be left at home alone for eight hours as long as they have access to a clean litter tray, fresh water, and have been fed a meal prior to being left alone. In time, it may even be possible to leave cats for longer periods, and with litter tray cleaners and automatic waterers and feeders, cats can be quite self-sufficient but still should be supervised with some regularity.

Other Considerations

We are going to spend an entire chapter on pet health care afford-ability, but it is still worth exploring the concept of cost when it comes to selecting an *almost* perfect pet and to do so before you find yourself in the position of being a new pet owner. This is important because most consumers don't know how much to budget for the care of a pet over its lifespan. People will be able to quote statistics about what it costs to raise a child to adulthood but have no idea of the costs of caring for a pet over its typical lifespan. Buckle up, because such information can be quite sobering, and you can take a glance at the affordability chapter whenever you need a reminder of what it costs to raise a pet.

It's a sad fact that many people purchase a pet on impulse and may spend what others would consider an exorbitant amount of money on the acquisition. The fact is that when you wander into a pet store—just to have a look—you are bound to see a furry little face that you want to take home with you. Just like the advice that you should never go gro-cery shopping when you are hungry, you should not go into pet stores when you are in the susceptible consideration phase but not yet fully prepared and committed. If you have children and they are wanting a pet, this is doubly important since it is likely that they will find a crea-ture that is difficult to resist—it's inevitable (you know it's true). It's best not to put yourself in that situation until you are much further in the process and know exactly what you want.

Spending on pet care is an important consideration because it can affect the selection process more than just the purchase price. If you have limited funds or are concerned with the number of animals already on the planet that need good homes, you might want to consider a shelter or a "rescue" organization. There are also a lot of pets available for free to a good home within most communities. In days of yore, this type of information might appear in the classified section of a newspaper but now can largely be accomplished with a simple Internet search or found in online marketplace listings. So, if the purchase price of the pet itself is not a limiting factor, consider the other expenses that might affect your decisions. If it will be a challenge to purchase enough quality pet food, you may elect to adopt a cat or small dog, where those costs will be less, rather than using lower-quality food for a larger dog. If you will regret having to pay for grooming services, avoid pets with inherent grooming costs because of their fur types, and select instead a more wash-and-wear variety of pet that may just need grooming a few times a year. It is best to think about all these issues before you head out the door "just for a look" where adorable little puppy eyes or pouncing kittens will pull at your heartstrings.

Health care will be covered in more detail elsewhere in this book, but just a few thoughts that apply to the selection process. All pets will require regular veterinary checkups, vaccination, and parasite control. That is relatively easy to budget for with some basic queries to your veterinary team. Some other health care costs can be approximated based on what you are looking for in a pet. There is no doubt that pets that are popular on social media often exhibit conformation extremes of some form (squashed faces, short legs, long bodies, very tall, deep chests, wrinkles, improper tooth alignment, etc.), and while they might be darlings of the Internet age, potential pet owners need to be aware that these types of animals may also have considerable medical needs that can have long-term consequences for the animal and be quite expensive for the owner. For example, pets with squashed faces (known as brachycephalic) not only may have profound difficulty breathing, but some eventually require corrective surgery to attempt to mitigate the problems associated with their conformation. If you select a pet with such conformation issues, do your research in advance so you can understand the future costs that might be associated with your choice so you can plan accordingly. There's also an ethical consideration which we might consider—whether propagating animals with such conformational issues is in the best interest of these animals rather than just providing features for our amusement. It's a personal choice and one you need to consciously make. There's no need to feel guilty about the features you find attractive, but it is worth appreciating in advance that many pet lovers have strong opinions on both sides of the issue.

Similarly, it would be nice to purchase pets that have no risks of developing health care problems, but this is not a realistic goal any more than having a child that is devoid of health risks. The concepts of selecting pets that might be at reduced risk for some of these problems is definitely feasible, and we'll cover that in more detail, but no matter how careful you are in selecting a pet without health care problems, it is not possible to eliminate all such risks. Still, we'll spend a considerable amount of time in this book helping to reduce those risks as much as possible. That's the *almost* perfect way!

Because most pet owners acquire and then pay for a pet with their discretionary after-tax money, cost is often a factor in maintaining an *almost* perfect pet. There's also no doubt that if people had pet health insurance starting from when a pet is about 8 weeks of age that it would be much easier to budget for unforeseen health care costs. Still, it is important that costs be viewed in perspective, or pet ownership will end up becoming a luxury affordable to only the wealthy. This would be a true pity, because pets have benefits for all of us and options exist for most budgets, as long as expectations are reasonable.

Attitudes about health care costs have actually changed somewhat since the outbreak of COVID-19. Most health care professionals, including veterinary team members, have protocols and standards of care about approaches, but compromises were implemented during the pandemic out of necessity. For example, strict rules about personal protective equipment (PPE) had to be relaxed due to scarcity, even if it was acknowledged that such compromise was suboptimal. Telehealth visits became more commonplace. Other compromises were also made. So, while it is acknowledged that there are ways of delivering health care at a level that is considered the gold standard, there is often the realization that accommodations are sometimes also needed. Many health care leaders have realized that in some instances there is a need for what is sometimes referred to as "incremental care," and this also applies for pet owners who want to do right by their pet but may not be able to afford the level of care that others might select.

Once again, there are costs associated with pet ownership, but it would be very harsh indeed to say that those with more limited means are not entitled to the benefit of sharing their lives with pets. Just like child-rearing, pet ownership should not be reserved solely for the rich. Pet ownership can be accomplished on almost any budget and that includes how much to spend to acquire a pet. With so many pets needing loving homes, and many available for free or low cost, there is no need to break the bank to acquire a pet. However, it can be extremely worthwhile to consider your selection appropriately to minimize the costs of maintaining the pet through its lifetime.

The Selection Process

Once you have committed to the lifelong nature of pet adoption, you have ensured your home is properly prepared, and you are aware of any financial limitations you'll need to consider regarding pet ownership, you are ready to proceed with the selection process.

The pet selection process is incredibly important. You and your new pet will be family for many years. Just like when you choose a life partner, choosing a pet to share your home should be a lifelong commitment, so it is important to select thoughtfully. Considering the importance of the decision, there are surprisingly few resources to turn to for guidance. Most books start their advice when you already have a pet. In most instances, veterinary teams are not consulted in the acquisition of a pet, so prospective pet owners often begin and complete this process without appropriate health care advice. In fact, veterinary teams often lament the situation when new pet owners come in with a pet of dubious heritage that was purchased for a considerable sum (with papers?) and evidence of congenital and hereditary problems that could have been avoidable with appropriate counseling.

As an informed consumer, you can be different. You can get assistance in selecting an animal that will fit your lifestyle. Are you looking for a big pet or a small one? Does it need to be good with children? Is it important that it be mellow, or are you looking for a long-distance running partner? The very first step may be deciding between a dog and a cat. Interestingly, this is usually not a tough decision because most would-be pet owners have strong preferences one way or another. In general, if you are looking for a pet that can be independent and requires less attention, then cats are probably the top choice. If you want a companion that you can interact with on your own terms and timetable and that could participate with you in activities, then a dog is probably the better choice. While many could be happy with either a cat or a dog (or both), it is very interesting that many people feel drawn to one species or another and potentially may bond to them in different ways.

Once the decision has been made between dogs and cats, consider using an online selection tool or app or talking with a veterinary team member to help with breed selection. Such selectors can help suggest pets based on their size, exercise needs, grooming requirements, and other characteristics (see Table 2.1). After making a selection, you

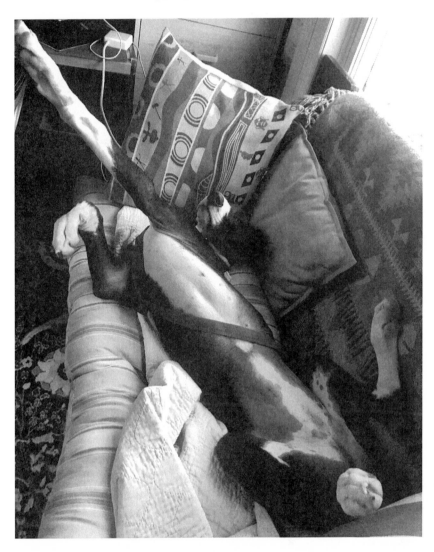

We decided to designate one item of furniture that the dog could sit on. It allowed her a view outside as well as a place to stretch out once in a while. Here she takes full advantage of it (courtesy Janice Adams).

can then pursue where you might find suitable animals, health guarantees that should be requested from the seller, and terms that include a no-questions-asked money-back guarantee following veterinary examination. Prospective pet owners can also do their shopping armed with questionnaires that inquire about health issues in the animals or their parents and genetic testing that might have been done to mitigate health care risks. Information on recommended tests to consider on a breed basis are available for both dogs and cats. You can also learn about breed predispositions to a variety of diseases from several resources, including those online (see Recommended Reading). Taking the time to make an informed decision goes a long way toward creating a better outcome and substantially less risk of "buyer's remorse." After all, the goal is a long-term, stable, loving pet-human relationship.

Organization	Website
Animal Planet (Dog)	www.animalplanet.com/breed-selector/dog-breeds.html
Animal Planet (Cat)	www.animalplanet.com/breedselector/catselectorindex.do
American Kennel Club (dog)	www.akc.org/dog-breed-selector/
DogTime (dog)	http://dogtime.com/quiz/dog-breed-selector
Hills (cat)	www.hillspet.com/cat-care/new-pet-parent/choosing-right-cat-breeds
Iams	www.iams.com/breedselector/
Optimum Pet (cat)	www.optimumpet.com.au/cat-advice/cat-selector
Pedigree (dog)	www.pedigree.com/getting-a-new-dog/breed-match
Puppyfinder (dog)	www.puppyfinder.com/dog-breed-selector
Purina (dog)	www.purina.com/dogs/dog-breeds/dog-breed-selector
Purina (cat)	www.purina.com/cat-breed-selector
Select a dog breed	www.selectadogbreed.com
Select Smart (dog)	www.selectsmart.com/dog/
Select Smart (cat)	www.selectsmart.com/CAT/
Vetstreet	www.vetstreet.com/breed-finder
Whiskas (cat)	www.whiskas.co.uk/breed-selector

Table 2.1. A sampling of dog and cat breed selector tools available on the Internet.

So Many Choices

Potential pet owners don't need to rush the process because there is no shortage of pets that need good homes. Dogs and cats both make great pets (and many other animals as well, but that is well beyond the scope of this book), but they come in a variety of sizes and shapes, with different characteristics and often with different health care needs. That's why research is so important.

Once the decision between dogs and cats has been made, there is typically then a discussion that ensues about whether to select a purebred, mixed breed, or hybrid (designer breed). This is discussed in more detail in its own chapter, but just a brief word here as it applies to the selection process.

People are often drawn to purebreds (e.g., Siamese, Poodle, Himalayan, Golden Retriever, etc.) based on their standardized characteristics, specific attributes and sometimes—to put it bluntly—their snob appeal. The main benefit of selecting a purebred is that those characteristics, including behaviors and health risks, are usually fairly predictable. There may be a mean-spirited and vicious Golden Retriever out there somewhere, but that is not the expectation—we expect Golden Retrievers to be gentle and loving. When it comes to deciding what you want the adult size to be, that's often quite predictable with purebreds—at least purebred dogs. If you want to select a breed that would be happy to go on long hiking trips with you, that's quite predictable. If you prefer an animal that would be content sharing the couch with you for long periods of time—that's also predictable. In fact, it is predictable which animals would be most prone to certain hereditary conditions, which are more or less likely to provoke allergies in members of the household, those with a heightened tendency to snoring or drooling, and what the likely grooming needs will be. So, the ability to predict what you are going to get is definitely easier with a purebred. In fact, with many purebreds available from breeders, it might even be possible to view the parents and siblings of your potential selection, so you have even more specific information.

Mixed-breed animals may be of more questionable heritage, but they are no less loving and no less worthy of a great home. They are typically also much cheaper to acquire and come with the bonus of providing a home to an animal in need. Since the heritage of mixed-breed animals is generally unknown, it's true that it is harder to predict adult size, grooming needs, temperament, and many other characteristics. But, in good news, mixed-breed pets (mutts, moggies) may also have lower prevalence of certain inherited conditions. There are, however, some misconceptions about purebreds and mixed breeds when it comes to health issues. Some believe that mixed-breed pets are healthier because there is less likelihood of inheriting those "bad" genes that can confer risk of certain genetic diseases. This is sometimes referred to as hybrid vigor, or heterosis. However, this concept is somewhat of a myth. While mixed-breed animals may not be as prone to some of the rare breed-specific genetic disorders (e.g., progressive retinal atrophy, muscular dystrophy, hemophilia, etc.), they can still get some of these conditions (although more difficult to predict), and they are still prone to many of the most common hereditary disorders that are seen in all breeds (e.g., hip dysplasia, thyroid disorders, allergies, etc.).

In addition to purebreds and mixed-breed animals, we are now seeing more and more so-called designer breeds of dogs and cats, which are specific crosses of certain purebreds to attain specific attributes in the cross. Designer breeds (hybrids) may have predictable features, but they don't necessarily "breed true." They result from the breeding of two different purebreds. So, if you cross a Standard Poodle with a Labrador Retriever, you'll get a Labradoodle, but if you breed two Labradoodles, you won't get a purebred Labradoodle—you'll get a mutt with some Labrador Retriever and Poodle characteristics. Actually, purebreds can eventually result when breeders select animals of specific attributes to deliver predictable features, so on an evolutionary basis, new breeds eventually do get created from hybrids. Many of today's purebreds have resulted from the intentional breeding of animals with specific characteristics, often by crossing other breeds to eventually yield a new one. So, for instance, in Australia, certain Labradoodles have been bred for their social nature and are often referred to as cobber dogs (cobber being an Australian term for friend). Hybrids are also popular with cat lovers, and many are regarded like purebreds (e.g., Bengal, Serengeti, Cheetoh, etc.). An interesting feature of some of these cat hybrids is that they might actually involve crosses with non-domesticated species of cats, not just different purebreds.

Whether you select a dog or cat, a purebred, mixed breed or hybrid, look for the features that best meet your social, emotional and financial needs. When raised correctly in a problem-free manner, all can be wonderful companions.

Sources of Pets

There are a variety of sources from which pets can be acquired today, so do not panic or worry that you will have forever missed an opportunity if you don't adopt the first furry face you fall in love with (which, if you're like most people, is every single one). Take your time. Try to make the very best choice for you.

If you've decided that you want a purebred or hybrid, the best source will be breeders. Anyone who breeds dogs or cats may consider themselves to be professional breeders, but most breeders who are doing this with improvement of the breed in mind will be associated with a major breed association, produce very few litters a year, and will likely scrutinize you more than you will them to make sure their animals are going to a good home. The advantage of dealing with conscientious breeders is that they will often be able to provide access to other family members of your potential future pet, particularly the parents, and hopefully they have been participating in health registries, have the results of DNA testing for the animals bred, and have generous policies (often the case) for returning animals if things don't work out. Breeders that produce animals for competition, such as the show ring, will likely have members of the litters that they consider exemplary (show quality) and that they would want to use in their breeding programs, but there are also many other purebreds in a litter that are wonderful but might not meet the breeder's particular criteria for breeding stock but that nonetheless would make a wonderful companion (pet quality). Don't be in a rush, because many conscientious breeders might have waiting lists for availability of offspring of future litters.

One of the disadvantages of breeders is that they can be difficult to find. Many breeders work out of their homes rather than storefronts, so you will have to research them online. The best place to start is often with the parent associations (e.g., American Kennel Club, Canadian Kennel Club, The Kennel Club, Cat Fancier's Association, The International Cat Association, etc.), which typically maintain a directory of member breeders. That alone is not a guarantee of conscientious breeding practices, but it helps determine potential candidates for further scrutiny. There is currently not a universally recognized certification program for breeders, so anyone who chooses to mate two animals can consider themselves to be a breeder, so it behooves would-be pet owners to do their research carefully. As you might expect from a largely unregulated field, there are breeders who do an excellent job of screening breeding pairs for both exceptional health as well as conformation, but there are also breeders who may not be as diligent in this regard. Buyer beware!

We single out conscientious breeders (realizing that there is no regulated certification or licensing program for breeders) because there are also instances of what are sometimes referred to as "backyard" breeders, or those involved with puppy and kitten "mills" that are intent on producing animals strictly for sale and profit. Sometimes they sell through pet stores, and sometimes they sell direct to the public, but often these animals are not the best representatives of the breeds they have been identified as (even if they have "papers"), and breeders may not be focused as much as they should on the genetic health of these animals. This is a generalization only but worthy of consideration.

There are, of course, other sources of purebreds and hybrids, including "rescue" organizations. These groups accept purebreds in need and typically foster them with people very familiar with the breed and dedicated to placing these animals in appropriate homes. If you want to help an animal in need and still have a purebred or hybrid, this may be a good place to start, and the individuals fostering these animals are often very knowledgeable about the breeds and their requirements. In many cases, they will be able to share the reason for the animal's relinquishment to the group and recommendations about the pet's potential issues and how they might best be managed. As one might imagine, pets get relinquished for a variety of reasons, but make sure those reasons wouldn't apply to you as well. In the end, if your goal is to have an *almost* perfect pet, it is best not to tackle problems you don't feel comfortable addressing.

Pet shops are often a very convenient place to see dogs and cats for adoption but are often a relatively expensive option, and the original source of those animals may not be shared with would-be adopters. Many of the largest retail pet supply shops no longer sell dogs and cats directly but may partner with shelters and other organizations to place pets in good homes. While there is much variability in the health quality of animals sold at pet shops, in most cases it is not possible to see the parents or the results of their genetic testing or health registry entries, so you are purchasing with more uncertainty and often with limited return options should problems arise. Some pet shops do a great job, but each should be scrutinized on its individual merits.

Shelters typically represent community-based facilities for pets that have been abandoned or relinquished. These are important organizations for caring for animals in need. Many of the animals in shelters are mixed breeds, but purebreds are also present. In some jurisdictions, especially where there are breed exclusions in place (such as for a variety of breeds considered "pit bulls"), there may be large numbers of such breeds available. Shelters are often the cheapest place to adopt animals and often do the best job they can with the funds available to them. Some shelters are designated as "no kill," and while there is no official definition for this term, it generally implies that there is a live release rate or "save rate" of at least 90 percent. Of course, these facilities have the same size and space limitations as other shelters, so they typically need to be more selective in which animals they will accept for relinquishment. In the end, it is not possible to save all strays and re-home them, and all shelters need to deal with the grim reality of what happens when animals lose favored-pet status and no longer have a home. From a problem-free perspective, shelter staff may have limited historical knowledge about the animals in their care, including health and behavioral information. They often try to do their best with intake profiles if a pet has been relinquished and the previous owners provide truthful information, but gaps often exist. However, shelters are often very generous in their willingness to accept animals back if problems are encountered in the pet's new home.

In the digital age, there are often databases of pets in need of homes and even peer-to-peer options in which those whose situations have changed (e.g., moving somewhere where they can't take a pet) will post the availability of pets, their back stories, and provide access to existing medical records. Listings for pets can also be found in online marketplaces or located with a simple Internet search. Once again, there is no shortage of pets in need of homes, so there is no need for you to rush the process.

Next Steps

Once you've decided whether you want a purebred, hybrid or mixed breed and where you intend to find one, there are still considerations to be made. You can decide whether you want a puppy/kitten or an older individual, if you have a preference for a male or female, and whether you have any behavioral characteristics that will be important to you (e.g., retrieving, endurance, tendency to bark, etc.). Think carefully about your choices because many of these traits are highly entrenched, so if you initially think an energetic dog may motivate you to jog with some regularity, you need to be prepared that the dog will still need this activity after you have decided that this is a resolution you no longer intend to keep.

For most pet owners, temperament is one of the most important characteristics for an animal you will be bringing into your home. While there are a variety of temperament tests and shelter assessments that have been developed, few have been validated for this purpose, and so

Four cats, one bed (courtesy Katrina O'Gahan).

it is still easier to judge these qualities in slightly older animals. Still, if you want to adopt a little bundle of fur, you may not be able to completely predict adult temperament, but testing is still worthwhile, and you should commit to appropriate training from the start.

When it comes to selecting a healthy individual, most adoption facilities will give you a grace period to have the pet examined by a veterinarian, but make sure the seller is offering a full money-back guarantee and not just a credit toward adopting another animal there. Also be aware that veterinarians will be able to identify some congenital issues (umbilical hernias, kneecaps that aren't seated properly, etc.) but that many conditions are just not clinically evident in young animals (e.g., hip dysplasia, many inherited heart and eye diseases, etc.). The best assurance you have is to collect as much information as you can about the parents of the pet being adopted, especially health records, DNA testing results and health registry entries. If possible, have the seller provide specific information about what they know about the health of the individual and the family health history (see Table 2.2). This is some of the most important information you'll need to raise an *almost* perfect pet.

While this will be covered in more detail in the chapter on early detection, it is worth noting here that genetic testing can be a great way of knowing about specific hereditary problems that might be encountered. In fact, if the parents have been tested, their results should indicate the likelihood of their offspring being affected. So, if both parents are "clear" for a genetic disease such as progressive retinal atrophy (a form of inherited blindness), then theoretically their offspring should have almost no chance of being affected (unless there was a rare spontaneous new mutation or the reported parents were not the actual parents). Such offspring might be designated as presumed "clear" based on parentage.

DNA testing is a major advance, and animals can be tested as early as 1 day of age (although most are tested around 12 weeks of age), but it may take a few weeks to get the results back, and the majority of real health concerns do not have DNA testing available (e.g., hip dysplasia, thyroid disorders, diabetes, etc.). So, DNA testing provides useful information but not necessarily quickly and not necessarily for all the conditions that pose the most risk for animals. These tests are covered in more detail in the chapter on early detection.

Even though definitive DNA tests are lacking for many important conditions, health registries also exist and can be a great way to get assurance that pets about to be adopted can be scrutinized as much as possible for their likely health status, often on the basis of entries made for parents and other family members. There are many health registries, known as schemes in some countries, in which breeders report

Golden Retriever Adoption Questionnaire

INFORMATION TO BE PROVIDED BY SELLER

Name of Business: Website:

Address: Telephone:

Name of Dog (Registered):

Date of Birth: Weight: □ kg □ lb   Color:

Identification: Microchip _____   Tattoo _____   Collar/Tag _____

Registration (e.g., AKC, UKC, CKC, etc.):

□ Show Quality   □ Pet Quality   □ Breeding   □ Non-breeding

Question	Yes	No	Don't Know	Documents Provided
Did parents have pre-breeding health screening?				
Are parents' health screens in a public registry?				
Are this animal's health screens in a public registry?				
Has this animal had genetic health screening?				
Have parents had genetic health screening?				
Has this animal received regular veterinary evaluations?				
Any irregularities determined by veterinary evaluations?				
Are all vaccinations current?				
Any exposure to infectious diseases?				
Is recent parasite evaluation available?				
Is this animal currently free of parasites?				
Is this animal on integrated parasite control?				
Any evidence of problem behaviors in this animal?				
Is there a history of problem behaviors in the family?				
Any evidence of allergies in this animal?				
Is there a history of allergies in the family?				
Has this animal been evaluated for orthopedic disorders?				
Have parents been evaluated for orthopedic disorders?				
Is this animal free of congenital heart diseases?				
Are both parents free of heritable heart diseases?				
Is this animal free of heritable eye diseases?				
Are both parents free of heritable eye diseases?				
Any evidence of hypothyroidism in this animal?				
Is there any history of hypothyroidism in the family?				
Any evidence of diabetes mellitus in this animal?				
Any evidence of diabetes mellitus in the family?				
Any evidence of seizure disorders in this animal?				
Any evidence of seizure disorders in the family?				
Any evidence of bleeding disorders in this animal?				
Any evidence of bleeding disorders in the family?				
Any evidence of cancer in this animal?				
Any evidence of cancer in the family?				
Medical-behavioral money-back guarantee provided?				

Signature: Date:

Table. 2.2. Example of an adoption questionnaire

the health findings for their breeding animals to an independent organization that allows would-be adopters and other breeders to see the family history of individuals for a variety of specific diseases and results (not only DNA test results but also radiographic evidence for hip dysplasia, eye examinations by board-certified veterinary specialists, cardiac evaluations, etc.). Examples of health care registries include the OFA (www.ofa.org), the American Kennel Club's Bred with H.E.A.R.T. program (https://www.akc.org/breeder-programs/akc-bred-with-heart-program/requirements/health-testing-requirements/), the British Veterinary Association's Health Schemes (https://www.bva.co.uk/canine-health-schemes/), and Officially Recognized Canine Health Information Database (ORCHID) for the Australian National Kennel Council (http://orchid.ankc.org.au/). This is how breeders contribute to improving their breeds and how would-be pet owners can increase the likelihood of adopting an *almost* perfect pet!

Case Example

Kimberley Donaldson came to visit ABC Veterinary Hospital after hearing from a friend that the hospital offered pre-adoption counseling. She and her husband had a four-year-old child, and they were thinking of getting a Siberian husky (they had seen a cute puppy of this breed in the pet store but resisted the temptation to buy it at that time). From the selection counseling session, it was determined that the Donaldsons lived in a two-bedroom apartment, both adults worked long hours, and their lifestyle was decidedly sedentary between work and child-rearing. By the end of the session, Kimberley had acknowledged that an energetic Siberian husky might not be the best breed for their circumstances and narrowed their choices to a Miniature Schnauzer or a Bichon Frisé and would make the final decision with her husband while armed with the breed information provided.

A staff member also provided some resources for finding an appropriate dog of either breed, including a local breed rescue, online breed-specific adoptions, and a list of breeders available from a national breeders' registry. The hospital provided a frequently asked questions (FAQ) document regarding pet adoption and basic care, forms for the prospective puppy seller to complete, and forms the practice would need once the final decision was made. A new puppy kit was provided (along with a container that the owner would use to bring a fecal sample on the first actual visit) to check for parasites. Kimberley was also invited to visit the Thursday evening "puppy kindergarten" class that was offered by one of the hospital staff, and they would introduce her to their basic temperament-testing regimen and go over the socialization and training classes offered. A quick introduction was made to Dr. Smith, whom she would see at the first scheduled visit, and she was invited to call back with any other questions. Kimberley was assured that, although it wasn't quite as involved as raising a baby, ABC Veterinary Hospital would be there to help her through the process every step of the way. The client-to-be left the practice armed with a much better understanding of pet ownership and decidedly more assured about how to approach the adoption process.

About three weeks later, Kimberley came in with Schnitzel, an 8-week-old Miniature Schnauzer, and dutifully brought in a fecal sample in the container previously provided. Schnitzel was a fine, healthy specimen, with only a minor umbilical hernia that could be fixed at the time of neutering. Kimberley had read most of the material that was provided and had some questions about which pet health insurance plan might be best for Schnitzel. Dr. Smith started Schnitzel out on a sensible dietary regimen and reiterated some of the breed risks, such as pancreatitis and calcium oxalate bladder "stones" that warrant being careful of what Schnitzel is being fed. The discussions of vaccination schedules, genetic screening, parasite control, nutrition, and proper socialization ensued, and then the long-term health care plan was reviewed.

Recommended Reading

Ackerman, L.J., ed. 2021. *Pet-Specific Care for the Veterinary Team.* Hoboken, NJ: Wiley.
_____. 2020. *Proactive Pet Parenting.* Problem Free Publishing.
_____. 2011. *The Genetic Connection, 2nd Edition.* Lakewood, CO: AAHA Press.
"Advice | International Cat Care." n.d. Icatcare.org. https://icatcare.org/advice/?per_page=12&categories=cat-breeds.
"Canine Health Schemes." n.d. British Veterinary Association (BVA). https://www.bva.co.uk/canine-health-schemes/.
Dulabs, Kylee. 2017. "Pet Ownership Costs Guide for 2019." The Simple Dollar. TheSimpleDollar.com. March 6. https://www.thesimpledollar.com/save-money/pet-cost-calculator/.
Fivecoat-Campbell, K. 2020. "Adoption Marketing: Marketing to the New Adopters of Shelter and Rescue Animals." *AAHA Trends* 36 (2): 51–55.
Landsberg, G., W. Hunthausen, and L. Ackerman. 2013. *Behavior Problems of the Dog and Cat.* 3rd ed. Edinburgh: Elsevier.
Partners for Healthy Pets. http://www.partnersforhealthypets.org/.
"Poisonous Plants." 2015. ASPCA. https://www.aspca.org/pet-care/animal-poison-control/toxic-and-non-toxic-plants.
"2011 AAHA/AVMA Preventive Healthcare Guidelines." 2011. Aahanet.org. https://www.aahanet.org/Library/PreventiveHealthcare.aspx.
"What Genetic Diseases And/or Conditions Should My Breed Be Screened For?" n.d. OFA. https://www.ofa.org/browse-by-breed.

3

Purebreds, Mixed Breeds and Everything in Between

So, you are ready to take the plunge and bring a new four-legged friend into your family. Bravo! There are so many rewards in sharing your life with a pet. Before you head out on your search for the "perfect" choice, however, let's think a bit more about your options.

As we discussed in Chapter 2, being a proactive pet owner means planning ahead, so it is important to carefully consider your options— purebreds, mixed breeds, and hybrids—in more detail. What are the advantages and disadvantages of each, and what might your choice mean to the goal of maintaining a problem-free pet?

As you head out in search of your new family member, you need to be prepared for a variety of options. In fact, the options are growing, right alongside our knowledge of various animals' predispositions to diseases. It has never been more important to understand and appreciate the distinctions, as this can impact health care risks and appropriate early screening for potential hereditary conditions.

There is not a census for pets, so it is not possible to know for certain the proportion of purebreds in the pet population, but as a rough approximation, roughly half of dogs are mixed breeds, while the other half are either purebreds or hybrids. Most cats—perhaps even 90 percent of the total cat population—are mixed breeds. That should help put things in perspective, even if we don't have official tallies to report.

Purebreds

Purebred pets are those with a documented pedigree or ancestry— the breeds that are recognizable by their physical characteristics. There are literally hundreds of dog breeds and dozens of cat breeds in the world today. Purebred is the term used to refer to those recognized breeds, and pedigrees are just the recorded ancestry of particular members of a recognized breed—a sort of family tree. Many countries have organizations that recognize breed status and record pedigrees (e.g., American Kennel Club, The Kennel Club, United Kennel Club, etc.), and it is quite possible that some breeds recognized as purebreds by one organization may not be recognized by another. Even if the breed is recognized by different associations, they may be recorded under different names (e.g., Doberman Pinscher versus Doberman). When pet owners state that their pet came with "papers," it just means that the parents claimed on an animal's registration application appear in the association's ledgers; it is not a testament as to the quality of the individual being registered and usually does not even establish with certainty that the parents listed on the application were the legitimate parents of the animal being registered (although this can be confirmed by genetic testing). In many cases it relies on the integrity of the person filing the application. There are also international organizations dealing with purebreds, such as The Fédération Cynologique Internationale (www.fci.be) for dogs and The International Cat Association (TICA) (www.tica.org) and the Cat Fanciers Association (www.cfa.org) for cats. You can look through the websites of some of these organizations to see the wide number of purebreds recognized, information about breed standards, and often also information on health concerns in specific breeds.

One of the most useful features of purebreds, from a problem-free pet perspective, is that purebreds tend to have more predictable behaviors and predispositions to disease, as was discussed in Chapter 2. Many behaviors are highly engrained in a breed (e.g., retrieving, herding), and pet owners may have certain expectations in this regard. It is also easier to predict features such as personality in purebreds, adult size and, as mentioned, breed predisposition to certain diseases. In addition, there are a variety of genetic screening tests now available, and most are applicable to diseases recognized in only certain purebreds (although some can also be detected in mixed-breed and hybrid animals as well).

Because certain health problems have been associated with certain breeds (such as progressive retinal atrophy in the Irish setter or polycystic kidney disease in the Persian), there is sometimes a mistaken belief that purebreds are less healthy than mixed-breed animals. It is important to appreciate in this regard that it is not the purity of the breed that causes susceptibility to disease but rather a presence of so-called "liability genes" that can get inadvertently concentrated in some breeding lines. Fortunately, one of the challenges associated with purebreds may also be a source of their salvation. There are now hundreds of DNA tests that are available to identify some of these genetic diseases, most applicable to breed-related disorders, and such tests allow the virtual elimination of such diseases if breeding stock are appropriately screened. So, while progressive retinal atrophy in the Irish setter is a recessive genetic cause of blindness, it is possible to select breeding animals that should never produce a litter with affected puppies. Similarly, for cats, there is a dominant genetic variant for polycystic kidney disease, which is most common in Persians. We now have a DNA test that can identify those with the gene variant so that prospective parents can be appropriately selected to avoid the trait in their offspring. So, purebreds may be at increased risk for some rare and funky genetic diseases, but we now have the tools for identifying some of these and eliminating risk of them occurring in future generations. This is a major breakthrough that can help us avoid some potential risks when selecting a purebred.

We'll discuss genetic tests in more detail in other chapters, but when it comes to certain disease genes that inadvertently get concentrated in certain purebred lines, it is worth mentioning that some of these genetic variants are often very breed specific. So, when it comes

This breed does not develop a heavy winter coat, so sometimes in cold weather a little help is necessary. Rifka is wearing a water-resistant jacket with reflective stripes under her car harness (courtesy Janice Adams).

to progressive retinal atrophy (PRA), it is important to realize that this is not a single disease seen in a single breed. Progressive retinal atrophy is a common term for the final endpoint for many different forms of genetic diseases that target the retinal tissues at the back of the eyes and cause them to degenerate over time. There are literally dozens of different genetic variants, each associated with different mutations on different aspects of genes that impact retinal function in a variety of breeds. The different genetic variants are typically seen in specific breeds and might have different types of inheritance (recessive, dominant, X-linked, etc.) and different clinical presentations (some presenting early in life, others later in life, etc.). It's important to realize this, because many DNA tests are not only variant specific, but they may only be seen in certain breeds as well. So, the DNA test for PRA in the Irish setter is different from the DNA test for PRA in the Siberian husky, which is different from the DNA test for PRA in the Abyssinian, which is different from the DNA test for PRA in the Bengal cat. DNA testing is often very accurate, but it is only applicable to specific variants (mutations) and often only in specific breeds. In fact, some breeds, such as the Miniature Schnauzer and Abyssinian, have more than one type of PRA to which they are susceptible. Fortunately, there are also multiple DNA tests available for those specific variants.

Hybrids

Hybrids are becoming more common in society as breeders and pet owners attempt to select for specific features by crossing certain purebred breeds. Hybrids are the product of crossing one distinct purebred with another, hopefully to create animals that share the desirable traits of both contributing breeds. Unlike purebreds, hybrids are not always consistent in their features, because there tends to be more variability when intentionally breeding two different purebreds. While some breeders have attempted to create new purebred breeds from the offspring of these crosses, in general the hybrids involve the continued interbreeding of specific purebreds to attain the desired crosses. That is, if you want a "Morkie," it is only going to result from the breeding of a purebred Maltese and a purebred Yorkshire Terrier; it takes two different purebreds combined to create a hybrid. The situation is a bit more nuanced in cats. While there are many canine hybrids being promoted (see Table 3.1), some feline hybrids have also been developed (see Table 3.2), and some of these are now recognized as purebreds by some registries. These include the Havana Brown, Ocicat, Oriental Shorthair,

Tonkinese, Bengal, Chausie, Savannah, Pixie-Bob and Toyger. Some of the cat hybrids are also notable because they may have involved crosses with non-domesticated cat species.

While initial crosses were touted as being healthier than the purebreds from which they were derived (so-called hybrid vigor), it is now recognized that these crosses can still concentrate liability genes and may develop their own predispositions to disease. Some of these diseases can even be detected with genetic screening in these hybrids.

Hybrids are typically created because breeders are trying to achieve a combination of features from those different breeds. So, the story goes that Labradoodles were initially created as guide dogs that have the features of a Labrador Retriever but the fur of a Poodle so that shedding is reduced (in an attempt to lower the risk of allergies in human caregivers). Unfortunately, purebred mixing for specific attributes does not always result in the desired physical or behavioral characteristics. Prior to Labradoodles, a variety of hybrids, such as cockapoos (cross between a Cocker Spaniel and a Poodle), were popular in their own right. In many cases, hybrids have become more fashion accessory than functional, and benefits of the mix are not always evident. It's a personal preference and choice.

Mixed Breeds

Mixed breeds are those that result from genetic interplay in animals of uncertain ancestry (and often uncertain parentage). They differ from both purebreds and hybrids in that they are typically not intentionally bred. Most commonly, mixed-breed pets result when a non-neutered animal gets access to and then mates with another non-neutered animal, and they produce a litter.

Mixed-breed pets have always posed a challenge to disease risk prediction, since without knowing breed contributions to a mixed-breed pet's ancestry, it can be difficult to predict any breed's predisposition to disease. This has been partially offset today by the ability to determine likely breed contributions on the basis of genetic testing. This is different from the genetic testing for disease variants and instead looks for genetic markers that can be associated with a variety of different breeds to help compile a picture of what breed markers may be assembled in a particular mixed-breed animal. The genetic testing will not determine breed ancestry with absolute precision, but it may be accurate enough to allow veterinary teams to consider some disease predisposition in individual pets. Genetic testing can also be used for disease screening of

Affenwich	=	Affenpinscher	x Norwich Terrier
Airedoodle	=	Airedale	x Poodle
Ausky	=	Australian Cattle Dog	x Siberian Husky
Aussiedoodle	=	Australian Shepherd	x Poodle
Baussie	=	Australian Shepherd	x Boston Terrier
Beabull	=	Bulldog	x Beagle
Biton	=	Bichon Frisé	x Coton de Tulear
Bogle	=	Beagle	x Boxer
Borkie	=	Bichon Frisé	x Yorkshire Terrier
Bowzer	=	Basset Hound	x Miniature Schnauzer
Cadoodle	=	Collie	x Poodle
Cavachon	=	Bichon Frisé	x Cav. King Charles Spaniel
Chorkie	=	Chihuahua	x Yorkshire Terrier
Chug	=	Chihuahua	x Pug
Cock-A-Poo	=	Cocker Spaniel	x Poodle
Corkie	=	Cocker Spaniel	x Yorkshire Terrier
Crustie	=	Chinese Crested	x Yorkshire Terrier
Daug	=	Dachshund	x Pug
Dorkie	=	Dachshund	x Yorkshire Terrier
Double Doodle	=	Goldendoodle	x Labradoodle
Eskland	=	American Eskimo	x Shetland Sheepdog
Goldendoodle	=	Golden Retriever	x Poodle
Jack-A-Bee	=	Beagle	x Jack Russell Terrier
Jug	=	Jack Russell Terrier	x Pug
Labradoodle	=	Labrador Retriever	x Poodle
Malt-A-Poo	=	Maltese	x Poodle
Mauxie	=	Dachshund	x Maltese
Morkie	=	Maltese	x Yorkshire Terrier
Muggin	=	Miniature Pinscher	x Pug
Peke-A-Boo	=	Bolognese	x Pekingese
Peke-A-Poo	=	Pekingese	x Poodle
Pekehund	=	Dachshund	x Pekingese
Pinny-Poo	=	Miniature Pinscher	x Poodle
Pitsky	=	American Pit Bull Terrier	x Siberian Husky
Poochon	=	Bichon Frisé	x Poodle
Poogle	=	Beagle	x Poodle
Pookimo	=	American Eskimo	x Poodle
Puggle	=	Beagle	x Pug
Rotterman	=	Doberman Pinscher	x Rottweiler
Schnoodle	=	Miniature Schnauzer	x Poodle
Sharbo	=	Boston Terrier	x Chinese Shar-Pei
Snorkie	=	Miniature Schnauzer	x Yorkshire Terrier
Spanador	=	Cocker Spaniel	x Labrador
Yorkinese	=	Pekingese	x Yorkshire Terrier
Zuchon	=	Bichon frisé	x Shih Tzu

Table 3.1. Just a few of the crosses that result in dog hybrids

Bengal	=	Domestic cat	x	Asian Leopard Cat
Bristol	=	Domestic cat	x	Margay
Chausie	=	Domestic cat	x	Jungle Cat
Cheetoh	=	Ocicat	x	Bengal
Havana Brown	=	Domestic black cat	x	Siamese
Highlander	=	Jungle Curl	x	Desert Lynx
Jungle	=	Bengal	x	Chausie
Jungle Bob	=	Pixie-Bob	x	Jungle cat
Kellas cat	=	Domestic cat	x	Scottish wildcat
Panterette	=	Pixie-Bob	x	Asian leopard cat
Pixie-Bob	=	Domestic cat	x	Bobcat
Punjabi	=	Domestic cat	x	Asian wildcat
Safari	=	Domestic cat	x	Geoffroy's cat
Savannah	=	Domestic cat	x	Serval
Serengeti	=	Oriental Shorthair	x	Bengal
Tonkinese	=	Siamese	x	Burmese
Toyger	=	Domestic cat	x	Bengal
Ussuri	=	Domestic cat	x	Amur leopard cat

Table 3.2. Just a few of the crosses that result in cat hybrids

certain medical problems and may even predict a variety of traits, such as the pet's likely size as an adult, coat characteristics, etc.

It's tempting to try to predict the breed composition of mixed-breed animals based on physical characteristics seen in the pet, but it is important to realize that this is not very accurate. When we adopt mixed-breed dogs and cats, there is often a temptation to ask the shelter staff, the veterinary team, or anyone else who will render an opinion, what breeds are likely in the animal's background. It's a fair question, but the fact is that when even experienced pet professionals offer a guess based on the shape of the head, the pet's size, the curl of the tail, or the color combinations, studies show that they are wrong at least as often as they are right. The only time more specific speculation is warranted is if the parents of the mixed-breed animal are known with certainty (e.g., neighbor's male pet jumped the fence and impregnated female pet).

In day-to-day life, speculating on a pet's ancestry is entertaining and harmless. However, guessing a pet's breed composition for medical purposes based on speculation about physical traits might lead us to consider—or more importantly, not consider—relevant risks for that specific pet. Presenting speculation as fact (i.e., a collie mix, Himalayan cross, etc.) is a concern when it is entered into veterinary medical records, as veterinary teams may use that information to recommend disease screening. Instead, in medical records we are better to stick with what we actually know (like using the term "mixed breed") and avoid introducing bias into the system by guessing the breed composition. Instead, when we have a pet that is of mixed heritage, and we really don't know with any certainty anything about the actual ancestry, it's best to just acknowledge this and admit our pets are "mixed." If preferred, there are also a lot of cute terms we can use instead, such as mutts for dogs or moggies for cats. Most people in our communities today are not of pure lineage and neither are our pets, so it's no slight to acknowledge the obvious. Consider other terms if they sound better, but having a varied ancestry is nothing to be ashamed of.

One other option exists if you hate the idea of having a term like mixed breed appear in your pet's veterinary medical record for all time. As was alluded to earlier, there are now DNA tests that help refine the breed composition question, at least to some extent. These tests provide some interesting information regarding the conservation of genetic markers but also have entertainment value in trying to unravel the mystery of your pet's ancestry. Such tests are great if you consider the results in context and appreciate that there are no specific DNA tests for any breed. The tests work by looking at many genetic markers which have statistical associations with certain recognized purebreds. It depends on the database and the number of representative animals in it. That's why you might send the same test to multiple laboratories and get somewhat different results, and why you might look at your pet and the results and think those results couldn't possibly be true (for example, how can this dog be the size of a small horse and the test says he is mainly Chihuahua?). Just like with human heritage tests, don't expect the impossible—they can only measure how closely certain genetic markers track to what populations they have defined in their databases. So, you might be an amateur genealogist and know that at least three generations of your ancestors were born and raised in Canada, but none of that shows up in a DNA heritage test. That's because there is no gene that reflects geography. When you move to a country, no matter how long you live there, nothing changes in your DNA. Similarly, there is no gene that reflects breed—there is no Beagle gene nor Siamese gene. In fact, even some purebreds may not be recognized as purebreds by such tests, depending on how closely their DNA markers match those in the reference population. Keep in mind that DNA heritage tests work by trying to match an individual's genetic markers with those of an ancestral population, at least as defined by the database accumulated. So, DNA tests may provide interesting information, but they do not magically enable us to determine breed contributions with certainty. After all, there is a good possibility that a mixed-breed pet had mixed-breed parents and even mixed-breed grandparents and so on, so there may not be any actual purebreds in the recent breeding history. Heritage tests will still determine genetic markers in the mix that match those in their reference populations and report results accordingly.

While purebreds and hybrids tend to have higher relative risk for some genetic disorders (especially traits attributable to single-gene mutations), it is important to realize that mixed-breed animals may still constitute a significant proportion of common health concerns in the total pet population (e.g., allergies, diabetes mellitus, osteoarthritis, obesity, etc.). This is no different from the situation in human medicine. There may be some ethnic groups with a higher prevalence for certain medical conditions, but that doesn't mean that most of us shouldn't be concerned with conditions that often run in families (high blood pressure, heart disease, cancer, etc.). The lesson to be learned from this is that all pets have risks for medical issues on the basis of their family history but that certain family histories may be more accessible than others. We do the best we can with the information we have. Knowledge of risk is helpful for planning, but it is not the sole criteria when choosing a new family member.

Sometimes, there is a tendency to recommend mixed-breed pets to prospective owners based on the fact that there are many more of these available in shelters that need homes. It is wonderful to rescue a mixed-breed dog or cat. Historically, mixed-breed pets were regarded as lower status than purebreds by many pet owners. Fortunately, times have changed. Many pet owners are proud of their animal's mixed-breed heritage, whether it is planned or happenstance. Geneticists have started to reject terms like "mixed breed" or "crossbreed" in favor of terms like "randomly bred" or "non-intentionally bred" to reflect the fact that intentional versus non-intentional breeding most influences genetic outcomes. That's really just a talking point for geneticists and not really a factor in the day-to-day life of living with a beloved pet.

Most pet owners have little concern about the labeling of their mixed-breed companions. Owners are happy enough with embracing comfortable terms for the products of such matings for dogs (mutt, mongrel, xbred, etc.) and cats (moggies, mutt cats, polycats, etc.). The terms domestic shorthair and domestic longhair are often used for cats of mixed ancestry, classified by their coat length. Such distinctions have become more important as so-called designer breeds have arisen from the intentional mating of two different breeds to achieve a hybrid. It is important to consider that it is not the unintentional mating of two animals that confers health; often, it is the intentional act of selecting two individuals with preferred traits (and few to no disease genes) to hopefully produce offspring with desirable (usually physical) outcomes (size, color, conformation, etc.). This is not necessarily something that can be achieved just by chance. After all, existing breeds themselves are the result of artificial selection, using genetic pressure by intentional breeding to create traits based on conformation, coat characteristics/colors, and behaviors. It just so happens that in some of that selection pressure, certain heritable conditions also got concentrated in those animals. Certain influential ancestors that were commonly included in pedigrees because of their desirable "good" genes may also have served to concentrate certain "bad" genes in specific purebred populations.

It is also important to realize that there are many reasons why some prefer to bring purebreds and hybrids into their homes. You do you. After all, there are often traits that people prefer in their pets, whether those traits reflect pets they have owned in the past, pets they have seen in movies or on the Internet, or recommendations they have received from influencers (veterinarians, friends, breed selectors, etc.). All pets, regardless of their heritage, deserve to be in loving homes. Whichever you choose to adopt, help keep them healthy, happy and *almost* perfect throughout their lives.

Hybrid Vigor: Is It Real?

In any discussion of health issues in dogs and cats, there is sometimes an assumption that animals of mixed heritage are likely to be healthier than purebreds because of something known as hybrid vigor. Hybrid vigor, or heterosis, is a term meant to imply that there are potential health benefits associated with the crossbreeding of different animals and that mixing up the gene pool somehow dilutes the impact of bad genes that might be concentrated in purebreds. However, it's really the advantage of having a large gene pool rather than a mixed gene pool that confers genetic benefits, and many pets, including purebreds, mixed breeds and hybrids, can carry so-called liability genes (genetic factors that contribute to the manifestation of complexly inherited conditions) for many different heritable disorders (hip dysplasia, atopic dermatitis, patellar luxation, cryptorchidism, feline lower urinary tract disease, etc.). Since many of these common diseases are associated with ancient disease liability genes in the species, many that preceded the relatively recent evolution of most purebreds and hybrids, those genes are widely disseminated in the entire pet population and can be seen in any pet. This is significant because, while the odds of a specific purebred

Let's all sleep together (courtesy Katrina O'Gahan).

developing a defined heritable problem may be higher than it occurring in a mixed breed (by virtue of the fact that there are so many more mixed-breed animals than any specific purebred), it is not unusual that most cases are actually seen in these mixed breeds compared to any specific purebred.

We might think of purebreds going back in history for thousands of years but, in reality, most purebreds were created by intentional breeding in just the last few hundred years by concentrating the genes of certain ancient ancestors and removing individuals that didn't conform to a certain "standard" and preventing them from participating in the gene pool. However, this lack of genetic diversity does not necessarily make these animals less healthy. In fact, problem genes can become concentrated in randomly bred animals as well as intentionally bred animals, and there are many examples of non-domesticated species proceeding to extinction without any apparent benefit from hybrid vigor. Nobody was breeding dodo birds poorly; they went extinct on their own in the wild and that genetic freedom did not save them. In the end, it is not the purity of the breeding animals that affects health outcomes; it is the relative accumulation of disease liability genes in the breeding population of purebreds, hybrids and mixed breeds.

The Big Picture

Even in pets that are of mixed heritage, inherited diseases happen when animals with disease liability genes have the opportunity to breed and contribute their genetic material to future generations. The most common conditions seen (e.g., allergies, diabetes, thyroid disorders) are influenced by multiple genes and often multiple environmental factors. This nuanced multifactorial pattern of disease risk has sometimes been colorfully described by scientists as follows—genes may load the gun, but environment pulls the trigger. That is, you might have a genetic predisposition to certain diseases, but most chronic diseases are not entirely controlled by genes; they are often profoundly influenced by environmental and lifestyle factors. There are also, however, diseases that are transferred as single genetic traits (monogenic traits) in which a gene variant is inherited from each parent and influences specific processes. In many cases those disease traits are recessive, and so individuals that carry only one gene mutation (genes occur in pairs) from either parent appear outwardly normal; with recessive disorders, it's only in animals in which both genes in a pair are affected that the problem becomes evident. Because of this, normal-appearing "carriers" with only one undesirable gene variant can still be successful genetic influencers and pass both good and bad genes to their descendants. Thus, if a particular animal (purebred, hybrid or mixed breed) is successful at producing offspring but has an underlying risk of health issues that aren't apparent (that is, the pet appears fine), those beneficial and not-so-beneficial traits are likely to be passed to future generations. On the other hand, in comparison to recessive traits, dominant traits are observable even if a genetic variant is transferred from only one parent.

The problem with most genetic diseases is that the gene mutations don't become apparent until diseases are recognized in individual animals (unless genetic screening is done). This happens because many disease genes that were present in the ancient dog and cat populations are still present in purebred, hybrid and mixed-breed animals today. Where a difference is observed is in the purebred populations in which some of the rare genetic diseases (e.g., hemophilia, cerebellar ataxia, dystrophic epidermolysis bullosa, gangliosidosis, etc.) managed to inadvertently get concentrated in specific breeding lines, often because an "influencer" with otherwise good features was intentionally bred and happened to have some bad genetic traits in addition to the good ones intentionally concentrated. Because carriers of recessive traits appear unaffected themselves, it is usually not until enough carriers are present in the breeding population that the likelihood increases that two carriers get bred together so that offspring with the disease variant become detectable, having inherited a disease variant from both normal-appearing parents.

Because so many common conditions (atopic dermatitis, crypt-orchidism, diabetes mellitus, hip dysplasia, thyroid disorders, bladder "stones," etc.) are so widely disseminated, all pets should be appropriately screened. It is true that the prevalence may be higher in certain purebreds than the general population, but since the actual number of mixed-breed animals in the total population is much larger than the population of any one breed, it is worth screening all dogs and cats, not just purebreds, for those common disorders while screening only specific breeds at risk for those rarer disorders seen almost entirely in purebreds and hybrids.

Accordingly, mixed-breed pets should be screened in the same manner as purebreds and hybrids for the conditions most commonly seen in all animals. Screening for the rarer and breed-specific disorders (e.g., intervertebral disk disease, cystinuria, muscular dystrophy, etc.) can be reserved for those animals at higher risk.

The good news for potential pet owners is that it is possible to completely avoid most of the disorders for which genetic testing is available if you select a pet from a litter in which the parents have already been tested. Most household pets today are not going to be intentionally bred, and the majority are neutered, so they don't typically contribute their genes to future generations. Thus, the purpose of screening is for the health benefits of your particular pet and not necessarily for the benefit of future generations, because your pet likely won't be bred. Because of this, even if a pet has one undesirable variant in a gene pair for a recessive disorder, that one mutation is not enough to cause disease in the individual and that individual can still make a great pet. So, the situation is completely different if you are just worried about your own pet's health versus the concerns you might have if you intended to breed and contribute your pet's genes to future generations.

There is one more aspect of genetic testing that might be beyond the scope of this book, but we're going to mention it anyway. Nowadays, it is easy to run a genetic panel that will literally test for hundreds of genetic variants with a single sample. This provides great value and a lot of results, but you likely need some help from your veterinary team in putting the results into context. That's because not all mutations (variants) or markers that are meaningful in some breeds are necessarily meaningful in all breeds. Some are more difficult to interpret unless there is a known gene association with clinical disease in specific

Bonnie (courtesy Katrina O'Gahan).

breeds. So, we know that the SOD1 test for a disease called degenerative myelopathy is significant in a handful of breeds in which it predicts animals likely to be affected with a debilitating spinal disease; we are less sure what it means when the test is positive in a breed or mixed breed in which that association between the mutation and the disease has not been documented. When this happens, wait for your veterinary team to help you interpret the results before you panic. A "carrier" or even "affected" result may not mean what you think it does when it occurs in a breed for which there is no known disease association.

To put things in perspective, there are a variety of rare genetic diseases that may become not so rare when concentrated in certain lines of purebreds, but also a lot of more common conditions that are at least partially inherited and that can be seen in any dog or cat (see Table 3.3). When it comes to testing, there are more likely to be DNA tests for the rarer disorders, since they are more likely to be controlled by mutations in a single-gene pair. The more common disorders, on the other hand, are likely to have more complex inheritance (multiple genes, environmental factors, etc.), and they are more likely to require screening based on blood work, urine tests, imaging, etc. The same is true for humans. We are familiar with single-gene disorders such as cystic fibrosis, sickle cell disease, and muscular dystrophy, and they are definitely worth screening for, but when it comes to the most common diseases we see in people, these single-gene disorders are far less common than more complexly inherited disorders such as high cholesterol, allergies, diabetes, high blood pressure, depression, etc. One group is easier to test for if the

Dog	Cat
Behavioral issues	Behavioral issues
Cancer	Cancer
Mitral valve disease	Feline Lower Urinary Tract Disease
Hip dysplasia	Osteoarthritis
Cranial cruciate ligament rupture	Eosinophilic syndromes
Patellar luxation	Kidney failure
Hyperadrenocorticism	Hyperthyroidism
Hypoadrenocorticism	Inflammatory bowel disease
Hypothyroidism	Upper respiratory infections
Diabetes mellitus	Diabetes mellitus
Lens luxation	Odontoclastic resorptive lesions
Urolithiasis	Urolithiasis

Table 3.3. Conditions commonly seen in all types of dogs and cats

genetic variants are known, but the other group actually poses higher risks to the entire population.

Final Thoughts

One of the major reasons for so much discussion about purebreds, mixed breeds and hybrids is that everyone seems to have an opinion about which one prospective pet owners should choose. In reality, your choice is a personal decision. There is sometimes a temptation to make a politically correct choice, but when you are actually selecting a pet that you will share your life with for a decade or more, it's absolutely acceptable to have your personal preferences.

Yes, it's true that there are a lot of pets already in the world that are in need of homes and that there may not be a specific need to breed more. It's also true that some individuals just enjoy the features of purebreds, may have fond memories of growing up with one, or are drawn to specific aspects of their behaviors or characteristics. The hybrids have appeal for individuals who are looking for something novel or the features promised in such a combination. There is no need to feel guilty. Whichever type of pet you choose, love it and pledge to work toward *almost* perfect status.

Case Example

Jezebel Garcia is a two-year-old Frug (a cross between a purebred French Bulldog and a purebred Pug, also known as a Frenchie Pug). Her mom, Gloria Garcia, chose her because she loved the adorable "designer dog" that she first learned about online. Gloria brought her spunky new pet to Dr. Aronson at ABC Veterinary Hospital for routine health assessment and vaccination. Dr. Aronson determined Jezebel to be a healthy specimen but recommended orthopedic screening for hip dysplasia, in addition to some other routine diagnostic testing.

Gloria was surprised by the recommendation, believing that not only was hip dysplasia a condition of large dogs, but that since Jezebel was a hybrid (she preferred the term designer breed), she assumed that the risk for genetic diseases would be very low. Dr. Aronson and the veterinary team spent time educating Gloria about hip dysplasia. They explained that not only was hip dysplasia a condition that could be seen in any size and breed of dog but that actually both Pugs and French Bulldogs were at increased risk for the condition. They recommended orthopedic screening for all dogs at 2 years of age, and while there was a good chance that Jezebel could be clear on radiographs (x-rays), it was still worth assessing her for it so that if there were problems, they would start addressing them early.

Gloria said she would take some time to think about it, and the hospital team provided her some information on the topic and some links to online resources. Gloria scoured the Internet for everything she could learn about her new favorite designer breed. After learning more, Gloria decided that the screening was in Jezebel's best interest, as early detection of any problem would allow for better management if a problem were to be discovered. As it turned out, Jezebel did have some early evidence of hip dysplasia, and the team went over an action plan for how they would help deal with any consequences of the situation. Gloria was thankful that she had decided to be proactive, based on pet care customized to the specific needs of her adorable pet. She was appreciative that the hospital team had provided her with everything she needed to be an informed pet health advocate.

Recommended Reading

Ackerman, L. 2020. *Proactive Pet Parenting: Anticipating Pet Health Problems Before They Happen*. Problem Free Publishing.

Ackerman, L., ed. 2021a. *Pet-Specific Care*. Hoboken, NJ: Wiley.

_____. 2011. *The Genetic Connection, 2nd Edition*. Lakewood, CO: AAHA Press.

Bell, Jerold, Kathleen Cavanagh, Larry Tilley, and Francis Smith. 2012. *Veterinary Medical Guide to Dog and Cat Breeds*. Teton Newmedia.

Bellumori, Thomas P., Thomas R. Famula, Danika L. Bannasch, Janelle M. Belanger, and Anita M. Oberbauer. 2013. "Prevalence of Inherited Disorders Among Mixed-Breed and Purebred Dogs: 27,254 Cases (1995–2010)." *Journal of the American Veterinary Medical Association* 242 (11): 1549–55. https://doi.org/10.2460/javma.242.11.1549.

Donner, Jonas, Heidi Anderson, Stephen Davison, Angela M. Hughes, Julia Bouirmane,

Johan Lindqvist, Katherine M. Lytle, et al. 2018. "Frequency and Distribution of 152 Genetic Disease Variants in Over 100,000 Mixed Breed and Purebred Dogs." Edited by Tosso Leeb. *PLOS Genetics* 14 (4): e1007361. https://doi.org/10.1371/journal.pgen.1007361.

Gough, Alex, Alison Thomas, and Dan G. O'Neill. 2018. *Breed Predispositions to Disease in Dogs and Cats*. 3rd edition. Hoboken: Wiley Blackwell.

4

Personalizing Health Care for Pets (Pet-Specific Care)

Just like people, all pets are different … and their health care needs are different, too. To achieve problem-free pet status regarding health, you'll need to be able to customize care to the needs of your particular furry friend. Yes, all pets will need regular veterinary examinations, vaccination and parasite control, but most pets have unique risk factors that should be addressed if we want to keep them healthy and happy for as long as possible.

In standard models of health care, pets often receive routine care until they get sick, and then pet owners seek veterinary attention. That's a very reactive model and is unsatisfactory for several reasons. The fact is that other than trauma and infectious diseases, most medical problems don't occur suddenly, and while they are brewing, there are usually no outward clues. So, pets that eventually develop chronic conditions such as diabetes mellitus, kidney disease, arthritis and heart disease often appear relatively fine until the body can no longer compensate, and only then the problem becomes evident. Also, pets can't really communicate when they first start feeling less than optimal, so we don't often notice a problem until the condition has been going on for quite a while. For example, we may not notice the prediabetic pet when it is just drinking a bit more water, but it really gets our attention when it starts having "accidents" in the house, and by that point, the diabetes is typically well established. It's easy to miss increased blood pressure (hypertension) in cats as they age, and sometimes blindness occurs before the problem is recognized and treated. Make no mistake about it—over a lifetime, chronic problems account for more quality-of-life issues than all other medical problems combined (infections, accidents, etc.).

Most pet owners can appreciate that cats are not small dogs, and they can also understand that the care of a Great Dane is likely different from that of a Chihuahua. Still, there is not a lot of information out there explaining how pets have very individual health care needs and that the care they receive should be personalized. In fact, even pets of the same breed and living in the same home may have different health care needs.

Personalizing health care is all about being proactive rather than reactive and appreciating what risks are most relevant for an individual animal. We'll go into more detail about why it is important to identify problems as soon as possible in the chapter on early detection, but in this chapter we're going to explore how to know what you should be on the lookout for in your particular pet. Pet-specific care might be regarded as "the right care, for the right pet, at the right time."

Pet-specific care involves approaches that allow predictions to be made as to an individual's susceptibility to issues, possible prevention, prospects for early detection, the course of that disease, and a disease's likely response to treatment. That care is all about managing risks, and so it is important to appreciate why those risks exist and what can be done about them. Of course, we also have health care risks, and sometimes we don't necessarily heed those risks, but there is always the prospect that we might do better with our pets (and children) than we do with ourselves. If you have a family history of heart disease, if you smoke, if you are carrying too much extra weight—all of these can be risk factors, and it is in our best interest to recognize them and do what we can to reduce or eliminate those risks. Our pets are no different.

The goal of pet-specific care is to prevent disease, if at all possible, or to decrease the impact of the disease on the pet, thereby improving the pet's quality of life. This is typically accomplished by identifying risk factors so we can be proactive in instituting lifestyle modifications to hopefully change the trajectory of the disease. It also involves increasing veterinary surveillance so that problems can be detected at the earliest opportunity, hopefully while they are still just emerging, and when there are typically the most options available for successful management.

If you think this approach is very similar to new models of human health care, you are absolutely right. Medicine is changing with the realization that everyone has slightly different susceptibility to disease (and response to medications) and requires individualized screening and counseling. If you have certain genetic factors for specific conditions, you will have different screening recommendations than someone who does not have those factors. If you smoke, you have different health risks than those who don't (although secondary and even tertiary exposure to smoke can adversely affect people and pets). If you have a family history of certain issues, you have risk factors that will be different than those who do not.

Pet-specific care is a powerful tool to stay ahead of problems, but it is not a new concept in health care. In fact, you are probably familiar with it under a different name. Pet-specific care may also be referred to as

- personalized medicine;
- precision medicine;
- pet-centric care;
- client-centric care;
- lifelong care;
- lifetime of care;
- theranostics;
- stratified medicine;
- predictive medicine;
- patient-specific medicine;
- P4 medicine;
- genomic medicine; or
- individualized medicine.

Whatever name you prefer, the concepts of pet-specific care are the same—understanding an individual's risk for developing problems, preventing them when possible, identifying them before they become problematic through early detection and, if they do develop, treating them appropriately with the pet's well-being in mind.

Why Embrace a New Approach?

You might wonder why there is a need for a different approach. After all, veterinary teams have been doing a pretty good job of taking care of pets for years without this pet-specific approach. That's true, but times have changed and, just as we expect human medicine to change to better meet our needs and care expectations, we can expect our pet's veterinary care to evolve, too. Recognizing that people are not all alike, human health care has embraced personalized medicine as an improved model of care. Shouldn't we want the same for our beloved furry family members? The new pet-specific care approach is focused on providing appropriate care by moving from a reactive approach where we wait until problems occur and then treat them, to a proactive approach focused on prevention and early intervention that supports better health outcomes for our pets. Pet-specific care allows our beloved furry family members to enjoy happier and healthier lives.

In the abstract, it may be hard to understand the difference between the reactive model of care and the proactive model of pet-specific care. So, let's illustrate this philosophy with a common example—arthritis (joint inflammation). Arthritis is a common debilitating condition in people as well as pets and, in most cases, it progresses over time. In our pets, some of the most common reasons for arthritis are underlying hereditary conditions such as hip dysplasia, elbow dysplasia, cranial cruciate disease, and an inflammatory disease known as osteochondritis dissecans. These underlying conditions affect specific joints, causing inflammation and pain. Over time, permanent crippling joint damage occurs. It is important to note that both humans and animals can often accept and adjust to both the discomfort and inconvenience in the early stages of arthritis, but that is often the best time to intervene—before permanent damage occurs.

In the current reactive model, the care process will likely proceed along a familiar route. Initially, you might notice that your pet has difficulty rising from bed or has some discomfort when jumping on or off the furniture or shows other signs of mild discomfort. You might even be relieved when it seems to be a bit better after a walk or exercise—until after resting, when the problem is evident again and may even be worse. In cats, you might not notice anything amiss, even in cats with active arthritic disease. Arthritis tends to progress slowly, so sometimes you don't get a full appreciation that the situation is worsening. At some point, you visit your veterinary team with your pet, they do radiographs (x-rays), and they may tell you your pet has permanent arthritic changes in the joints and underlying evidence of a developmental disease (such as hip dysplasia) that was the likely cause. There are a variety of medications that can be used to help control the pain and inflammation, and if that is not adequate, there is always surgery. That's the current reactive model.

Pet-specific care offers a proactive approach. If we know that most cases of arthritis (specifically osteoarthritis, which is also known as degenerative joint disease) occur because of underlying developmental orthopedic diseases that are often inherited, we can approach the situation differently. We do not have to passively wait for problems to occur. Instead, we can screen for those underlying disorders early—before they end up causing arthritis and permanent joint damage. To start, if we follow the advice in the pet selection chapter, we will try to adopt pets that have a lower risk of developing these inherited developmental disorders. Then, we could either screen all pets by 2 years of age for evidence of developmental disorders (some tests even allow screening for hip dysplasia by as early as 4 months of age), or at the very least, screen those breeds known to be at especially high risk, as we will explore in the chapter on early detection. Or, we might screen most pets by 2 years of age but do very early screening in pets with a family history or of a breed known to be at increased risk.

Nubs stretching out (courtesy Katrina O'Gahan).

If we can identify pets early enough, we can plan interventions such as dietary change, weight reduction, exercise programs to strengthen supporting muscle groups, nutritional supplementation, and physiotherapy to delay the inflammatory problem from actually doing permanent damage to the joints. Arthritis tends to be a progressive degenerative disorder, so the further into the future we can push its effects, the better off we are. The differences between these two models of care are enormous—in the traditional, reactive model, permanent damage has typically occurred before we even begin to provide care, while in the proactive pet-specific care model, we are able to focus on supporting a healthy, pain-free life for the pet for as long as possible, perhaps indefinitely.

While the example of arthritis is convenient, it is important to realize that this type of chronic process is common with many common disorders seen in dogs and cats, including periodontal disease, heart disease, kidney disease, and many others. For some of these disorders, such as periodontal disease, early intervention done before there is irreversible damage can change the entire trajectory of the disease. That's why routine dental care is so important for us as well as our pets. For other conditions, such as heart disease, it is not always possible to completely eliminate risk, but early intervention provides the most chance for successful long-term management.

As discussed above, arthritis often results from wear and tear on the joints, but in pets it is not unusual that there are underlying inherited contributing disorders. In a perfect scenario, we can determine the risk for those underlying problems based on family history, but that is not always available. So, we typically rely on general orthopedic screening, perhaps with an increased focus on pets believed to be at higher risk based on breed predisposition. It's worth mentioning here that when it comes to inherited orthopedic diseases, it is important that we use actual medical evidence about risk and not our personal bias. Many people tend to think of hip dysplasia as a condition of large dogs, but this is actually a misconception. It's not the size of the animal that increases the risk of hip dysplasia but whether or not there is a genetic predisposition and family history. Hip dysplasia is common in some large breeds (e.g., German Shepherd Dog, Rottweiler, Great Dane, etc.) but is also seen in smaller dog breeds (e.g., Pug, French Bulldog, Shih Tzu, etc.) and even cats. The risks start with having a genetic predisposition based on family history, and then a variety of nongenetic factors (diet, growth rate, exercise, etc.) determine how the condition progresses (remember the old adage: genes may load the gun, but environment pulls the trigger). The relative balance of nature and nurture is not typically known for most animals, and the heritability of a condition like hip dysplasia can vary from 25 percent to 75 percent.

Other than inherited problems, are there other situations that should make us more vigilant for the increased probability of arthritis in our pets? Yes! In addition to underlying problems that may be heritable (such as hip dysplasia), pets with prior history of trauma (hit by car, fractures, etc.), those with other medical conditions that may predispose them to osteoarthritis (nutritional imbalances, infections of the bones and joints, hormonal disorders, etc.) and even those that are overweight or obese may be at increased risk and benefit from early screening. These risk factors should prompt us to evaluate for osteoarthritis earlier and more consistently, but since all pets can develop arthritis, and it usually presents first in young adult to middle-aged pets, routine screening should probably be done for all pets earlier rather than later.

Maintenance Schedules

In Chapter 1, the concept of maintenance schedules was introduced. When you buy a new car, it comes with a maintenance schedule of when service is required on the basis of regular use of a specified vehicle. You probably wouldn't be surprised that the maintenance of a Porsche might be different from that of a Toyota and that actual maintenance is likely to vary based on how the vehicle is used. Pets are no different, and they benefit from a schedule of when and what care is anticipated, given the circumstances of a specific pet and owner. The schedule should be based on general prevention guidelines, but it should also be personalized with information about your individual pet and its lifestyle. It is also important that schedules be periodically updated because health care is a dynamic process and situations change. An example of a maintenance schedule can be seen in Figure 4.1.

It may seem complicated to create a maintenance schedule for each of your pets, but it really isn't, and your veterinary team can provide a lot of support to help get the job done. The first place to start is with preventive medicine and that involves the visits recommended by your veterinary team for routine care, sometime referred to as wellness visits. That typically also includes specific times for tasks such as microchip implantation, genetic testing, and reproductive control, for which your veterinary team can provide more specific age recommendations. Some of these wellness visits will warrant vaccination, or possibly vaccine titers, which are tests that help predict when vaccine boosters are needed. The next step is to include all the testing required for parasite control, which might include fecal testing for internal parasites, heart-worm testing, and blood tests to screen for tick-transmitted diseases. Finally, the schedule is populated with early-detection testing based on individual risk factors. Most pets at some point will need screening for orthopedic diseases, and many pets will warrant surveillance testing for a variety of diseases for which they may have risk factors. Now—that really wasn't so difficult—was it?

Playing Detective

At its core, pet-specific care is about balancing risk and reward. If we can determine that a pet may be at increased risk of developing a problem, and if early intervention can help us achieve better long-term outcomes, then the effort is worthwhile. On the other hand, if the like-lihood of benefit is low, or if the risk is low, then we are better to con-centrate our efforts elsewhere. So, for example, if you are raising your pet in Tucson, Arizona, and it develops lameness that may be consis-tent with arthritis, your veterinary team might find it worthwhile to also screen for the fungal disease coccidioidomycosis (known locally as Valley Fever), which is common in this part of the world and can infect bones and joints. On the other hand, if you live with your pet in Man-chester, New Hampshire (or London, England, or Toronto, Canada), there is little need for testing for this particular fungal infection unless you have traveled to somewhere with your pet where it might have been exposed.

Pet-specific care is all about managing risks, so the very first step typically involves assessing pets for risks based on their individual cir-cumstances. In most cases, this assessment first happens during puppy and kitten visits, often at around 8 weeks of age. Your veterinary team may pose several questions about your lifestyle—not to be nosy but to have a better idea of what risk factors may be pertinent for your pet. You can see an example of a risk assessment form in Figure 4.2. If your veter-inarian doesn't use a particular risk assessment form, there are many for you to choose from on the Internet, and it will help focus your attention on the cause-and-effect relationship that exists between our individual pets and the problems for which they might carry risk. Sometimes we can substantially reduce risk with lifestyle changes (for example, we can almost eliminate the risk of infection with feline leukemia virus if our cats are not allowed to be in contact with other cats), and in other cases

Age	Human Age (Approx.)	Needs
2-8 weeks		Fecal parasite testing; parasite control
8 weeks		Congenital disease screening (cataracts, umbilical hernia, malocclusion, luxating patellae, heart murmur, etc.); Risk Assessment; Start monthly parasite prevention; Microchipping, Start pet health insurance
6-16 weeks		Initial vaccination series
12 weeks		Genetic screening (including GR PRA 1 & 2, progressive rod-cone degeneration, Ichthyosis A, dystrophic epidermolysis bullosa, neuronal ceroid lipofuscinosis, osteogenesis imperfecta, skeletal dysplasia, degenerative myelopathy, etc.)
16 weeks		Create Personalized care plan based on risk assessment, genotypic and phenotypic assessment
26 weeks	6 years	Neutering surgery, dental evaluation, fecal parasite testing, congenital disease screening; heartworm prevention
1 year	12 years	Adult re-evaluation; vaccine boosters/titers as needed; parasite check; baseline hemogram, biochemistry, thyroid screening and urinalysis; cardiac evaluation
1.5 years	16 years	Mid-year evaluation; dental evaluation with radiographs/cleaning as needed
2 years	19 years	Adult re-evaluation; vaccine boosters/titers as needed; parasite check; orthopedic screening (hips, elbows), cardiac and ophthalmologic evaluation
2.5 years	24 years	Mid-year evaluation; dental evaluation with radiographs/cleaning as needed
3 years	26 years	Primary re-evaluation; vaccine boosters/titers as needed; parasite check; baseline hemogram, biochemistry, thyroid screening and urinalysis; cardiac evaluation
3.5 years	28 years	Mid-year evaluation; dental evaluation with radiographs/cleaning as needed
4 years	32 years	Primary re-evaluation; vaccine boosters/titers as needed; parasite check; ophthalmic evaluation
4.5 years	36 years	Mid-year evaluation; dental evaluation with radiographs/cleaning as needed
5 years	40 years	Primary re-evaluation; vaccine boosters/titers as needed; parasite check; baseline hemogram, biochemistry, thyroid screening and urinalysis; cardiac evaluation
5.5 years	44 years	Mid-year evaluation; dental evaluation with radiographs/cleaning as needed
6 years	48 years	Primary re-evaluation; vaccine boosters/titers as needed; parasite check; senior evaluation
6.5 years	52 years	Mid-year evaluation; dental evaluation with radiographs/cleaning as needed
7 years	54 years	Primary re-evaluation; vaccine boosters/titers as needed; parasite check; senior evaluation
7.5 years	56 years	Mid-year evaluation; dental evaluation with radiographs/cleaning as needed
8 years	60 years	Primary re-evaluation; vaccine boosters/titers as needed; parasite check; senior evaluation
8.5 years	63 years	Mid-year evaluation; dental evaluation with radiographs/cleaning as needed
9 years	66 years	Primary re-evaluation; vaccine boosters/titers as needed; parasite check; senior evaluation
9.5 years	69 years	Mid-year evaluation; dental evaluation with radiographs/cleaning as needed
10 years	72 years	Primary re-evaluation; vaccine boosters/titers as needed; parasite check; senior evaluation
10.5 years	75 years	Mid-year evaluation; dental evaluation with radiographs/cleaning as needed
11 years	78 years	Primary re-evaluation; vaccine boosters/titers as needed; parasite check; geriatric evaluation
11.5 years	80 years	Mid-year evaluation; dental evaluation with radiographs/cleaning as needed
12 years	82 years	Primary re-evaluation; vaccine boosters/titers as needed; parasite check; geriatric evaluation
12.5 years	84 years	Mid-year evaluation; dental evaluation with radiographs/cleaning as needed
13 years	86 years	Primary re-evaluation; vaccine boosters/titers as needed; parasite check; geriatric evaluation
13.5 years	88 years	Mid-year evaluation; dental evaluation with radiographs/cleaning as needed
14 years	90 years	Primary re-evaluation; vaccine boosters/titers as needed; parasite check; geriatric evaluation
14.5 years	92 years	Mid-year evaluation; dental evaluation with radiographs/cleaning as needed
15 years	94 years	Primary re-evaluation; vaccine boosters/titers as needed; parasite check; geriatric evaluation
15.5 years	96 years	Mid-year evaluation; dental evaluation with radiographs/cleaning as needed
16 years	98 years	Primary re-evaluation; vaccine boosters/titers as needed; parasite check; geriatric evaluation
16.5 years	100 years	Mid-year evaluation; dental evaluation with radiographs/cleaning as needed
17 years	102 years	Primary re-evaluation; vaccine boosters/titers as needed; parasite check; geriatric evaluation

Figure 4.1. Example of a maintenance schedule for a specific pet

we may need intervention (e.g., vaccination) or surveillance (periodic testing) and treatment.

All animals have certain risks that pertain to their individual circumstances. By acknowledging and prioritizing risks, we can craft meaningful personalized action plans (maintenance schedules) for each pet. This also helps us budget for likely care to be needed or consider

Risk Assessment Form

Pet's Name: Date of Birth:
Breed:
Gender: ☐ Male   ☐ Female   Neutered: ☐ Y   ☐ N

Has genetic testing been run on your pet or its parents? Results?   ☐ Y   ☐ N
Has this pet or its parents been included in a breed registry   ☐ Y   ☐ N
for heritable diseases (hip dysplasia, eye diseases, etc.)? Results?
What other testing has been done to date?

Any family history of any of the following (please check all that apply)?
☐ Arthritis   ☐ Atopic dermatitis (allergies) ☐ Glaucoma   ☐ Heart Disease
☐ Kidney Disease   ☐ Seizure disorders   ☐ Thyroid disorders ☐ Urinary tract "stones"

Family history of any other specific medical conditions?   ☐ Y   ☐ N
Please list.

What food are you currently feeding?

What medications/supplements are you currently giving?

What parasite control are you currently providing?

Are you doing any home dental care (brushing, rinses, etc.)?   ☐ Y   ☐ N
Your perception of your pet: ☐ Below ideal weight ☐ Ideal weight ☐ Above ideal weight

Does your pet ever sleep with you, or share your bed?   ☐ Y   ☐ N
Does your pet ever travel outside this immediate region?   ☐ Y   ☐ N
Does your pet come in contact with other people's pets?   ☐ Y   ☐ N
Does your pet ever visit a groomer or boarding facility?   ☐ Y   ☐ N
Does your pet ever go to pet shows or other pet events?   ☐ Y   ☐ N
Does your pet ever go to parks/fields/gardens/wooded areas?   ☐ Y   ☐ N
Is your pet a patient at more than one veterinary hospital?   ☐ Y   ☐ N
Does your pet ever have an opportunity to drink from water outdoors, such ☐ Y   ☐ N
as from ponds, puddles, water bowls, rivers or creeks?

What other types of pets do you have in your household?
☐ Dogs   ☐ Cats   ☐ Birds   ☐ Others _____

Figure 4.2. Example of a risk assessment questionnaire for pet owners

other options, such as pet health insurance. Regarding pet health insurance (which will be covered in more detail in the chapter on affordability), it is important to realize that coverage will only be granted if insurance is in place before a problem is actually diagnosed. Once a problem has been identified and is considered "preexisting," it will be excluded from coverage in almost all insurance policies. Accordingly, it is most beneficial to put insurance in place while pets appear completely healthy and when there is nothing that would be considered preexisting.

Predisposition to Disease

For most pets, family history, genetics and breed predisposition are significant contributors to disease susceptibility. This is true whether the pet is a purebred, hybrid, or mixed breed. For many purebreds and hybrids, there is often specific medical risks that can be identified. This may be a bit more complicated for hybrids (designer pets), but predispositions have been identified for many, and there is some possibility that they could have inherited issues seen in both contributing purebred parents. In many instances, when a pet is mixed breed (mutts and moggies) and the parents have not been identified with certainty, it may be difficult to discern any type of predisposition because we rarely have family history. Also, while genetic testing is very helpful in this regard, it is also important to realize that the hereditary health problems that are most common in both dogs and cats of all breeds (e.g., allergies, thyroid disorders, heart diseases, cancers, etc.) are typically more complexly inherited, and definitive DNA tests for these conditions are not as commonly available or diagnosis-specific.

Exposure risks are another significant contributor to disease susceptibility. This category includes both problems that are common regionally and risks our pets have from exposure to others that could be carrying diseases. For example, a pet exposed to many other pets will be at increased risk for infectious diseases (e.g., distemper, parvovirus, rhinotracheitis virus, etc.) and, potentially, parasite transmission (roundworm, hookworm, fleas, etc.). A pet that has access to wooded areas may be exposed to ticks that may introduce tick-related infections to the pet (Lyme disease, ehrlichiosis, Rocky Mountain spotted fever, etc.). Many infectious and parasitic disorders can vary in prevalence based on region, so make sure your veterinary team is aware if your pet travels outside of its typical residential region.

Geography plays a significant role in disease susceptibility, partially because it influences infectious diseases that are present in the area, or the vectors (insects, vermin, etc.) that are associated with their transmission. For example, heartworm is transmitted by mosquitoes, so if you are in an area that has both mosquitoes and heartworm, mosquitoes can feed on a pet infected with heartworm and then pass the infection to other pets through their bites ... even if your pet never goes outside (we've all spent half an hour trying to kill a mosquito that entered our home uninvited. You know it's true). To keep pets problem free, it is not important that you are necessarily aware of all the diseases in your area but that you share your lifestyle information with your veterinary team, so they can help keep both you and your pet adequately protected.

When creating maintenance schedules, as mentioned above, it is also important that your veterinary team knows whether or not your pet is likely to travel outside your immediate residential region, so they can help you plan appropriately.

Susceptibility to medical problems is also influenced by life stages and preexisting conditions. For example, an umbilical hernia is more likely to be evident in a young pet, while most cases of glaucoma present during adulthood. Regarding preexisting conditions, we have already discussed how a pet with early evidence of hip dysplasia will be more

Being proactive is important. Since this breed can develop joint problems later in life, we provided her with soft but supportive beds right from the beginning (courtesy Janice Adams).

likely to develop arthritis later in life. That's why we want to identify those pets early, when we have a better chance of putting programs in place of making it less likely the pet will experience debilitating problems in its future. When it comes to life stages, there are published guidelines (see Recommended Reading), but these do change from time to time, and they are not consistent even between dogs and cats. We can most easily appreciate the life stages that describe the care needed in early life (puppy and kitten life stage) as well as old age (senior life stage), realizing that there is some variability between breeds, especially for dogs. The puppy or active growth stage might be completed by 6–8 months in some smaller breeds but extends from 1–2 years in some larger breeds. Similarly, the senior life stage usually includes the last 25 percent or so of anticipated life span, which can differ markedly between breeds, typically based on their size. Because cats are more uniform in their adult size, it is possible to assign life stages on a species-wide basis, even though there is some breed variability evident.

A pet's gender, as well as whether it has been neutered, will also influence risk. Some diseases are exclusively seen in one gender over another (such as prostate disease in males or uterine infection in females), but there are also so-called sex predispositions in which some problems may be more commonly seen in males or in females, even if the reason is not apparent. On the other hand, some disorders and traits are transmitted genetically on the sex chromosomes. For example, hemophilia is a disease of defective blood clotting and extensive bleeding and is inherited via mutations on the X chromosome. Such conditions are more often seen in males since they only have one X chromosome (the other is a Y chromosome) and are unable to mitigate the effects of the mutation with a second normal X chromosome. The tortoiseshell coloring in cats (patches of orange, black and white) is also transmitted on the X chromosome, and since it takes two X chromosomes to cause tortoiseshell coloring, this coloring is almost exclusively seen in females (females having two X chromosomes, while males only have one).

Neuter status also affects risk. Females spayed before their first heat have a reduced risk of breast (mammary) cancer later in life, while neutered males have a lowered risk for prostate disease. We even have guidelines to suggest the most appropriate age for neutering on a pet-specific basis, based on adult size and risk for developing developmental orthopedic diseases (such as hip dysplasia) and the pet's risk for certain cancers. For cats, there is typically a universal recommendation to spay or neuter by 5 months of age, but the situation can be much more complicated in dogs, especially purebreds. While the risk of breast (mammary) cancer is reduced when pets are spayed before their first estrus ("heat"), some dogs with heritable risk for certain orthopedic diseases may benefit from having the surgery performed after they have completed their main growth phase. To complicate matters even further, for some breeds, adjusting the age at which they are neutered can impact their risk for certain cancers. This can vary by breed, size (risks can be different for size varieties of the same breed, such as miniature, standard, toy, etc.), gender (risks can be different for males and females), as well as other factors. For example, there might be evidence that males of a specific breed should be neutered at 6 months of age, while females of the same breed should wait to be spayed until 2 years of age, depending on risks of cancers, orthopedic diseases, urinary incontinence, etc. This can make general rules problematic, at least for dogs, so discuss with your veterinary team the best time to consider such surgeries for your particular pets. Once again, the situation seems to be clearer for cats in which spaying/neutering by 5 months of age not only prevents unwanted pregnancies (which can occur as early as 4 months of age), but it also decreases the risk of mammary (breast) cancer, virtually eliminates uterine infections (pyometra), often increases longevity, and can decrease some undesirable behavioral problems.

Even conformation (remember the smushed faces we were talking about?) and non-disease traits can be associated with predisposition to disease. For example, cats with white fur may be at higher risk for developing sun exposure cancers such as squamous cell carcinoma; color dilution alopecia causes patchy hair loss and is more common in dogs with diluted coloring patterns, such as "blue" Dobermans, etc. Dogs with long backs, such as Dachshunds, are more prone to intervertebral disk disease. In pet-specific care, all this information is factored into the schedule of care to promote prevention if possible, early detection of concerns, and appropriate treatment for improved health outcomes and quality of life.

Family History

Family history is an incredibly important concern when it comes to health risks, but we often don't have this information when it comes to our pets. If pets are purchased from conscientious breeders who record such information with health registries, this can provide a treasure trove for veterinary teams and pet owners, but in the vast majority of cases, no such information exists. In that situation, we are going to have to do the best we can with the information we do have available.

As we'll learn in the chapter on early detection, DNA testing can fill in a lot of blanks for specific genetic conditions, especially those that are transmitted simply through a single-gene pair. However, for the majority of health care problems in dogs and cats (such as diabetes, arthritis, allergies, etc.) that are transmitted in a more complex fashion (multiple genes and/or the influence of environmental factors), DNA tests are unlikely to indicate anything other than risk. So, while it may not be entirely fair, if we don't have family history and we don't have DNA testing for some of the most common things, we often rely on suspicions on the basis of how common problems are in the breed in general (at least if we are dealing with purebreds or hybrids). This is typically referred to as breed predisposition.

Breed predispositions are generalizations, because most health problems run in families, not the entire breed, but with a lack of more specific information, it is sometimes necessary to use breed generalizations when planning proactive health care. So, we might acknowledge that the risk for a condition such as hip dysplasia is higher in a breed like the German Shepherd Dog, but this does not mean that all German Shepherd Dogs will get hip dysplasia or that all German Shepherd Dogs are even susceptible to hip dysplasia. However, if we were considering a screening protocol for hip dysplasia, and we didn't have more specific information about family history, we would certainly want to ensure that breeds at higher risk got appropriately screened, since their risk would be considered higher than that of some other breeds and mixed breeds. See Figures 4.3 and 4.4 for some breeds and some of the conditions for which there is a known or suspected breed predisposition.

As you might imagine, it can be scary when the veterinary team advises screening your pet for a nasty-sounding disease, even when your pet appears completely healthy, but that is an entirely appropriate response to risk. It doesn't mean that your pet will actually get any of these problems, but you want the veterinary team to be on the look-out for them nonetheless. So, if you own a Cavalier King Charles Spaniel, don't panic if the veterinary team shares with you that the breed can be prone to a variety of ills, including mitral valve disease (heart disease), keratoconjunctivitis sicca (dry eye), macrothrombocytopenia (a bleeding disorder), primary secretory otitis media (glue ear), and syringomyelia (a spinal disorder) among others, and instead be reassured by the fact that they are aware of breed predisposition and are prepared to counsel you accordingly. All pets (yes, all pets—purebred, hybrids, and mixed breeds) have health care risks, just like people. Breed predispositions just inform us about risks that seem to be higher in particular groups. They do not mean that your pet will actually develop any of these problems.

Breed	Breed Predispositions
Labrador Retriever	Centronuclear myopathy*, Cystinuria*, Degenerative myelopathy*, Elbow dysplasia, Exercise-induced collapse*, Hip dysplasia, Nasal parakeratosis*, Osteochondrosis dissecans, Progressive rod-cone degeneration*, Skeletal dysplasia Type 2*, Tricuspid valve dysplasia
German Shepherd Dog	Acral lick dermatitis, Elbow dysplasia, Degenerative myelopathy*, Exocrine pancreatic insufficiency, Hemophilia A*, Hip dysplasia, Hyperuricosuria*, Masticatory myositis, Perianal fistula*, Renal cystadenocarcinoma/ Nodular dermatofibrosis*
Golden Retriever	Atopic dermatitis, Elbow dysplasia, Hemophilia A, Hip dysplasia, Hypothyroidism, Ichthyosis*, Juvenile cellulitis, Muscular dystrophy*, Patella luxation, Progressive retinal atrophy (GR_PRA1 and GR_PRA2)*, Progressive rod-cone degeneration*, Sensory ataxic neuropathy
English Bulldog	Anasarca, Brachycephalic syndrome, Entropion, Factor VII deficiency, Fold dermatitis, Hip dysplasia, Hyperuricosuria*, Hypothyroidism, Laryngeal paralysis, Multifocal retinopathy (CMR1)*, Pulmonic stenosis, Sacrocaudal dysgenesis, Ventricular septal defect
Beagle	Cataracts, Cryptorchidism, Diabetes mellitus, Factor VII deficiency*, Glaucoma (POAG)*, Hip dysplasia, Juvenile polyarthritis, Musladin-Leuke syndrome*, Night blindness*, Patellar luxation, Pulmonic stenosis, Pyruvate kinase deficiency*, Retinal dysplasia
French bulldog	Atopic dermatitis, brachycephalic syndrome, cataracts*, corneal ulcers, Factor VIII deficiency*, Factor IX deficiency*, Histiocytic ulcerative colitis, Necrotizing meningoencephalitis, Hyperuricosuria*, Multifocal retinopathy*, Cone-rod dystrophy I*
Poodle	Cataracts, Epilepsy, Factor VIII deficiency*, Legg-Calve-Perthes disease, Mucopolysaccharidosis*, Neonatal encephalopathy*, Organic aciduria, Oxalate urolithiasis, Progressive rod-cone degeneration*, Sebaceous adenitis, von Willebrand disease*
Rottweiler	Cervical vertebral instability, Cruciate ligament rupture, Fragmented coronoid process, Gastric dilatation/volvulus, Leukodystrophy, Membranous glomerulopathy, Myotubular myopathy*, Patent ductus arteriosus, Polyneuropathy and neuronal vacuolation*, Short tail*
Yorkshire Terrier	Atlantoaxial instability, cataracts, Cryptorchidism, L2-Hydroxyglutaric aciduria*, Lymphoproliferative disease, Necrotizing meningoencephalitis, Patellar luxation, Patent ductus arteriosus, Primary lens luxation*, Progressive rod-cone degeneration*
Boxer	Brachycephalic syndrome, Cardiomyopathy*, Cystinuria, Factor II deficiency, Hyperadrenocorticism, Neoplasia, Progressive axonopathy, Pulmonic stenosis, Short tail*, Sphingomyelinosis, Subaortic stenosis, Ulcerative colitis

Figure 4.3. Some common dog breeds and a few of the conditions to which they are predisposed. An * indicates that DNA testing is available.

Breed	Breed Predispositions
Persian	Acne, Brachycephalic syndrome, Cardiomyopathy, Cerebellar degeneration, Chediak-Higashi syndrome, Deafness, Hip dysplasia, Intervertebral disk disease, Polycystic kidney disease
Maine Coon	Cardiomyopathy*, Hip dysplasia, Middle ear polyps, Patellar luxation, Polycystic kidney disease*, Polydactyly, Pyruvate kinase deficiency*, Spinal muscular atrophy*
Himalayan	Asthma, Cataracts, Hip dysplasia, Polycystic kidney disease, Portosystemic shunting, Progressive retinal atrophy (PRA-pd)*, Ulcerative keratitis, Urolithiasis (calcium oxalate)
Burmese	Cardiomyopathy*, Craniofacial Defect*, Cutaneous asthenia, Diabetes mellitus, Gangliosidosis (GM1 & GM2)*, Glaucoma, Hypokalemic polymyopathy*, Urolithiasis (calcium oxalate)
Ragdoll	Arterial thromboembolism, Cardiomyopathy*, Eosinophilic sclerosing fibroplasia, Mucopolysaccharidosis VI*, Polycystic kidney disease* Progressive retinal atrophy (PRA-pd)*
American Shorthair	Cardiomyopathy, Craniofacial deformity, Hip dysplasia, Mucolipidosis, Polycystic kidney disease, Porphyria, Progressive retinal atrophy (RdAc)*, Pyruvate kinase deficiency*
Siamese	Asthma, Cardiomyopathy, Cerebellar abiotrophy, Factor IX deficiency, Glaucoma, GM1 Gangliosidosis, Lens luxation, Pancreatitis, Patellar luxation, Porphyria*
Abyssinian	Cardiomyopathy*, Diabetes mellitus, Idiopathic cystitis, Myasthenic syndrome*, Patellar luxation, Progressive retinal atrophy (RdAc & Rdy)*, Pyruvate kinase deficiency*
Birman	Audiogenic reflex seizures, Chediak-Higashi-like syndrome, Mucopolysaccharidosis VI*, Polycystic kidney disease, Polyneuropathy, Progressive retinal atrophy (PRA-pd)*
Bengal	Cardiomyopathy, Cataracts, Polyneuropathy, Progressive retinal atrophy (PRA-B & RdAc)*, Pyruvate kinase deficiency*, Urolithiasis (urate)

Figure 4.4. Some common cat breeds and a few of the conditions to which they are predisposed. An * indicates that DNA testing is available.

Horses and Zebras

There is an old medical axiom that states that if you hear hoof beats outside your window, the sounds are more likely to be from a horse than a zebra (unless you live on a game preserve in Africa, of course). This means that for most issues that arise, you should make sure the most common problems are addressed before you dig too deeply for strange and exotic things that could be causing the trouble.

As we are personalizing health care for our pets, let's not forget the simple things that have a major impact on health management, such as nutrition, weight management, exercise, dental care, vaccination, behavioral care and enrichment, and parasite control. We'll cover these in more detail in different chapters, but it is well to remember not to forsake these pillars of wellness. It is easy to be led astray by what sounds exotic or we come upon it in news or postings, and this is where Internet searches can yield frightening results, but now more than ever it is important to avoid misleading information and to keep things in perspective.

Personalizing Cost of Care

There is an entire chapter coming dedicated to affordability of pet health care, but it is worth mentioning here that personalizing care is not only pet-specific but also owner-specific. It's wonderful to consider pets as family members, but sometimes it is not possible to just say, "do whatever is needed—cost is no object." Of course, people sometimes say that, but they don't necessarily mean it. In many cases, cost is a very real consideration. With veterinary care, medical decisions are made by caregiving pet owners, not the pets themselves. Everyone wants to do what is right for their pet, but sometimes that care is beyond the financial wherewithal of some pet owners. Pet health insurance is a great equalizer in this regard, but if it is not in place when a problem happens, coverage of that particular problem will likely not be possible after the fact.

It is a somewhat harsh realization that health care often needs to be customized, not only to the needs of the pet but to the financial needs of the pet owner. Thus, sometimes there is a need to consider a potential "spectrum of care," and it is better to have such discussions with veterinary teams sooner rather than later. Nobody really wants to have this type of discussion, sometimes because of the guilt of not being able to afford recommended care for a beloved pet, but also because nobody likes to admit that they have financial limits, but it is important that veterinary teams know if there are constraints so they can propose appropriate approaches given any limitations.

Providing pet-specific care allows us to do what we can to keep our furry companions safe and healthy, but it is important to realize that it is not possible to predict all health outcomes for pets. The purpose of planning and personalizing care is to try to anticipate potential issues and plan accordingly.

Letting Go

One of the most difficult things to do with a pet who has been a best friend for many years is to be able to say goodbye as their problem-free life comes to an end. This is difficult on several fronts. It is always heartbreaking to let go of a loved one, regardless of the circumstances. However, it is often more difficult when it comes to pets for many different reasons. One of them is predictable but no easier just because you are

Leira relaxing in the sink (courtesy Antoinette Falzone).

aware of it. If you have fully embraced the role of pet parent, then you likely share the common emotion that comes with surviving the death of a child surrogate. We expect our human children to outlive us, but for pets that live a more abbreviated lifespan, we really need to be able to come to terms with the fact that no matter how well we care for them, and how much they mean to us, their time on this earth is often all too brief.

Because we completely fulfill the role of pet parent, when pets are at the end of their lives, they can't tell us when they would prefer to go or when they no longer want extraordinary measures keeping them alive. They can't say when they are no longer enjoying their existence, when they are ready to depart this world, and it often leaves us with guilt that we need to make these decisions for them. Add to this the fact that as health begins to ebb, there is often considerable expense associated with diagnostics and therapeutics, and this can be a time fraught with second guessing and guilt and worries about whether spending more money will do anything to improve the eventual outcome.

One other devastating aspect of a pet approaching the end is that family, friends and acquaintances may not fully comprehend the grief we experience going through the process. Other pet parents will be quick to empathize, but for those who have never experienced such a bond, they may not understand the profound sense of loss, and often isolation, that accompanies the demise of a pet. After all, if a pet has been with you through good times and bad, has been your trusted confidante, and has always provided judgment-free support, it would be astonishing if you did not experience grief as you would for any close family member.

You can take some solace in the fact that you shared a loving existence with your pet, that your pet will not judge you for whatever decisions you make on their behalf, and that we have hospice options if needed and humane methods of peacefully bringing a beloved pet's life to an end without any suffering. Do take solace from these facts, but be prepared that you will still need to go through the same stages of grief as anyone else experiencing a devastating loss.

In the same vein as other problem-free strategies, end of life is something that we need to acknowledge for all living beings, and our pets are no exception. Be aware of the anticipated lifespan for your particular pet and what types of interventions you would be comfortable with ... before anything happens. Making decisions during times of crisis is extremely difficult and not always in the best interest of either you or your pet.

There is often a false belief that you will just "know" when the time is right for euthanasia, but this is very misleading if you don't have a plan. There are several quality-of-life assessments that can be done in end-of-life scenarios with just an Internet search, and they help pet parents use objective criteria to determine when pets are not enjoying life much anymore, typically looking at measures of pain, mobility, happiness, bodily functions, and other criteria. It's not possible to determine the absolute "correct" time, but with such surveys, it is possible to know when a threshold has been crossed and when the time is nigh.

Taking a logical approach to such a difficult situation also allows a certain amount of planning in what otherwise would be a chaotic time. Think about what remembrances you might want to have—whether it involves photos, family member visits, casts of paw prints, or online memorials. Talk to your veterinary team about their options and recommendations and also discuss what you would like done with the body after euthanasia (cremation? burial?). Also remember that your pet isn't judging you, so if you make a decision to have the euthanasia on a Friday afternoon so you have the weekend to mourn with like-minded pet parents before facing coworkers who may not understand what the fuss is all about for a pet—absolutely make things happen on your schedule.

When it comes to euthanasia itself, the process is usually quite peaceful. Typically, there is a catheter placed in a vein, a relaxing agent is given so the pet settles into a sleep-like state, and then a special solution is given that slows and then stops the heart. It's often over in just a few minutes.

No matter how tough you think you are, or how detached, expect that you will indeed need to grieve the loss of your pet. However, if you have been living with a problem-free philosophy, please remember to celebrate the bond you shared with your pet. Death is an eventuality that none of us can avoid, so while it is natural to be sad, don't ignore the wonderful memories that accompanied your pet's life with you. Pets don't feel sorry for themselves, and don't be surprised if your pet trusted you completely to make decisions on their behalf ... right up until the end. As part of the grieving process, it is also possible that you will have feelings of guilt for not having acted soon enough (if only I had taken her in when I first started noticing problems) or for not following all recommendations (perhaps if I had agreed to the more aggressive course of therapy), then the outcome might have been different. Such feelings are to be anticipated but can be kept in perspective if we maintain a problem-free philosophy and make the best decisions we can with the information we have available to us. We can never know what might have been, and we can't change what has already occurred, so it is best to make peace with the situation when we know we did the best we could. That often doesn't make it any easier at the time, but eventually we'll be able to see the situation for what it was. If you are finding it difficult to deal with the passing, many communities also offer grief counseling for pet owners. Your veterinary team can often provide recommendations or you can find resources with a quick Internet search. If you need help getting started, consider a free resource such as rainbowsbridge.com.

Case Example

Bella is an 18-month-old spayed female Golden Retriever who belongs to Larry and Jerome, who were considering adopting a baby but thought they would first practice with a pet. Bella had started licking and chewing at her paws, and they were pretty sure it was due to atopic dermatitis (allergies), since the veterinary team had told them previously that this was common in the breed (a breed predisposition).

At the time, they thought it was strange that pets could develop allergies, but after researching it further on the Internet, they realized it was actually quite common. In fact, when they had asked the veterinary staff if there was anything they could do to be proactive in case Bella did develop allergies, the hospital team introduced them to behavioral approaches to condition Bella to willingly accept bathing and ear cleaning, so the medicated baths now recommended were not going to be an issue. They also received a medication that would help with the itchiness and were glad to learn that it was safe for long-term use, since they intended on keeping Bella healthy and happy well into old age.

The hospital team reminded them that there was also a breed predisposition for hip dysplasia and that Bella was due for orthopedic screening in a few months. The owners had created a checklist from the health care schedule originally prepared for them and had already done their research on those disorders and how to proceed if Bella was affected. They knew from health registries that Bella's parents and grandparents did not have evidence of such problems and were reassured by that but also understood the need to screen Bella individually. They also had gotten pet health insurance for Bella and did so when there was no evidence of preexisting conditions, so they felt well prepared for whatever was in store.

Recommended Reading

Ackerman, L., ed. 2021. *Pet-Specific Care for the Veterinary Team*. Hoboken, NJ: Wiley.
_____. 2020. *Proactive Pet Parenting: Anticipating Pet Health Problems Before They Happen*. Problem Free Publishing.
_____. 2019a. "An Introduction to Pet-Specific Care." *EC Veterinary Science* 4 (1): 1–3.
_____. 2019b. "What Veterinary Healthcare Teams Should Know about Genetic Testing." *AAHA Trends*.
_____. 2011. *The Genetic Connection, 2nd Edition*. Lakewood, CO: AAHA Press.
American Animal Hospital Association. 2012. *Evolving to a Culture of Prevention: Implementing Integrated Preventive Care*. Lakewood, CO: AAHA Press, 1–23.
Bell, Jerold, Kathleen Cavanagh, Larry Tilley, and Francis Smith. 2012. *Veterinary Medical Guide to Dog and Cat Breeds*. Teton Newmedia.
Bushby, Phillip A. 2021. "Is There an Optimal Age for Cat Spay or Neuter?" *Today's Veterinary Practice* 11 (1): https://doi.org/https://todaysveterinarypractice.com/is-there-an-optimal-age-for-cat-spay-or-neuter/.

Giuffrida, Michelle A., Dorothy Cimino Brown, Susan S. Ellenberg, and John T. Farrar. 2018. "Development and Psychometric Testing of the Canine Owner-Reported Quality of Life Questionnaire, an Instrument Designed to Measure Quality of Life in Dogs with Cancer." *Journal of the American Veterinary Medical Association* 252 (9): 1073–1083. https://doi.org/10.2460/javma.252.9.1073.

Hamburg, M.A., and F.S. Collins. 2010. "The Path to Personalized Medicine." *New England Journal of Medicine* 363 (4): 301–304.

"Hereditary Diseases." n.d. World Small Veterinary Association. https://www.wsava.org/Guidelines/Hereditary-Disease-Guidelines.

Partners for Healthy Pets. http://www.partnersforhealthypets.org/.

Quimby, J, S. Gowland, HC Carney, et al. 2021. "AAHA/AAFP Feline Life Stage Guidelines." *Journal of Feline Medicine and Surgery* (2021) 23, 211-233. DOI: 10.1177/1098612X 21993657

Salt, Carina, Penelope J. Morris, Richard F. Butterwick, Elizabeth M. Lund, Tim J. Cole, and Alexander J. German. 2020. "Comparison of Growth Patterns in Healthy Dogs and Dogs in Abnormal Body Condition Using Growth Standards." Edited by Juan J. Loor. *PLOS ONE* 15 (9): e0238521. https://doi.org/10.1371/journal.pone.0238521.

Simpson, Robert John, Kathyrn Jo Simpson, and Ledy VanKavage. 2012. "Rethinking Dog Breed Identification in Veterinary Practice." *Journal of the American Veterinary Medical Association* 241 (9): 1163–66. https://doi.org/10.2460/javma.241.9.1163.

Urfer, Silvan R., Mansen Wang, Mingyin Yang, Elizabeth M. Lund, and Sandra L. Lefebvre. 2019. "Risk Factors Associated with Lifespan in Pet Dogs Evaluated in Primary Care Veterinary Hospitals." *Journal of the American Animal Hospital Association* 55 (3): 130–137. https://doi.org/10.5326/jaaha-ms-6763.

5

Pet Health Care Delivery in an On-Demand World

Pet owners love their pets, but they are also consumers, and most consumers today have high expectations about getting the services they want, when they want them, and how they want them. The average pet owner today has 24/7 access to a smart device, and many stream services on demand, do banking and investing online, have access to expedited delivery, and have become accustomed to summoning transportation when needed, preordering their meals and beverages, and even having them delivered.

On the other hand, many veterinary hospitals today still reflect a type of "mom and pop" retail experience. Unlike many drug stores, hardware stores, and bookstores that have been eclipsed by large retail enterprises, many veterinary clinics are still community-based businesses working out of a relatively small retail footprint. Yes, there are corporate-owned practices and large specialty and emergency hospitals, but most veterinary hospitals are independent facilities that offer most services needed, such as appointments, surgery, imaging (radiographs, ultrasound, etc.), laboratory, dispensing pharmacy, etc.

Most veterinary hospitals have standard retail operating hours, and when closed, they usually leave instructions for pet owners to seek assistance at an emergency facility after hours. In most cases, when there is an emergency, the emergency clinic will not have access to your pet's medical records, and the emergency clinic will likely not be able to contact your veterinary team directly, so it is important that you plan for such a situation from the start. If you have been honing your problem-free skills, you will be prepared with the information that might be needed, such as vaccination history, any diagnoses that have been made, recent laboratory results, and all medications being administered to your pet.

It is important to realize that almost all veterinary hospitals will need payment at time of service, and if an animal needs to be admitted and treated, a substantial portion of the anticipated final bill will need to be paid in advance. This can surprise some pet owners, so better to be aware of this up front. Most veterinary hospitals are small businesses that function on fairly tight margins, so most do not have the ability to extend credit. It's important to be prepared.

Modern consumers might find it tempting to consider meeting their pet's health care needs on the Internet. After all, it's available 24 hours a day, seven days a week, there are a lot of pet-related resources to be seen, and many are inexpensive or even free. It's true that there is a lot of non-curated information available on the Internet, and if you've got the time to review the information provided on almost limitless websites, you might find useful information, but it is still not likely that you will get the resolution you are seeking, because you won't have a confirmed diagnosis nor access to appropriate medications. There are telehealth options that are becoming more commonplace, and in some communities there are even mobile veterinary services that will come to your home or place of work, but it is still rare to find satisfaction through an Internet search alone.

The Veterinary Team

For many community veterinary hospitals, the care team consists of a handful of veterinarians, hopefully some registered technicians (known as veterinary nurses, animal health technicians, and animal health technologists in different localities), assistants and caretakers, customer service representatives and perhaps a few managers. This small contingent of individuals typically run the entire hospital, and it is not unusual that owners of the hospital work within the hospital itself. Currently a minority of veterinary hospitals are corporate owned, and some are associated with other types of businesses (e.g., large pet supply companies, human pharmacies, large retailers, etc.) in what are sometimes referred to as retail-anchored practices. There are pros and cons to each type of hospital.

Most veterinarians working in these types of hospitals are typically considered as general practitioners or primary care doctors (first-opinion doctors in some countries). Unlike physicians in primary care human practice who typically just see patients and may do minor procedures, most veterinarians are involved with the total care of patients, from office visits to performing laboratory tests to supervising animals that are hospitalized to performing surgeries. It's very compartmentalized, but the veterinary team handles the vast majority of patients seen on a day-to-day basis within the hospital.

Most veterinary hospitals are divided into two areas: a front office area where clients are allowed and a back office area that is primarily reserved for the veterinary team. Clients typically have access to the reception area and examination rooms in the front office, but if a pet is admitted to the hospital or needs to go into a treatment area for a procedure, the pet will be escorted back by a hospital team member, while generally the pet owner will remain in the examination room or return to the reception area. It's understandable why pet owners would like to accompany their pet into the back area, and most veterinary team members are sympathetic, but it is still not allowed in most cases. One might suspect that pets would be calmer with an owner present, but the opposite is often true, and most hospital insurance policies advise against bringing clients into an area where infection control is tightly monitored, and it is not possible to guarantee safety or to assure the privacy of other client and pet information. So, even though it is tempting to want to stay with your pet, let the veterinary team do their jobs, and do your best to remain calm and follow their directions. It's in your pet's best interests.

While the veterinary team at a primary care hospital often does an admirable job with all the varied patient care needs presented on a daily basis, they sometimes need assistance with two particular types of patients—emergencies and those with more complicated medical situations. In those cases, it is possible that the veterinary team will suggest that your pet go to an emergency clinic or be referred to a veterinary specialist. Since certain terms are commonly used in human medicine to describe levels of health care provided, we might as well discuss them briefly here as they apply to veterinary medicine.

As mentioned earlier, most veterinary care is provided by primary care veterinarians, and most veterinary hospitals are equipped to handle the routine health care needs of most pets. When more specific levels of care are required, pets may be referred to secondary-care veterinarians, who are often specialists with specific expertise in different disciplines (such as dermatology, ophthalmology, oncology, etc.). Such specialists may function either within a larger hospital setting or, depending on the specialty, as separate offices or facilities. When pets require an even higher level of care—often that involves sophisticated equipment and expertise within a hospital setting—this typically constitutes tertiary care. In some instances, quaternary care may be an extension of tertiary care, such as for very specialized surgeries or investigative or experimental procedures.

Emergency or trauma centers may exist as separate or integrated units and may have their own designations regarding the level of trauma to which they are accredited, with Level 1 typically being the highest level of certification. This is different from the levels described above regarding primary through quaternary care, and there are organizations involved in certifying veterinary hospitals (e.g., https://www.veccs. org/facility-certification/veccs-facility-certification-vs-vetcot/). While some large veterinary hospitals may have their own emergency services and in some rural communities veterinary hospitals have to handle their own emergencies by necessity, emergency clinics are typically staffed to handle emergencies even when primary care veterinary hospitals are closed. As mentioned previously, most of these emergency facilities will not be able to access your pet's medical records or your veterinary team in after-hours situations, so you will need to ensure that you have access to pertinent information on your pet's behalf. It's the problem-free way.

Most veterinary specialists, also known as board-certified specialists since they are accredited by a recognized specialty board or college, will have completed advanced training and passed certification examinations within their area of expertise. If your pet has an issue for which either you or your veterinary team wants a second opinion, a "referral" will be requested, and you will likely need to take your pet to a separate facility for your specialty appointment. Today, there are veterinary specialists in many important disciplines, including dermatology, ophthalmology, internal medicine (cardiology, neurology, oncology), surgery, and others. The specialist will go over options for your pet's care and will also send a referral report back to your primary care veterinary team, so everybody is aware of the plan going forward.

The reason for knowing how veterinary clinics work is because you not only need to be a health care advocate for your pet, but because the different aspects of veterinary care are not necessarily seamless, you may need to be the conduit for managing aspects of your pet's care in different settings. Currently there is no centralized repository of medical records for pets, and most pet owners don't maintain an online portal that houses all their pet's relevant health care information. Options such as blockchain exist (see below), but to date they are not in widespread use across veterinary hospitals.

Sometimes it seems that human medicine and veterinary medicine are on divergent tracks, but the two have actually been moving closer together through what has been referred to as the One Health initiative. One Health is an approach that recognizes that the health of people is closely connected to the health of animals and our shared environment, and health care professionals have been diligently working cooperatively to achieve optimal health outcomes for all concerned. Areas of collaboration include diseases that can spread between animals and humans, antibiotic resistance, food safety, diseases spread by parasites (fleas, ticks, mosquitoes, etc.), genetic testing, and many others. Pet-specific care and personalized medicine are actually byproducts of this teamwork.

Telehealth

Telehealth has been used in veterinary medicine for decades, and yet changes in technology and advances in human medicine have changed the landscape in recent years. Regulatory changes, however, have not always kept pace, and this has been frustrating because certain things that can be done in human medicine cannot necessarily be done in veterinary medicine, even with access to the same technology. Different aspects of telehealth can also be referred to as telemedicine, virtual care, health care on demand, and connected care.

Human medicine functions on a different regulatory model than does veterinary medicine, and consumers may see programs in human health that have telemedicine more completely integrated into overall care. Thus, there might be programs integrated with insurance groups, public health and other endeavors that increase patient access and lower health care costs. Technologies can also be used to establish a valid physician-patient relationship in human medicine without the requirement of an in-person examination. While there has been some relaxing of the regulatory environment for veterinary telemedicine in the wake of COVID-19, in the past veterinarians were prohibited from initiating a medical relationship with pet owners on the basis of electronic means alone. So, if you have an existing relationship with a veterinary team, telehealth is a possibility, but there are still regulatory concerns about accepting new clients virtually and whether or not diagnoses can be made and treatments can be prescribed. These same restrictions do not exist in the same way in human health care (where television commercials promise you can establish an immediate physician relationship and get access to medications, for example), so there is the hope that everything will eventually get sorted out. The field and its applications are clearly evolving, but veterinarians and pet owners still need to abide by existing regulations until they are changed.

Roxie playing on the shore (courtesy Nora Carbonneau).

Telehealth is a broad category of services in which veterinary care is delivered remotely or virtually. For health care professionals, telehealth comes with a set of regulations as to what can be done virtually and what cannot be done without physically seeing the pet. You may speak to a member of the veterinary team by telephone, text (SMS) or video, and they are allowed to respond within the parameters of existing regulations.

It's important to realize that there are some things that can be accomplished by telehealth, but a lot of things that cannot. There are also some areas of medicine that are more amenable to such virtual means of care. As you might imagine, there are a lot of things that cannot be done, but it might still be possible for basic advice to be given, including the need to seek emergency care rather than trying to address all things virtually. So, it might be possible to have a conversation about how to manage a pet with fleas but more difficult to do anything useful when a pet is actively having a seizure—other than advise pet owners how to keep themselves safe and then seek more direct veterinary care.

If you are interested in telehealth options, discuss these with your veterinary team, so you understand what is available and the costs. Also realize that government regulations have been more lenient with human physicians, and veterinarians may have restrictions on what they can legally provide to pet owners. The situation is constantly evolving. In the end, veterinary teams are going to try their best to meet your needs within the confines of what is considered permissible by individual licensing boards, so it can be different from location to location.

Pet owners may have reasonable or unreasonable expectations about what can be accomplished without directly seeing a pet. As we have stressed from the beginning, speak to your veterinary team in advance so you have realistic expectations about what is possible with telehealth. In some cases, you may have a follow-up question to services that have already been provided (e.g., "Sheba chewed out one of the stitches from the procedure she just had, but it isn't bleeding. Do I need to bring her in?"). In other instances, you might want to know if you can avoid bringing a pet into the hospital ("Lily has had a bout of vomiting. Can I just give her the medicine we've been given previously, and I'll bring her in if she doesn't get better?"). If no recognized veterinarian-client-patient relationship exists, it still might be possible for veterinarians to answer basic questions that would not constitute providing specific medical advice for any specific pet (e.g., "what is mange?," "can dogs get chicken pox?," "my cat is bleeding. Should I bring her in there, or go to an emergency clinic?," etc.). In general, veterinary teams can answer generic questions about health (sometimes known as teletriage or teleadvice) for pets they haven't seen, but are limited in what can be said about specific diagnosis and treatment unless there is a permitted consultation, which typically reflects an existing veterinarian-client-patient relationship and the pet having been physically seen within the past 12 months.

Teletriage might also include providing advice for a pet that has consumed poison, whether that involves instructing pet owners to call a poison control hotline or advising them to go to the nearest emergency clinic. There are also now a variety of applications for pets using wearables, including remotely measuring pulse, respirations, temperature, position, and activity level, and this also constitutes teletriage, but this typically happens within a sanctioned veterinarian-client-patient relationship.

From a technical standpoint, there are essentially two different ways that virtual health can be delivered—synchronous and asynchronous. Synchronous consultations occur on a real-time basis, and technology is typically used to provide an audiovisual encounter. In most cases you are probably using your own smart device to communicate, using a teleconferencing app, or are at a telehealth kiosk, but in some cases visiting veterinary team members may be remote from your home and act as telepresenters on your behalf, providing more hands-on evaluation and communicating with veterinarians at the hospital. With asynchronous telemedicine, sometimes referred to as "store-it-forward" care, the consultations do not happen in real time. You typically submit questions, images, videos, laboratory results, etc., for the veterinary team to comment on, and they respond at a later time. While this lacks some of the personal touch of synchronous consultations, it is often much easier for both busy pet owners and veterinary team members to accommodate in their schedules. Whichever form of telehealth communication is selected, it is worthwhile to have realistic expectations of what can be accomplished by such a consult so as not to be disappointed with the results. Nobody is going to be able to talk you through providing emergency surgery at home, but there is value in having direct communication about the type of care that is recommended for your specific pet.

The onset of COVID-19 has greatly changed the landscape for telehealth. In many cases, it has also changed the nature of routine office visits, since during peak infectivity there had to be options for keeping owners safe while still performing essential veterinary care. This often meant having veterinary team members escort the pet into the building for evaluation while keeping pet owners out of the hospital as much as possible and maintaining physical (social) distancing for everyone's safety.

Other than teleconsultations, the most common forms of telehealth relate to things like prescription requests based on virtual examinations, recheck evaluations, after-hours care, post-surgery checkups, patient monitoring through wearable devices and other technologies, and even following up on hospice care patients and others for which in-hospital visits are not possible or not feasible. Finally, nearly half of all pet owners are not currently bringing their pets to the veterinary clinic with any regularity, so virtual care removes one barrier to them being able to seek veterinary advice, as long as appropriate veterinarian-client-patient relationships are in place.

Remote Monitoring

Technology is now available that allows remote monitoring of pets, and this can be an important resource when considering virtual care. The most common forms of remote monitoring are wearable collars, but other options for remote monitoring include glucometers, blood pressure devices, heart monitors and even sensors that can allow hearing actual heart sounds, as well as other features.

Wearable collars with sensors are the most common form of remote monitoring. These collars can typically measure position (lying, sitting, standing), activity, pulse, breathing, and even heart rate variability. The measurements are generally collected continuously and in real time. For many of the devices, the veterinary health care team can access the information any time of the day or night through a cloud-based server.

There are a few reasons why you might choose to monitor your pets remotely. For pets with existing medical issues, especially chronic problems, wearables allow measurements to be taken continuously and analyzed in real time. For certain devices, systems can be set up to send alerts when specific thresholds are exceeded, such as when the heart rate gets too high or too low. This can alert you and the veterinary team when action is required, including bringing your pet in for medical care or taking it to an emergency facility.

One of the most useful features of wearable collars in animals without medical issues is that they can allow your veterinary team to determine actual

Leira at rest (courtesy Antoinette Falzone).

resting heart and respiration rates for pets, which may be difficult if not impossible to collect during office visits. You may not fully appreciate why this is challenging, but many pets are anxious or stressed during visits to a veterinary hospital, and heart and respiratory rates taken during those visits may be significantly altered. However, in the comfort of a pet's own home, such measurements are much more likely to be indicative of actual resting rates. It might also be possible to use wearables to infer relative stress levels in pets in different circumstances, including boarding facilities and other environments.

Another important development in remote systems is continuous glucose monitoring for diabetics, which is available for both dogs and cats. Glucometers are available that can be used to sample interstitial fluid (a thin layer of fluid around body cells) for glucose determinations, but it can be difficult to collect enough samples over time to approximate a glucose curve in pets on insulin therapy, which is typically what veterinary teams would prefer to measure. Similar to the human devices, veterinary continuous glucose monitors have a sensor that is inserted under the skin to read blood glucose levels. A garment is typically used to cover the device so that it is not dislodged. It should not be surprising that pets will often paw at the garment and try to remove it until they get used to it being in place. In general, the devices sample the capillary fluid every five minutes or so, and once analyzed can provide a more complete picture of glucose status. Without such home testing, it would typically take hospitalization of the pet and sampling of the blood glucose every few hours to determine when blood glucose levels peak and drop. Older remote systems offered only analysis of past glucose concentrations after disconnecting the sensor and uploading the data. Newer systems measure and display glucose readings in real time, allowing direct intervention and altering treatment accordingly.

Remote monitoring can also play a key role in wellness care. With overweight and obese animals constituting a near-epidemic in many communities, exercise is often recommended as part of the solution. Fitness wearables, in most cases accelerometers, can be used to track effectiveness of a prescribed regimen, and additional devices such as connected scales can be used to monitor weight at home between office visits. It's not unusual that people wear these devices to help "track their steps" on a daily basis, and soon it might not be so unusual for pets to use them that way as well. Wearable devices with accelerometers can also be used in rehabilitation after surgery or injury and can provide the veterinary health care team with real-time data of recovery progress.

One other exciting development in remote monitoring is the development of digital litter boxes. New technologies provide more than just self-cleaning cat litter. Some can proactively monitor important health features, such as waste amount, frequency and duration, which can be helpful when trying to determine how often a cat is using the litter box, and other important measurements. Some can even monitor body weight.

Expect that in the years ahead remote monitoring will be an ever-more important part of pet-specific care and that at some point it may make sense for you and your pet.

Pet Portals

Pet portals are private, secure websites that allow you to store your pet's information online and typically access certain information from your veterinary hospital. Pet owners typically have a secure login, and they can then see information about their pet and often add information as well.

Most pet portals associated with veterinary hospitals will also provide certain information from the medical records (such as vaccination details, medications prescribed, etc.), and there may be other useful

Peaches takes a break (courtesy Lanna Palmer).

features such as being able to request an appointment, print out a record for a boarding facility or pet sitter, refill a prescription, purchase non-prescription items, set up reminders for medications being given (such as monthly flea and tick control), receive alerts and notifications from the veterinary hospital, etc. There is typically also a library of pet health information that has been reviewed and curated for your use by your veterinary team. Many portals also have an associated "app" for use on mobile devices.

While pet portals may not provide enough details to share with other veterinary professionals (see blockchain below), they are often a great way for you to keep much of your pet health information in one location and be able to access it day or night. However, to take full advantage of a pet portal, ensure that you actually avail yourself of the opportunity and upload relevant information to your site so it is available whenever you might need it.

Blockchain

If you have ever used Bitcoin or other forms of cryptocurrency, you are probably familiar with the concept of blockchain, but you may not know that it is also demonstrating real benefits in many aspects of human health care and is bound to gain more prominence in veterinary medicine as well. Its main benefit is that it holds the promise for allowing secure privileges to various aspects of a medical record.

Blockchain just refers to an online database shared across a network of computers, but it differs from other databases in a number of important ways. For security, once a record has been added to the chain by a legitimate entity (such as a veterinary clinic, laboratory, or specialty center), it is very difficult for others to change (or hack). For consistency, the network makes frequent checks to ensure that all copies of records are the same across the entire network. Otherwise, your pet's medical record exists solely within your veterinary hospital's record system and its backup devices. There's probably not a great risk that your veterinarian's digital medical records would be hacked, but it's possible. However, the other problem with the current system is that the medical record cannot be easily shared with others, even with your permission, and others cannot easily add to those records (e.g., specialists, emergency clinics, laboratories, etc.).

In a blockchain, individual records are bundled together into blocks and then linked sequentially within a digital chain. Each block contains a unique code, called a hash, that identifies where it belongs when assembled into a chain. These hash codes are created by a mathematical formula and contribute to the security of the system. In the final step, when the blocks are added to the chain, the hash codes connect the blocks in a specific order. Any change to the original record, no matter how minuscule, would be detected and would warrant the generation of a new hash code. That change to the hash code alters the blockchain, making it extremely difficult for hackers to make changes that are not immediately detected within the network. It's not impossible, but attempting to change all the hash codes within the chain would require phenomenal computing power, making it much more secure than other systems.

The other useful feature of a blockchain database is that it is decentralized across many computers, so there is no one computer on which the records reside, making hacking much less likely and also making it less likely that records could get inadvertently deleted, destroyed or stolen from the veterinary hospital. Those with appropriate permission can access the blockchain information and add to the database, and the system sets up tests of trustworthiness before anyone is allowed to add to the chain. Trusted individuals are allowed to add to the chain and have private "keys" that are nearly impossible to hack. However, public keys can also be generated for information sharing, and so you as the pet owner can see the information in the record even if you don't have access to directly change results. This is now quite common in human hospital systems with patient access. Blockchain also allows full audit trail capability, which means there is complete documentation of the creation, modification and attempted deletion of records.

Without blockchain, current systems for sharing electronic data among doctors, pet owners, referral hospitals, laboratories and insurers are still quite error prone. Incorrect information can emerge as patient data gets reentered time after time by different individuals, and it is difficult to conserve changes made by one party into everyone's version of the medical record. You've probably experienced this when various offices have asked you for the same information you have already provided, and each time that happens, there is the potential for errors to creep into systems. So, for example, if a pet is seen by both a primary care and a specialty clinic, changes made to the medical records at either facility are not immediately captured in the medical records of both facilities and require multiple steps to send, receive, and enter information; errors and omissions are possible at all stages.

Blockchain can be used to provide all pet owners and providers with identical content. The decentralized-ledger approach to information management gives all parties simultaneous access to a single record of strongly encrypted data. It also creates an audit trail each time any data in the record are changed, helping to maintain the integrity of the system and its information. Eventually, blockchain could be used to provide secure and accurate medical information for all individual pets. You, as pet owner, could then access information in your pet's medical record and be assured that all modification attempts would be securely recorded, annotated, and are relatively tamper proof. If a pet has received treatments from multiple doctors at different facilities, all that information could be accessed from the blockchain, and there would be an audit trail for any changes made.

Blockchain is great in principle, but the success of any such system depends on the participation of many medical providers, or there are few benefits over those seen with traditional electronic medical records. So, while blockchain is great in large medical organizations with thousands of doctors and millions of patients, it's somewhat more complicated in veterinary hospitals with a few doctors and perhaps a few thousand patients.

Of course, one of the reasons blockchain will be important for veterinary hospitals is that with so many private hospitals unaffiliated with one another and potentially using different practice management software, there can be many "islands of information" with very few opportunities for "data bridges." That is because most veterinary hospitals don't share information with each other, so there are very few opportunities for them to analyze large data sets and determine trends. Blockchain can help address this and make it easier to deliver pet-specific care. For example, it is difficult to know the overall prevalence of a condition such as diabetes mellitus in the pet population, never mind in a population of Pugs or Burmese cats, which are presumed to be at higher risk. When we don't have large datasets, we typically need to rely on published studies suggesting "breed predisposition," which are not necessarily large nor robust studies (but they might be the best information available). Blockchain itself does not perform analytics, but permissions could be granted for analytics to be performed on such data. This could be extremely powerful in veterinary medicine in which large numbers of small hospitals exist globally, but a large database could potentially be mined for a wealth of information relative to pet-specific care (such as breed predispositions, disease prevalence, epidemiology, trends, etc.) without infringing on the privacy of any individual pet or owner. For example, we would have access to information such as whether certain medical problems are more common in certain breeds compared to others, the prevalence of disease in the general population, know whether reference intervals for laboratory tests are the same in all breeds, and even basic information such as the actual lifespan of different purebreds compared to hybrids and mixed-breed animals. Blockchain is the likely future of medical recordkeeping, but we're not quite there yet in veterinary medicine.

Case Example

Blair Donaldson is a three-year-old neutered male Dalmatian who has been previously diagnosed with seasonal allergies (atopic dermatitis) and was being administered a once-daily medication to control his itching. His owner, Jean, has been very conscientious, and they (preferred pronoun) were very proud of their hands-on approach to problem-free pet parenting. Blair has been well controlled for the past several months with daily medication but started scratching significantly in the last few hours. Since Blair had previously experienced severe reactions (hot spots) from his scratching, Jean immediately telephoned ABC Veterinary Hospital to bring him in without delay before the situation got any worse.

Julie, the customer service representative who answered the phone, was very concerned about Blair and recalled how tragic Blair seemed after his hot spot (a very inflamed patch of skin which can quickly become traumatized by scratching). Julie would book Blair for an appointment the next day, which was the first availability, but asked if Jean might be interested in a telehealth consult that could be scheduled for that afternoon, when Julie would try to create some time between existing veterinary appointments.

When Dr. Green and Jean connected on that telehealth call, it was very apparent that Jean was concerned and was afraid of what Blair might do to himself if the scratching could not be curtailed.

Dr. Green suggested that the likely culprit was ragweed pollen in the environment, which was wreaking havoc with many allergic pets in the practice as the pollen count was at an all-time high for the season. He advised that Blair be given a cool-water soak for at least ten minutes, gently toweled dry by blotting rather than rubbing, and then a mild itch-relieving spray be used on affected areas. During the bathing, Jean was going to do a thorough check for fleas and other parasites and verify with their roommate that Blair's parasite control product had been administered on schedule. It was advised that Blair remain indoors with windows closed and air conditioner on, and it was recommended that an over-the-counter antihistamine be considered (suitable products and doses were provided). It was unlikely that the antihistamine would have a major impact on the itchiness, but it might help a bit and also have some sedating effects, which might make Blair more sleepy and less likely to do damage to himself. The plan was to repeat the cool-water soak and spray before bedtime, but if Blair was not significantly more comfortable by then, to give another dose of his allergy medication just this once to keep him comfortable overnight, and they would address whatever issues remained at the appointment scheduled for the next day.

Jean was relieved that there was now a plan in place and felt the telehealth consult provided them with peace of mind and a strategy moving forward.

Recommended Reading

Ackerman, L. 2020a. Blockchain in *Five-Minute Veterinary Practice Management Consult*. Edited by L. Ackerman. 3rd ed. Hoboken: Wiley.

_____. 2020b. Telehealth in *Five-Minute Veterinary Practice Management*. Edited by L. Ackerman. 3rd ed. Hoboken: Wiley.

_____. 2019. "Why Should Veterinarians Consider Implementing Virtual Care?" *EC Veterinary Science* 4 (4): 259–261.

Casey, Michael, and Paul Vigna. 2019. *The Truth Machine: The Blockchain and the Future of Everything*. New York: Picador; St. Martin's Press.

Geron, T. 2018. "One Remedy for High Health Costs: Blockchain." *The Wall Street Journal*, May 29.

"Home." n.d. One Health Initiative. https://www.onehealthinitiative.com.

Katayama, Maki, Takatomi Kubo, Kazutaka Mogi, Kazushi Ikeda, Miho Nagasawa, and Takefumi Kikusui. 2016. "Heart Rate Variability Predicts the Emotional State in Dogs." *Behavioural Processes* 128 (July): 108–12. https://doi.org/10.1016/j.beproc.2016.04.015.

Miller, MC. 2019. "The Telehealth Trend." *AAHA Trends* 35 (4): 29–34.

"One Health." 2019. Centers for Disease Control and Prevention. https://www.cdc.gov/onehealth/index.html.

"The Real-Life Rewards of Virtual Care—How to Turn Your Hospital into a Digitally Connected Practice with Telehealth." 2018. American Animal Hospital Association, American Veterinary Medical Association.

Surman, Sean, and Linda Fleeman. 2013. "Continuous Glucose Monitoring in Small Animals." *Veterinary Clinics of North America: Small Animal Practice* 43 (2): 381–406. https://doi.org/10.1016/j.cvsm.2013.01.002.

"Telehealth & Telemedicine in Veterinary Practice." n.d. American Veterinary Medical Association. http://www.avma.org/telehealth.

6

Prevention

The Best Medicine

In medicine, it is hard to imagine any concept more important than prevention, and yet it often does not get the attention it deserves. Preventing problems from happening in the first place is the cornerstone of raising an *almost* perfect pet. After all, what could be better than putting in the effort upfront to keep your pet healthy, rather than have to deal with problems that could have been avoided?

Controlling the Situation

One of the most important aspects of prevention is appreciating that we have more control over situations than might at first appear. We have discretion over what and when our pets eat, how they are exposed to environmental situations, where and when they travel, and almost everything with which they might come in contact. It's an awesome power we have and one that we can wield to keep our pets safe from harm.

Just think about it. Every time your pet goes outside, you have control over how that should happen. If you go for a walk, is your pet on a leash, halter or other such device? That's great, because even if your pet is very obedient and never wanders off, the same cannot be said for other people's pets. Leash laws have greatly decreased traumatic injuries, such as pets being hit by cars, and they also help decrease the risk of our pets having altercations with other animals (including wildlife) and of biting incidents. Now, we would be remiss in a book on *almost* perfect pets to not mention that how you restrain your pet depends a lot on your pet. A pet that is content and well controlled on a standard leash is a pleasure to take anywhere. However, if you have a pet that tends to lunge ahead or otherwise misbehave at walk time, you might consider

93

a head halter, which gives gentle directed pressure to encourage more appropriate behavior without any form of punishment. If you have a pet that is prone to having difficulty breathing with anything that puts pressure on the throat, a chest halter system may be a better choice, as these systems apply gentle pressure either to the chest or head rather than the neck. Many trainers actually prefer halters to collars for most pets. So-called choke chains or prong collars are no longer recommended for pet training. In addition, electronic "shock" collars refer to collars that deliver electronic stimulation of varying intensities remotely via a radio-controlled device. While at low levels the electric stimulation is unlikely to cause damage, most behaviorists and trainers favor more positive reinforcement training tools, and some retailers no longer sell these types of products.

The situation is a bit more challenging when it comes to car travel. Many pets—dogs more than cats—enjoy traveling in the car. While it may look cute to see a pet's head out the window, ears flapping in the wind, this is not recommended for many reasons. Pets traveling in the car should ideally be in crates to protect them from becoming projectiles in the case of accidents or sudden stops and starts. In an accident, unrestrained pets are likely to be disoriented, and when doors are opened, there is a greater chance that they will run into traffic. Harnesses also exist that can be used with seatbelts to restrict pets in a vehicle, but to date the results have not shown these devices to protect consistently. For cats, being in a cage or crate is clearly the best option, and cats may be calmer if the crate is then covered with a blanket. By the way, pets can get carsick, just as people can, and if that is the case with your pet, speak to your veterinary team, as there are medications that can help. In addition, pets should never be left alone in a car, and it is important to be aware that temperatures within a closed car can be significantly higher than outdoor temperatures. Every year pets die from such exposures.

We've discussed pet-proofing a home in the selection chapter, but just to reiterate here, you control most of the situations in which pets can find themselves in trouble. Take that responsibility seriously, and go through your home and consider where changes should be made to keep your pet safe. In addition, like any good parent, don't create dangerous scenarios by leaving your pets without appropriate supervision. You may think that they couldn't get into trouble when you step out for just a few minutes ... but you'd be wrong. Eventually pets will become more trustworthy as they understand the rules of the household, but any pets, no matter the age, can be tempted (food on counters, medications or cleaners in accessible cabinets, possessions in closets, etc.), and the results can be disastrous. No matter how well behaved your pet is, the easiest way to keep them safe is to ensure that you have adequately prevented them from getting access to things that are dangerous or other items you value highly.

When it comes to yards and gardens, there are other choices to be made. A fenced yard is the best option, but of course crafty cats and dogs can find their ways over and under fences, so pets should be supervised until their escape potential is clearly known. If pets are going to be allowed outside for any period of time, they should have access to shady areas and a source of clean water. Most pets appreciate some exposure to the outdoors, but it is important to understand that this often increases their risk for infectious diseases and parasites. For example, a variety of tick species can be found in the outdoor environment, and many carry disease agents. Mosquitoes are important carriers of heartworm and West Nile virus, and while mosquitoes are also present indoors, there are typically much higher numbers outdoors. Wildlife in yards can also serve as carriers of disease, even if they don't come in direct contact with our pets. Raccoons and possums can carry fleas, which can get transferred to our pets. So, fencing is an important option, but it does not provide complete protection, so supervision is still important.

Electronic fencing is increasingly popular with pet owners as an alternative to physical fencing, but it has significant limitations. Electronic or invisible fences set an acceptable perimeter with underground wires, and then a collar on the pet gives a mild shock when the animal approaches that perimeter. The concept is that the aversive stimuli are used so that the pet learns the boundaries and that it can avoid shocks by staying within those boundaries. The training method works in principle, but it does require you to use electric shocks on your beloved companion, an aversive practice most behaviorists do not recommend or condone. It also requires that your pet continue to wear the shock collar while outside to be sure that they do not forget the barrier training. Additionally, an electronic barrier does not protect your pet from other animals that can freely come onto your property (they aren't wearing a collar, so crossing the perimeter won't be deterred). It also does not provide as strong a barrier for your pet as a fence does because, when animals are stressed, scared or sufficiently enticed, they will endure the temporary shock, which ends once they are past the barrier and off your property. Still, when fencing is not possible, it's another option that can be considered.

Pets can also be at increased risk based on exposure to other animals (such as at a boarding facility, groomer, or even within a veterinary hospital) or environments (e.g., drinking from or swimming in ponds, walking in wooded areas, having access to disease vectors, etc.) or travel outside of the home area to another area in which a condition is prevalent or through owner indiscretion (accidental ingestion of chocolate by pet, sandbox not covered to prevent fecal contamination by other pets and wildlife, yard debris not cleared, which serves as a point of entry for ticks, etc.). It sounds daunting, but understand that you actually have a lot of control for preventing problems, as long as you have a firm understanding of risks and how to address those risks.

Controlling Infectious Diseases

Vaccinations have been important in controlling a variety of diseases in the dog and cat population, including fatal diseases communicable to humans, such as rabies. In fact, vaccination has become such a standard practice that many of the diseases that used to be common in pets, such as distemper and hepatitis in the dog, and feline panleukopenia and calicivirus in the cat, have become less common in the general pet population, other than in shelters and geographic clusters.

Most veterinary teams divide vaccines into those considered "core," which should be administered to all pets of a species, and "noncore,"

Ivan takes a grooming break (courtesy Tyra Sherry).

which are given based on certain risk factors. So, in the dog, vaccine components considered core are usually distemper, hepatitis and parvovirus, as well as rabies, which is regulated by law (as a major risk to humans). On the other hand, Lyme disease might be considered for vaccination as a noncore product, based on where the pet lives or if it is likely to travel to a location where it could come into contact with ticks carrying the disease. In cats, vaccine components considered core are feline viral rhinotracheitis, calicivirus and panleukopenia, with rabies regulated by law, while something like feline leukemia virus vaccine is given based on risk, such as exposure to other cats.

There are many considerations to be made regarding personalizing a vaccination protocol for a specific pet, including governmental mandates, local disease prevalence, safety of the vaccine, ability of the vaccine to prevent disease (efficacy), duration of immunity (how long the protection lasts), any risks posed by the vaccine itself, and any animal-specific issues to be considered (including age, state of health, other concerns, etc.).

In general, vaccines are avoided in animals less than 6 weeks of age, as immunization before this age may interfere with the natural protection young animals get from their mothers. It is important to let puppies and kittens nurse, since the first milk they receive (colostrum) tends to be rich in antibodies that the mother provides to her offspring. So, vaccine protocols usually begin when animals are 6–9 weeks of age, depending on their individual circumstances.

Most vaccines are given as an initial series every 2–4 weeks as indicated on their product labels and then periodically as needed. Guidelines have been developed for vaccination of both dogs and cats by a variety of organizations, but all rely on veterinary judgment because each pet is unique in its risk profile.

One hot-button issue within the profession itself is how often pets should be revaccinated. Veterinary teams are often caught between the recommendations that appear on the product labels of the vaccines they are using and the realization that some of the vaccines likely provide protection for a longer period than the manufacturer lists. Here's the dilemma. When the vaccine manufacturer got its government approval, they might have documented that animals remain protected when they receive a "booster" vaccine annually. Wonderful! However, it is likely that at least some of those vaccines would provide protection that would last longer than a year, at least in some animals. Also wonderful! The problem is that we don't know which animals need to be vaccinated more frequently and which might be able to skip a year or two. We do know that some breeds do not generate as much protection as others, so it often comes down to professional judgment by the veterinary team. Conservative veterinarians may want to revaccinate annually if that is what is recommended by the vaccine manufacturer, since protection will be assured, while others might want to give at least some vaccines every two or even three years based on the likelihood that protection will last more than a year in healthy animals. Other veterinarians will recommend running antibody levels (titers) for certain infectious diseases periodically as a crude measure of whether animals still demonstrate protection from previous vaccination. It's not precise but can be a reasonable indication of when protection is waning and when revaccination is indicated.

In an era of anti-vaxxers, it is not unexpected that some people would also be suspicious of vaccines for their pets. Vaccines are remarkably safe, but there are quite rare instances of complications, so don't be shy about having discussions with the veterinary team. Just as in human medicine, the benefits should always outweigh the risks, and when it comes to vaccination, the goal is to create a population of pet animals that are protected from serious infectious diseases. That being said, it is important to be aware of so-called "vaccine hesitancy" in which certain members of the public are fearful of the possible adverse consequences of vaccination and may choose not to vaccinate their pets. That creates public health risks (as it does in human medicine) because it leaves animals prone to developing serious diseases and spreading them to others. The public health aspect of vaccination relies on the concept of "herd immunity" where a population of vaccinated pets provide a buffer against the spread of disease. We can't necessarily control the vaccine status of stray and feral animals, nor of wildlife, so keeping pets vaccinated and safe is an important goal. Pet owners need to appreciate that some vaccines may be required by law (such as rabies) in certain countries and are not discretionary. While the anti-vaccination (anti-vax) contingent of pet owners is likely less than those fearful or reluctant about childhood vaccination, it is important to acknowledge their concerns, but use your own judgment about whether you want your pet to have social access to such unvaccinated and unprotected animals. Vaccination is an incredibly important aspect of keeping our pets healthy. The World Health Organization has recognized vaccine hesitancy as a global health threat, and it is important to realize that it is a concern for pet health as well.

The path to problem-free vaccination status is to appreciate risks in the environment and to work with your veterinary team on reasonable solutions. Not every infectious disease has an effective vaccine, and not every vaccine is appropriate for every pet. As discussed in the chapter on personalized health care, the process typically starts with a risk assessment for each pet and then considerations of the best ways of dealing with those risks.

One thing that became apparent with the onset of the COVID-19 crisis is that situations can arise in which there is an infectious disease but not yet an effective vaccine. In these cases, physical (social) distancing is very important at controlling the situation. Individuals with potential contact to infection but who appear to be free of the infection are quarantined, while those documented to be infected are isolated from the rest of the susceptible population. This is as true in animals as it is in people. Isolation and quarantine concepts apply whether animals are capable of being infectious or whether infectious agents can just piggyback on otherwise healthy-appearing pets.

Parasite Control

Parasite control is not only an important element in preventive care for pets, but it is also a critical public health issue since many of those parasites can cause medical issues in people as well. We typically divide parasite problems into those parasites that reside on the outside of the body (ectoparasites) and those that live within the body (endoparasites).

Surface parasites include a variety of bugs that live and feed on the skin, such as fleas, ticks, mites, lice, and mosquitoes. They not only can be pests, but some can transmit a variety of infectious diseases as well. Some can even transfer other parasites; for instance, fleas are a main source of tapeworm in pets. How does this happen? Well, fleas can contain certain tapeworm larvae, and when itchy pets chew at their skin, they may actually ingest fleas and tapeworms along with them. Ticks especially are responsible for several significant diseases in people and pets (Lyme disease, ehrlichiosis, Rocky Mountain spotted fever, anaplasmosis, babesiosis and many others).

Internal parasites include those that can live in the bloodstream, such as heartworm, but also a host of parasites that tend to live in the intestines, including roundworms, hookworms, and tapeworms. Whipworms can be found in both dogs and cats but are more often detected in dogs. Internal parasites are common in dogs and cats and are of public health significance as some can be transmitted to people (especially roundworms and hookworms). Because of this public health issue, all pets in contact with people should have parasite control, and in most cases this control should be year-round.

Parasite control has three aspects: surveillance (testing for parasites), routine use of preventives, and treating any infections/infestations as detected. Surveillance testing involves periodic screening for parasites on a regular basis. For example, heartworm screening is done with blood tests once or twice a year (depending on regional risk), while most intestinal parasites are detected by running tests on fresh feces, where parasite eggs can be detected. There are also immunologic tests for some parasites. It is important to realize that sometimes there is a lag period between when pets first acquire parasites and when they are detectable, since the parasites first need to migrate to specific parts of the body and go through parts of their life cycles before they produce eggs and larvae that become detectable. The time between when a pet gets infected with a parasite and when the parasite is capable of producing eggs or larvae that is detectable is known as the prepatent period, and it can differ significantly between parasites. For the dog with tapeworm *Dipylidium caninum*, the prepatent period might be three weeks, while for the heartworm parasite *Dirofilaria immitis*, it might be six months or longer. Accordingly, animals are typically routinely screened on a periodic basis. Routine screening for parasites in general is important, because while the most common parasites are ... well, common, there are also some dangerous relatively rare parasites that are only incidentally detected, and some can have tragic consequences in people (e.g., raccoon roundworm).

The use of preventive parasite-control products is monumentally important in keeping our pets healthy. These products are given routinely to pets to prevent parasites from becoming problematic or to halt the progression of parasite life stages so as not to progress to full clinical disease. Routine use of flea and tick control keeps these pests off of our pets. These products do not necessarily repel these parasites (some products do), but they can kill them before they have a chance to lay eggs. Some combination products work by interfering with different stages of the parasite life cycle. Heartworm preventives are routinely used in dogs and cats where this parasite is found geographically; they interfere with the heartworm life cycle so the immature forms of the parasites cannot progress to becoming adults. Since heartworm is transmitted by mosquitoes, using mosquito control products can also lessen the likelihood of heartworm infection, but it should not replace heartworm prevention products.

Because of the risk of some parasites being transmissible to people, there are typically guidelines that make recommendations regarding best practices for parasite control in dogs and cats. These are meant to help keep pets parasite free but also have a public health intention of preventing the spread of parasites to family members. Since it is not unusual for puppies and kittens to have parasites that are transferred from their mother during delivery and nursing, and since there may be a lag period (the prepatent period) before these parasites are actually detectable with testing, there is a general recommendation that all puppies and kittens be "de-wormed" in a series of treatments until they are able to be placed on more integrated parasite-control products.

It would be handy if one product could protect all pets from all internal and external parasites necessary for each geographic region. Unfortunately, there currently is no single medication that works on all parasites. Instead, pet owners must use a combination of products to achieve adequate protection. For each animal, the best product choices will depend on the local prevalence of parasites in your area and your pet's individual risk factors. The determination can be challenging for your veterinary team, who want to make the best recommendation for control of anticipated parasites while minimizing the need of providing too many different products. To accomplish this, teams usually plan on preventing the most dangerous parasites and then treating other parasites that may be detectable on periodic screening. So, for example, pets may be on integrated products that will help control fleas, ticks, heartworm, roundworms and hookworms but elect not to add additional products that would control tapeworms (a common variety of which is transmitted by fleas) unless there is a problem detected. Parasite-control products are considered very safe, but the team will try to strike a balance between risk and reward, as for any medical intervention. All medications should be used on the basis of a risk-benefit assessment, but the benefits from parasite control typically far outweigh the risks of using such products on our pets, especially when we factor in the risks of possible spread to family members. While it will receive more coverage in the chapter on medications, it is worth mentioning here that one of the main problems associated with parasite control is forgetting to administer the products on schedule. As you might imagine, it really doesn't help anything if you purchased the product, but you forgot to actually make sure it was given. There are parasite-control products that can be administered by tablet, topical application, and even injection, so use whatever reminder system that works for you to make sure they are given on schedule.

When it comes to parasite control, we also need to take personal responsibility for limiting exposure. To prevent the spread from roaming pets and wildlife, make sure that sandboxes and play areas are covered, as fecal contamination can be a problem. Keep lawns and yards well maintained and avoid accumulations of leaves and debris as these are nesting grounds for ticks. Have a plan in place for disposing of pet fecal waste (such as putting feces in plastic bags for disposal in a sanitary landfill, adding it to compost where the internal heat should be sufficient for killing parasites, or flushing dog feces down the toilet), understanding that parasites in the feces might be transmissible to family members. One of the most common fears is for the risk of toxoplasmosis in pregnant women. People can get toxoplasmosis from consuming contaminated water and raw foods, insufficiently washing fruits and vegetables (leading to inadvertently consuming contaminated soil) and through cat feces in which the parasite might reside (while potentially not causing the cat any harm). Because of this disease, it is not recommended that cat feces be flushed down the toilet since municipal water treatment systems will not always be sufficient to kill this parasite, but it can be handled in the other ways mentioned. It is best not to leave pet fecal material on the lawn, since that can directly affect public health, and if it gets carried away into storm drains, it can affect the water supply.

One of the most important things that can be done for parasite control, as well as for infectious diseases, is proper hygiene. While some parasites are capable of penetrating intact skin (such as hookworms contracted on a sandy beach through bare feet), most parasites are transmitted when parasite eggs in fecal matter get accidentally transferred to the hands and from the hands to the face and mouth. The best approach is to use year-round parasite control to keep our pets parasite free, but routine handwashing and/or the use of hand sanitizer is important to limit the unintentional spread of parasites and infectious agents. It works for limiting the spread of diseases between people and that applies to close contact with our pets as well. No need to be afraid of our pets, but good hygiene is always appropriate.

Exercise and Weight Management

While covered in more detail in the chapter on nutritional considerations, it is important to mention here that there is a near-epidemic of pets being overweight and obese, and the best way to deal with the situation is to ensure that pets are not overfed and that they have adequate exercise to burn off the calories they consume.

Adequate exercise does not mean excessive exercise, and just as we would not consider living a sedentary existence all week and then running marathons on the weekend, it's more important to have a regular exercise regimen that is sustainable and appropriate for your specific pet. For many pets, a brisk daily walk may be all that is needed, and having some activities in the home or yard. However, if you have selected a high-activity breed, be prepared to have sufficient outings to burn off some of that energy or you might have to contend with objectionable behaviors. In any case, the exercise program should be individualized for the needs of your particular pet in a manner that protects everyone's sanity.

Once again, this will be covered in more detail in the nutrition chapter, but appreciate that even if you think your pet being chubby is cute, it can have major health implications as it does in humans. In addition, for pets prone to developmental orthopedic diseases, such as hip dysplasia, keeping them lean during their most active growth phases is one of the best ways to limit damage from the disorder.

To be fair, it can sometimes be difficult to appreciate how overweight our pets may be. At present, most people don't weigh their pets regularly, so small increases in weight might not be immediately discernible, and we may face some surprises when pets get weighed at the veterinary hospital. We do have options, however. Weight alone can be deceptive, since heavily muscled individuals may weigh more than standard charts would indicate as normal, so veterinary teams

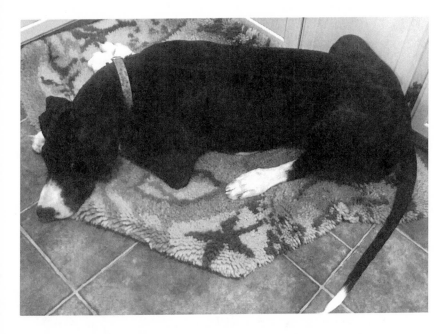

Early skill building in the dog can include commands like "down stay." Here a five-month-old Great Dane does so on her designated mat. The mat can be carried from place to place (courtesy Janice Adams).

often rely on body condition scores (BCS) and muscle condition scores (MCS) to provide objective measures of body mass, and these can be used at home as well. There are several different grading systems that are used that rank body condition on a scale (such as 1 to 9, or 1 to 5), some suggested by pet nutrition companies and others supported by veterinary organizations (such as https://wsava.org/global-guidelines/global-nutrition-guidelines/). These are simple measures that can be performed at home, even if you don't have access to a scale for your pet.

There are, of course, ways for you to measure your pet's weight routinely. If you have a pet you can easily lift, you can weigh yourself alone and then with your pet, the difference being attributed to your pet. If your pet is larger, most veterinary hospitals would be happy to weigh your pet and record weight trends, even if you don't have a scheduled appointment. Don't be surprised if your scale at home doesn't agree entirely with the professional scale at the veterinary office—that happens when we have our weight taken at the doctor's office too. Finally, these days it is easy and relatively inexpensive to purchase a digital pet scale for use at home. Do an Internet search, and you will be amazed at what you can find.

The great part about managing pet weight is that we, as pet owners, have full control over what gets consumed, so we really have no excuses. The difficult part is that often pet owners believe that "food is love," and it can be habit forming to see the devotion our pets have for us when we feed them. This is true, and for pets that are truly food motivated, we can use this to shape all kinds of positive behaviors (see chapter on mindfulness and pet care). Still, we do not need to let pets coerce us into giving them treats on their schedule (no matter how cute or persistent they are!), and pets love any social reward, such as playing games with them, cuddling with them, or even just paying attention to them—it doesn't need to be all about food.

Oral Care

Despite the fact that dental care is needed in dogs and cats as much as it is in humans, most pets do not receive the level of oral care required. Because of this oversight, dogs and cats commonly develop periodontal disease in which dental plaque adheres to the teeth, and bacteria within the plaque irritate the gum tissue and may even result in infection of the underlying bone. By 3 years of age, most dogs and cats have some evidence of periodontal disease and that can set them up for a variety of medical problems in their future, including kidney, liver and heart muscle changes.

Pet owners may be more concerned with a pet's bad breath or with unsightly calculus (tartar) visible on the teeth, but it is actually the progressive nature of periodontal disease and what's going on beneath the gumline that you can't see that poses the most risk for pets. It is important that such changes not be allowed to persist, since only the damage from the very earliest stages of periodontal disease can be effectively reversed. After that, the damage becomes progressive and irreversible. That is why it is so important that our teeth be thoroughly cleaned on a regular basis, and the same applies to our pets.

To prevent future problems, talk with your veterinary team about oral care strategies. They can do periodic dental cleaning under anesthesia to help with the situation, but it is important that you take responsibility for oral care at home, too. This care might include regular brushing with pet-specific toothbrushes and toothpastes (dentifrices), oral rinses with specially formulated antiseptics, and diets and chews specifically created for this purpose. You might never have pictured yourself brushing your pet's teeth, but with patient and gentle training, most pets will allow you to do it. Even if they don't realize that such cleaning is good for their health, you can rest assured that it is one of the most important ways to ensure that pets remain *almost* perfect well into their senior years.

Start with Healthy Stock

All pets, whether purebred or not, may be predisposed to certain conditions based on family history or certain genetic (or epigenetic) traits that they carry. This topic is covered in more detail in the chapter on early-detection strategies, but for now it is sufficient to realize that if you have a pet that is healthy to start with, then there are fewer surprises to catch up with us as we engage in health management (as opposed to disease management).

Not so long ago, predicting a pet's health was a bit of a gamble, but we now have much better tools for selecting animals less likely to have problems. There are more details in the chapter on appropriate pet selection, but let's take another brief look here.

Family history is a major determinant of health risks, so if we are interested in prevention, then it makes sense to select pets that are less likely to develop certain health issues in the first place. Even though we can't entirely prevent problems from happening, you might be surprised at what can be accomplished these days. If possible, try to adopt a pet from a place where you have access to information on family medical history. Many breeders participate in registries in which they record the status of their breeding animals for a variety of disorders known to exist in the breed. These registries are meant primarily for breeders to be able to improve their breeding stock by locating animals with desirable results for specific conditions, but the public has free access to these records of participating breeders, so you can use them to see the status of individual animals, including the parents and extended family of a pet you are considering purchasing. We often don't have this degree of transparency for our own parents and grandparents, so this is a phenomenal resource when breeders participate.

Today, we also have the possibility of DNA testing for literally hundreds of genetic variants (phenes, conditions and traits) in dogs and cats, which can tell us a lot about those disorders for which DNA testing is available. When breeders use such testing on their breeding animals, we can use the results to infer the health status of their offspring, since if the parents are clear for a genetic trait, it shouldn't be possible that animals in the litter would be affected. We can also run genetic testing on animals we plan on adopting, but it may take a few weeks to get the results. While pets can be given DNA tests by as early as 1 day of age, they are more commonly tested at around

Another important skill is the "wait" command, here modeled by Rifka as she waits for the release command after her food bowl has been put on the floor (courtesy Janice Adams).

12 weeks of age. DNA testing and health care registries can't tell us everything about the future health of an animal, but they are a great start.

Identification

You may not believe it could happen, but you could find one day that your pet goes missing. It can happen for a lot of reasons, including pets wandering off when a door or window is opened, bolting from a yard, car or other environment, or any number of other situations. Pets can also be stolen. If pets are found by someone else, they don't have the ability to ask those people to call home on their behalf, so you need to think of this in advance.

There are a number of permanent identification possibilities with pets, and while some prefer tattoos, the most common approach is with microchip implantation. The microchip doesn't act as a beacon if a pet goes missing, but if someone finds a lost pet and takes it to a veterinary clinic or shelter, they can use a scanner to retrieve information on the microchip, and when contacted, the microchip registry can inform the pet owner where their pet is located.

Microchips are placed with a relatively painless injection (they are about the size of a grain of rice), and they might be used to confirm the identity of animals, help unite them with their owners when they get lost, and may also be used to substantiate that certain laboratory results (such as genetic testing) are indeed for the animal claimed. Collars and tags are also useful, but they are not considered permanent identification because they can easily be removed.

In the event your pet ever goes missing, make sure you have the resources to help facilitate recovering your pet. This should include recent images of your pet, identifying features, and methods that will help confirm your pet's identity (microchip number and manufacturer, tattoo and registry, DNA "fingerprinting," etc.). Remember also that for people who might find your pet, they may have familiarity with only the most common breeds, so it is possible they might misidentify your pet if they just call in to neighborhood shelters. Ideally they will take your pet to a veterinary hospital or a shelter where the pet can be scanned for microchip identification, or they will look for tattoos and hopefully be able to trace them to a registry. Make the process as easy as possible by ensuring redundancy in your pet identification, where they have permanent identification such as a microchip, as well as collars that might contain identifying information (e.g., rabies tags, contact information, etc.).

Since collars and tags can be lost or removed, on their own they do not constitute permanent identification.

Body Modification

When it comes to body modification in pets, we're not talking about piercing or even tattoos for the purpose of identification. Body modification, which is the deliberate altering of appearance, typically for aesthetics, is still performed in pets but is becoming less acceptable and with fewer veterinarians participating in the procedures. The most common body modifications in pets include ear cropping, tail docking and declawing.

Ear cropping involves surgically removing portions of the ear flap and then bracing the ears on the head for a period of time so the ears are pointed and are directed upwards. The procedure is almost exclusively done in dogs and gives certain breeds a characteristic appearance (such as Doberman Pinschers, Schnauzers, Great Danes, Boxers, Cane Corsos, and the breeds collectively referred to as pit bulls) that is preferred by some. The surgery is typically performed in pups at 7–12 weeks of age, and the ears are then "taped" for a variable period of time so they maintain the proper orientation. Cropping is banned in many countries where it is considered a form of cruelty, but it still occurs. In fact, many pet owners just believe that these breeds naturally have ears that look like that, so it is just a matter of accepting pets that come in all sizes, shapes and conformations and having reasonable expectations. Whatever the reasons for why ear cropping was done historically, each pet owner needs to come to terms with whether they believe it is appropriate to surgically alter pets to achieve some cosmetic goal. By the way, if you prefer dogs with upright ears, there are many dog breeds that achieve that naturally, without surgery, including the Papillon, Australian Cattle Dog, Boston Terrier, Pembroke Welsh Corgi, German Shepherd Dog, Scottish Terrier, Siberian husky, and Norwich Terrier, to name just a few.

Tail docking involves surgically amputating parts of the tail and associated vertebrae. Similar to ear cropping, the procedure is almost exclusively done in dogs, where it gives certain breeds (Boxer, Corgi, Doberman Pinscher, Rottweiler, Cocker Spaniel, Poodle, etc.) an appearance that might seem preferable to some. The surgery (or nonsurgical alternatives performed by non-veterinary individuals) is typically performed in pups less than 14 days of age, and the length of the remaining tail is often dictated by breed standards. Docking is banned in many countries where it is considered a form of cruelty, but like ear cropping, it still exists, and many pet lovers might not realize that the "look" of certain breeds regarding their tails might have required surgical alteration. Whatever the reason that tail docking was done in the past (in ancient times it was once thought to prevent rabies, which clearly was never true), at present it is just regarded as a cosmetic surgery, which is illegal in many countries and yet is still performed. For pet owners that prefer dogs with short tails, there are many dog breeds in which this occurs naturally, associated with a variety of "bobtail" genes, including the Australian Shepherd, Brittany Spaniel, English Bulldog and many others. In fact, in response to prohibitions of tail docking in certain countries, some breeders are attempting to "outcross" to other breeds that are naturally tailless and to introduce this genetic trait to their breed of interest. Of course, even though tail docking is not commonplace in cats, there are several tailless varieties, including the Manx, Cymric, American Bobtail, and Pixie-Bob.

While ear cropping and tail docking are almost exclusively done in dogs, declawing was primarily reserved for cats. The rationale was that cats could cause damage and injury with their claws, and so surgically removing the claws might lead to lower chances of relinquishment by upset pet owners. That view has not been supported by research, and most behaviorists suggest that environmental enrichment and providing acceptable scratching alternatives is preferable for this natural tendency than surgical amputation. While trimming and filing nails can make them less likely to do damage (soft nail caps are also available), declawing actually involves amputating the toe bones to which the claws are attached, and this can have some adverse consequences. Declawing is banned in many countries in which it is considered a form of cruelty, and yet it is still performed in some places. In some situations, declawing has actually allowed cats to remain in a home, when otherwise they would be relinquished or abandoned, so the practice does have its proponents. A better approach if possible is to realize from the start that scratching is a normal cat behavior, often associated with predatory behavior and territorial marking. Prevention of problems should focus on providing acceptable options for kittens (such as multiple scratching posts) and supervising kittens and training them to use these devices appropriately. Synthetic pheromones (feline interdigital semiochemicals) are even commercially available to help attract cats to designated scratching areas. It's interesting to note that dogs can also do damage from scratching, but declawing has never been seen as a solution for this. Pet owners have become accustomed to routinely trimming and filing dog's nails and even applying soft caps to the claws. Perhaps such regular care will also become commonplace for cats and further minimize the need for surgical alternatives.

Case Example

Tori is the owner of Jasmine, a healthy five-year-old Himalayan cat. Jasmine and Tori had a close relationship, and since Tori had a flexible work schedule, she was able to spend a fair bit of time working from home and spending lots of time with Jasmine.

One day when Tori opened the front door for a delivery, she noticed a gray patch of fur in the bushes, which turned out to be a young cat (not quite a kitten, but it didn't appear to be full grown either). It did not resist at all when she approached, and it began to purr when she picked it up and began petting it. Tori was sure this little bundle of fur must belong to someone, so she decided to keep her safe and start looking for an owner.

Tori posted some notices in the neighborhood, as well as on local Internet feeds, and was sure that someone would respond. In the meantime, she was amazed at how well Jasmine took to the newcomer, and she didn't pull away when the newcomer nuzzled her or even when it shared her litter tray and food bowl. Tori decided to nickname the cat "Tag" for the time being, since it seemed to tag along with Jasmine wherever she went.

After a few weeks, nobody had claimed Tag, and Tori needed to decide what to do since her long-term plan was not really to keep two cats. While contemplating the possibilities and leisurely reclining on the couch with Jasmine and Tag, she noticed a patch of scaly hair loss on the top of Jasmine's head. She checked Tag as well but didn't see anything. However, as a concerned pet owner, she promptly called ABC Veterinary Hospital and made an appointment for the next day. She also mentioned about her new furry guest and was told to bring Tag in as well.

After some testing, the veterinary team concluded that Jasmine had ringworm, likely contracted from Tag. Tori was surprised, because Jasmine was fully vaccinated and was also on the parasite-control regimen recommended by the hospital. Tori was surprised to learn from her veterinarian that ringworm was not even caused by a worm—it is a fungal infection. The veterinarian suspected that Jasmine got the infection from Tag and collected a sample for fungal culture to confirm. When Tori asked how that could happen, since Tag had no symptoms, she learned that some cats can be "carriers" of ringworm and have no discernible problems themselves but can then transmit the infection to other pets and humans. Tori then shared that she also had a rash on her neck (where Tag liked to snuggle) and wondered if it could be related. In the end, Tori learned a valuable lesson about quarantine before exposing Jasmine to other animals. Perhaps most devastating was the news that ringworm spores could survive for up to 18 months in her home!

Recommended Reading

Ackerman, L. 2020. *Proactive Pet Parenting: Anticipating Pet Health Problems Before They Happen.* Problem Free Publishing.

Ackerman, L.J. 2011. *The Genetic Connection, 2nd Edition.* Lakewood, CO: AAHA Press.

"American Animal Hospital Association-American Veterinary Medical Association Health Guidelines Task Force." 2011. *Journal of the American Veterinarian Medical Association* 239 (5): 625–29. https://doi.org/https://www.aahanet.org/Library/PreventiveHealthcare.aspx.

Creevy, Kate E., Jesse Grady, Susan E. Little, George E. Moore, Beth Groetzinger Strickler, Steve Thompson, and Jinelle A. Webb. 2019. "2019 AAHA Canine Life Stage Guidelines*." *Journal of the American Animal Hospital Association* 55 (6): 267–90. https://doi.org/10.5326/jaaha-ms-6999.

"Declawing of Domestic Cats." 2020. American Veterinary Medical Association. 2020. https://www.avma.org/resources-tools/avma-policies/declawing-domestic-cats.

Epstein, Mark, Ned F. Kuehn, Gary Landsberg, B. Duncan X. Lascelles, Steven L. Marks, Jean M. Schaedler, and Helen Tuzio. 2005. "AAHA Senior Care Guidelines for Dogs and Cats." *Journal of the American Animal Hospital Association* 41 (2): 81–91. https://doi.org/10.5326/0410081.

Ford, R., L.J. Larson, K.D. McClure, et al. n.d. "2017 Canine Vaccination Guidelines (2017) AAHA." www.aaha.org. https://aaha.org/guidelines/canine_vaccination_guidelines.aspx.

Hazel, Susan J., Lori R. Kogan, V. Tamara Montrose, Michelle L. Hebart, and James A. Oxley. 2019. "Restraint of Dogs in Vehicles in the US, UK and Australia." *Preventive Veterinary Medicine* 170 (1): 104714. https://doi.org/10.1016/j.prevetmed.2019.104714.

"Home." n.d. Companion Animal Parasite Council. https://www.capcvet.org.

OFA (Registry). https://www.ofa.org.

Partners for Healthy Pets. http://www.partnetsforhealthypets.org.

Pereira dos Santos, José Diogo, Eva Cunha, Telmo Nunes, Luís Tavares, and Manuela Oliveira. 2019. "Relation between Periodontal Disease and Systemic Diseases in Dogs." *Research in Veterinary Science* 125: 136–140. https://doi.org/10.1016/j.rvsc.2019.06.007.

Pets and Parasites. https://www.petsandparasites.org/.

Quimby, J, S. Gowland, HC Carney, et al. 2021. "AAHA/AAFP Feline Life Stage Guidelines." *Journal of Feline Medicine and Surgery* (2021) 23, 211-233. DOI: 10.1177/1098612X21993657

Salt, Carina, Penelope J. Morris, Richard F. Butterwick, Elizabeth M. Lund, Tim J. Cole, and Alexander J. German. 2020. "Comparison of Growth Patterns in Healthy Dogs and Dogs in Abnormal Body Condition Using Growth Standards." Edited by Juan J. Loor. *PLOS ONE* 15 (9): e0238521. https://doi.org/10.1371/journal.pone.0238521.

Shaw, Jane R. 2019. "Evaluation of Communication Skills Training Programs at North American Veterinary Medical Training Institutions." *Journal of the American Veterinary Medical Association* 255 (6): 722–733. https://doi.org/10.2460/javma.255.6.722.

Stone, AES, GO Brummet, EM Carozza. et al. 2020. "AAHA/AAFP Feline Vaccination Guidelines." *Journal of Feline Medicine and Surgery* (2020) 22, 813-830. DOI: 101177/1098612X20941784

Weese, Scott. 2021. "New (Probably) Canine-Origin Human Coronavirus?" *Worms and Germs* (blog). May 20. https://www.wormsandgermsblog.com/.

7

Why Early-Detection Strategies Make Sense

Early detection is one of the core principles of raising an *almost* perfect pet. When we have the option of determining what issues may lie ahead, there is an opportunity to intervene early and sometimes even change the course of a disease process. It's always better to prevent a condition from ever occurring in the first place ... but the next best option is to identify problems early, when typically, there are the most options for doing something about them.

Without early-detection mechanisms in place, we are at a distinct disadvantage when it comes to health care. Not knowing what may be coming, we end up waiting until a problem has been brewing long enough to become evident, and then we need to react to it. Unfortunately, when we are forced to wait for something to become problematic, the process has time to advance, and we end up having fewer options for dealing with it.

When we think about it logically, the earlier we intervene when something appears to be going awry, the better the chances our interventions will be successful—not always, but the chances are better. Sometimes we encounter a devastating disease in which the prognosis does not change with intervention, but for some of the most common problems encountered in pets (diabetes mellitus, arthritis, allergies, heart disease, kidney disease, thyroid disorders, and many more), being proactive in diagnosis and management is clearly advantageous. Being proactive can help save lives, and there are usually many more treatment options when things are caught early.

If early detection is so important in health care and so commonly used in human medicine, then why isn't it as routine in veterinary medicine? In veterinary medicine, early detection is certainly routine for parasite screenings (heartworm testing, testing for gastrointestinal parasites, etc.) that have human public health significance. Veterinarians also generally screen pets before procedures requiring anesthesia and when pets become seniors. Yet, while humans are routinely screened for a wide variety of disorders, pets may not be routinely screened, even if they are at risk of serious disorders such as glaucoma, diabetes mellitus, high blood pressure (hypertension), hypothyroidism, hyperthyroidism, heart and kidney diseases and many other concerns. Typically, pets are only screened for potential chronic conditions if there is a specific concern that would warrant investigation or a known family history that has been uncovered. Why is early detection screening emphasized in human medicine but not to the same extent with pets?

Veterinary teams know that early detection is critically important to a pet's well-being. They are aware that detecting problems early and before clinical signs (symptoms) appear often increases treatment options and improves health outcomes. Teams are also familiar with the fact that many health conditions run in families, even though it may not appear clear-cut which ones pose the most risk in individual pets (unless there is a clear family history). It may seem hard to believe in this day and age, but it is still difficult to find legitimate resources that can be used for determining breed predispositions (where risk may vary with location and local gene pool), to understand and appreciate all the

Ivan at rest (courtesy Tyra Sherry).

health issues that could pose risks for individuals, to easily find guidelines that allow for the customization of care across so many individual situations, and to keep track of screening tests available when they appear to evolve with such regularity. After all, in human medicine we deal with essentially two genders and several ethnicities, and there is access to massive health databases. In veterinary medicine, there are two genders with a large percentage being altered (neutered), hundreds of breeds, hybrids and mixed breeds, major conformation alterations and standards (just think of the differences between toy breeds and giant breeds), and no centralized database of health care information. The variability within groups and between groups is mind boggling, difficult to conceptualize, and even more difficult to implement in terms of evidence-based early-detection protocols.

There are, however, two other barriers to routine screening—pet owner fear and cost. Interestingly, these same barriers exist in human medicine, but we have made stronger efforts to overcome them because of widespread recognition of the importance of early detection. Pet owners are sometimes frightened by the idea that their apparently healthy and happy pet could have a health issue, and avoidance of screening for such conditions is often a response to this fear. We see this same response in humans who are reluctant to seek care even when they have concerning symptoms. It's actually baffling why people wait so long to go to the doctor when they suspect that something is not quite right. The cost of screening is also a deterrent with those pet owners reluctant to spend money when there is no clear evidence of a problem. Veterinarians also may be reluctant to ask clients to pay for such tests, because if nothing abnormal is detected (which is the desired result), some pet owners may feel as though they got nothing for their efforts ... although truly not finding problems should actually be a cause for celebration. In human medicine, this issue can often be avoided, as most insurance plans offer preventive screening at little or no cost so that people will be less likely to skip these important early screenings. Insurance companies have realized that these tests are both important and cost effective at catching concerns early, promoting better outcomes and often lowering treatment costs. Pet owners need to be prepared to pay for routine testing with the realization that we hope the screening tests do come back without any problems detected. We do the testing for the peace of mind that comes with being proactive. It is better medicine, and if there is a problem, we've detected it early when we have the most options for intervention. Our default position is that we expect that everything will be fine; the screening test is meant to be proactive ... just in case.

Fortunately, being proactive does not mean that we need to run every test available for our pets. We can often narrow our focus to those conditions that are either common in the places we reside or travel (such as heartworm and a variety of diseases transmitted by ticks), where there is known or likely exposure, where there are known risk factors (including breed predisposition), or when genetic testing has identified a potential concern. So, if we know that pets have risk factors for problems like glaucoma, blood clotting disorders, certain heart diseases, developmental problems (such as hip dysplasia), diabetes mellitus, dental issues, thyroid disorders and even some cancers, it makes sense to include such screening in our pet's "maintenance schedule." Your pet's schedule will be tailored to your pet's specific risk factors and needs.

Genetic Testing

We are going to spend some time on genetic testing in this chapter, not because it is so commonly performed by veterinary teams, but because it is one of the few diagnostic tests that pet owners can submit themselves. As a pet owner, you are not going to be performing blood tests or checking heart function or taking radiographs (x-rays)—but it is quite possible you may run a DNA test on your pet independently, so we are going to spend a fair bit of time in this chapter explaining what genetic testing can do for you and what it can't.

Genetic testing involves collecting a tissue sample from pets (typically either a blood sample or a cheek swab) and submitting it to a special laboratory that will extract the DNA from nucleated cells and test for specific traits or conditions. There are literally hundreds of genetic markers and variants (mutations) that can be detected, and they can help us predict the likelihood of our pets developing any of these conditions. Phenes are traits or characteristics that are genetically determined, and while we will not be using the term appreciably in this book, you may variably see references to genetic phenes, mutations, variants, or traits, depending on whether you are surfing the web or reading research journals. They all refer to specific genetic tests and the conditions or traits with which they are associated.

The majority of DNA tests that are available assess pets for genetic diseases controlled or influenced by a single-gene pair. When we talk about gene pairs, it is important to realize that every individual has genes that occur in pairs—one variant of the pair inherited from each parent. It is the combination of these two variants that determines many traits (e.g., coat color) and, potentially, susceptibility to inherited diseases. In more than half of all diseases influenced by a single gene, it actually requires that affected individuals inherit an abnormal variant from both parents, and if they only inherit an abnormal variant from one parent, they would be a "carrier" of the trait but not suffer from the disease, because the other variant is normal and can compensate. In this case, the disorder is referred to as being "recessive" because it takes two abnormal variants (one from each parent) for the pet to be affected. In a smaller percentage of diseases, a single abnormal variant from either parent is able to cause disease, and such a disorder would be considered "dominant" because it can result in disease even in the presence of a variant that isn't abnormal.

Sometimes, we can get the benefits of genetic testing even without testing our pets if their parents have been tested by the breeder. Since genes are interpreted in pairs, and half the genetic information in each pair comes from each parent, if we have reliable genetic testing results from both parents, we will know what the possibilities are for puppies or kittens in the litter. For example, if both parents are "unaffected" or "clear" for the genetic variant causing the bleeding disorder von Willebrand disease Type I, then there should be no way that any of the offspring could be affected with this specific disease. Of course, this isn't foolproof, but it is helpful. When the results are not consistent (a pet develops a problem, but the parents don't carry the disease variant), it is possible that a spontaneous new mutation arose or that the laboratory made a mistake, but there is actually a more likely answer—human error. In these cases, it is almost always the case that one or both of the listed parents were not the actual parents of the pet tested. This happens in human medicine as well, when children come to learn that a parent is not a biological relative after DNA testing indicates an inconsistency. Of course, these errors are rare, so we can generally use DNA information from parents to determine disease risks in both pets and children. It's just important to realize that errors can still creep into the system even if the testing itself is rarely to blame.

Even without family history, and even if our pet's biological parents were not tested, we can learn a lot about our furry companions by performing DNA testing on them directly. DNA testing can be done on purebred, mixed-breed or hybrid cats and dogs. This testing can really be done as early as 1 day of age, but for practical purposes, it is typically performed at around 12 weeks of age. By this time, the pet has likely started its vaccination and parasite-control regimens, any congenital problems (those evident in young puppies and kittens) have been identified, microchipping has been done (which is required by some testing laboratories), and if pet health insurance has been purchased at around

8 weeks of age, it will be in effect with few or no preexisting problems being documented by the time the DNA testing has been submitted.

DNA testing is typically performed on either a cheek swab or a blood sample, and the sample can be submitted for either an individual test or a panel of multiple tests. DNA is extracted from the sample submitted, and for each trait or disease being tested and controlled by a single-gene pair, the result will specify the findings for each genetic variant of that gene pair, along with some interpretation of what the gene pair indicates about the individual animal and trait (e.g., affected, unaffected, carrier, etc.). It is most cost effective to run a panel of tests (dozens to hundreds), but this might require more interpretation since certain tests in the panel may not be directly applicable to your particular pet. That is, some of the tests may be applicable to rare disorders seen in only certain breeds, but if those tests are part of a panel, they will be run in all animals. In any case, you are going to need your veterinary team to help interpret the results because, although pet owners can submit tests directly to DNA testing laboratories, they are likely to need help understanding the significance of the results. For example, if a pet has a genetic marker indicating risk for a certain type of inherited glaucoma, there is not much you are going to be able to do with that information at home. In that instance, the veterinary team will want to schedule more direct testing (for perhaps years in the future), such as periodically scheduling screening for measuring the pressure of the fluid inside the eye (intraocular pressure) to confirm the suspicion of glaucoma, and then determining when intervention should be started. Before you start worrying about the DNA results, it is important to know that some pets with genetic risk factors never go on to develop an actual clinical disease. That's right—some DNA tests will identify a pet that has increased risk for developing certain problems, but that doesn't mean that actually developing the problem is a foregone conclusion. Your veterinary team can help you understand the DNA test results and what they mean for you and your beloved pet.

The purpose of DNA testing is that it can be used in young puppies and kittens and can help identify potential "risk" for future problems, even those that might appear much later in life. That also means that the tests can indicate "risk" but not necessarily that developing the problem is a certainty and that there are many common conditions (e.g., diabetes, allergies, hip dysplasia, etc.) for which DNA testing is not available or not very specific (because a trait may be influenced by multiple genes and/or affected by a variety of environmental factors) because the inheritance is more complex. Also, most of our pets today are neutered and not used for breeding, so we don't need to worry about protecting future generations, just keeping our pets healthy. This distinction is important because even if pets are "carriers" for certain diseases, it won't necessarily adversely affect their health or their ability to be wonderful pets.

Because the body has so many redundancies built into the system, it is also possible that an individual might have a genetic risk but never develop the actual disease. It is also possible that a pet has a genetic risk and has the disorder, but it really doesn't compromise the animal's health or well-being. For example, there is a genetic condition in the Labrador Retriever known as Exercise-induced Collapse (EIC), in which affected individuals collapse after intense exertion. Dogs with two normal variants are completely unaffected, and if a dog inherited a single abnormal variant from one parent, it would be a carrier of this recessive disorder but not show signs of disease. However, dogs that inherit an abnormal variant from both parents can be "affected" and suffer from this disorder. They can even die during severe episodes, so this is potentially a serious disease for those animals with a tendency to overexert or partake in strenuous activity. However, in a home environment in which you might go for walks or play fetch in the yard, you may never even be aware of the problem because your pet never overexerts. It's good to know about, and you'll probably keep your pet's exercise regimen fairly tame, but it might not have much impact on your family relationship or your pet's health.

Since DNA variants and the tests that measure them don't change with age, DNA testing can provide some indication of genetic health, at least as far as the tests available that can be performed at an early age. Similarly, most human infants get postnatal genetic testing, typically for a few dozen hereditary conditions (such as phenylketonuria, congenital hypothyroidism, cystic fibrosis, etc.) before they ever leave the hospital—not because the majority of children are expected to have these problems, but it provides peace of mind for the parents that some potential problems can be screened, and it provides early detection for the small percentage of children who have these genetic conditions. Having no problems evident on postnatal screening is expected for most (pets and children) and does not mean that there won't be any problems that develop in life, but screening has been done for the things that can be evaluated at this young age.

As already mentioned, the DNA tests that are most predictive tend to be for conditions resulting from variations in a single-gene pair, such as for most forms of muscular dystrophy in humans or different forms of progressive retinal atrophy in dogs and cats. In fact, if you were to look at a list of these single-gene disorders for pets, you might not be familiar with the names of many of the diseases (such as Bernard-Soulier syndrome, amelogenesis imperfecta, fucosidosis, hyperoxaluria, etc.) These relatively rare disorders are detectable because we have been able to isolate and identify the exact DNA mutation ... and test for it. For lots of other conditions that tend to run in families, the inheritance may be more complex and involve multiple gene pairs, as well as environmental factors. Sometimes we can identify a variant or marker that is "associated" with a risk factor, but in these cases the test only indicates a change in risk. That's why in human medicine there may be a DNA marker test for Alzheimer's disease, but it really only indicates a level of risk compared to the general population; it is not measuring something that actually causes the disease. In veterinary medicine, there are marker tests associated with risk for a variety of diseases, including some forms of inherited cardiomyopathy, dermatomyositis, and degenerative myelopathy.

By the way, you may think that breeders should just eliminate from breeding any animals that carry "bad" genetic traits, but it is not that simple. Each animal carries about 19,000 different genes, some "good" and others "bad," and so a balanced perspective is needed. If we eliminated all animals that carried a "bad" trait, we would likely seriously compromise the gene pool by narrowing it so much that we would move toward inbreeding and lose the important protective quality of genetic diversity. However, if carriers can be determined, such as with a DNA test, it is possible to breed animals that will never produce offspring that actually have the disease in question. That's what genetic counseling is all about—preserving genetic diversity without adversely affecting health.

Just to recap, when running DNA tests in pets, it is important to keep things in perspective. The preference is to acquire pets from sources that have already screened their breeding animals for hereditary problems. That way you know what you are dealing with before you even adopt a pet. If that is not possible, test as soon as it is practical. If you adopt a pet at 8 weeks of age and microchip it and start pet health insurance at that time, you can test at 12 weeks of age or whenever the insurance is in full force. Insurance companies really should not decline coverage on the basis of a DNA test, but no need to take any chances, so it is advised to get the insurance before testing. You can do DNA testing at any time in a pet's life, but obviously it is of most use when done early. DNA doesn't change over time, so you might as well get as full a picture as possible up front. As mentioned previously, when DNA tests are run, the expectation is that everything will likely come back normal. The purpose of running DNA testing is not to diagnose disease but for the peace of mind that comes from knowing that you screened for what you could at this young age. If an unanticipated risk is identified, that just gives you and your veterinary team time to craft strategies for how you'll deal with things.

Most of the DNA testing that is done is to determine risks for inherited traits and diseases, but there are additional applications that might also prove useful. Some DNA tests can also be helpful for cancer diagnosis and treatment. Liquid biopsies are blood tests that look for genetic material shed by cancers into the blood, which can be a noninvasive way of making a diagnosis. Actually, such liquid biopsies aren't used so much to detect cancers in healthy individuals but to help guide treatment based on the specific tumor markers identified. Matching certain tumor markers to appropriate targeted therapies can greatly improve outcomes. Such testing can also be done on actual tumor biopsies, but when tumors are widespread, liquid biopsies may be able to uncover multiple mutations, which can be instrumental in finding the best therapy for an individual. In addition to helping direct appropriate treatments, such tests might also be capable of identifying cancer at earlier stages. Stay tuned, as there are so many applications of genetic testing being used today.

One other thing that is relevant regarding genetic testing is that there are now tests available for mixed-breed animals to help determine what breed combinations might be in the mix. These tests provide some information that might have a bearing on health care, but really they are more for interest sake if you are trying to determine what breeds might be present in the mix. There are no genetic markers that are absolutely predictive for specific breeds (there is no collie gene or Siamese gene, for example), but many markers in aggregate might be consistent with contributions from certain breeds. This is the same type of testing that is popular in heritage tests for people, and like those tests, pet tests might suggest genetic markers that are often associated with certain breeds, but they do not present a reliable family tree of breeds. Many mixed-breed pets came from mixed-breed parents, and often from mixed-breed grandparents, so don't expect the impossible. These tests are entertaining, and they provide useful information, but they are not definitive.

Orthopedic Screening

Many common developmental orthopedic diseases (e.g., hip dysplasia, elbow dysplasia, osteochondrosis, etc.) can be inherited from parents that carry genes associated with these traits. It is worthwhile to screen pets for these common conditions because they can become debilitating. Of course, as discussed under genetic testing, we get the most benefit when breeding animals are screened, since we can then choose to purchase a pet with a known family history regarding such problems. Many breeders record the findings for their breeding animals in registries, and so it is possible to consider the results in different generations within a breeding line. This isn't foolproof, because most of these conditions have a complex pattern of inheritance and problems can even "skip" a generation, and genetics is usually only part of the puzzle. However, buying pets with registered family history is a great place to start.

When it comes to conditions such as hip dysplasia, there are certain breeds that have higher rates of occurrence (breed predisposition), but all pets can be affected since the "liability genes" associated with the disorder seem to have been spread widely in the ancestral population, at least for dogs. Because of that, any individual could be affected, even though certain breeds may be more likely to be affected based on family history.

Most of these disorders are not detectable in very young animals, but there are techniques available for screening individuals at high risk

Maggie at rest (courtesy Taylor Landry).

as early as 4 months of age. For most pets, general screening at 2 years of age is most practical, and for breeding animals, they can get certified registry numbers (certification of their hip conformation status, for example) at this age on the basis of veterinarians submitting radiographs (x-rays) to the registry for evaluation. Once again, since most household pets won't be bred, their results do not need to be sent to the registry, but screening is often done just to get an early start on management for animals documented to have risk for these problems.

There are no specific treatments for orthopedic disorders like hip dysplasia, but the goal is to manage potential consequences, especially arthritis. If a developmental disorder is identified early, then there are a lot of things that can be done in terms of nutrition, exercise and physical therapy to keep pets healthy and active and delay the onset of crippling changes to the joints and bones.

Specialist Evaluation

For some medical problems that are hereditary, there may be a need for specialist evaluation, especially in breeding animals. This is particularly important for eye diseases (ophthalmology) and for heart diseases (cardiology). Accordingly, some breed associations recommend that breeders of those breeds have their pets "certified" by veterinary ophthalmologists and/or cardiologists, and those examinations can be entered into registries. This is important because some of these diseases do not have genetic testing and may be difficult to identify without specific expertise. Once again, this isn't so much a necessity for owners of household pets, but breeders often need to get their breeding animals checked to be able to match with other breeding stock, so if you are planning on adopting a pet, it would be worthwhile to know if breeding pairs were screened for these problems.

Other Testing

Based on our health risk assessment, genetic testing and regular veterinary assessments, we can determine risk factors for a lot of conditions that would benefit from early intervention. For example, there are a variety of DNA tests in both cats and dogs that can identify pets with an increased risk for developing specific genetic forms of heart disease (cardiomyopathy). As discussed earlier, pets with such results will not inevitably develop heart disease, but it does indicate they are at higher risk and warrant more specific screening, even if such screening is not indicated for a few years. So, in those pets, we might recommend additional screening with an electrocardiogram, echocardiogram (ultrasound examination), or even cardiac monitoring at the appropriate time and potentially referral to a cardiologist.

Some testing is run as a matter of public health. For example, it is recommended that all pets be screened for internal parasites by periodic tests. This is true even if animals are on preventive therapy. So, it is recommended that pets have fecal examinations that would detect certain internal parasites (such as roundworms, hookworms and tapeworms), and some of these are capable of being spread to family members. There are also immunologic tests for some parasites and a variety of tests for the infectious diseases transmitted by ticks (more details provided in chapter on prevention). While some of these conditions cannot be transmitted directly from pets to people (such as heartworm, West Nile virus or Lyme disease), pets can act as sentinels, alerting pet owners to the fact that they too are exposed to the same vectors (mosquitoes, ticks, etc.) that can potentially be spreading these diseases.

There are many situations in which we are aware of increased risks for certain disorders, and we determine it is in our best interest to screen and get ahead of any problems developing. So, if pets have risk factors for any number of conditions, including glaucoma, arthritis, high blood pressure (hypertension), diabetes mellitus, hypothyroidism, hyperthyroidism, bladder "stones" (urolithiasis), dry eye (keratoconjunctivitis sicca) and many other issues—it makes sense to screen for them. These just get added to your pet's "maintenance schedule" after consultation with the veterinary team.

As long as we are discussing other forms of testing, it is important to mention that the timing of such testing is critical. DNA testing can be done at any time because DNA doesn't change over time, but the most benefit occurs when we have those results early in life. Orthopedic screening can be done according to guidelines, but most registries and schemes won't assign clinical status to animals less than a certain age. For most other tests, they are likely to be performed at certain ages (depending on the breed and genetic variant), depending on the natural progression of the disorder being tested. So, for example, you are probably aware of when people should start having colonoscopies, mammograms, etc. and also realize that physicians may alter those generalizations based on a person's family history and other risk factors. The same is true for pets, where some screening may be done in young animals, while other screening is only necessary at later ages unless individual history and risk factors indicate an alternate schedule would be appropriate.

Veterinarians can learn a lot about your pet's health from periodic blood and urine tests. Changes in laboratory values over time can alert pet owners and veterinarians to health concerns early, often before pets are showing clear clinical signs (symptoms) of problems. Periodic testing typically includes a panel of tests that looks at things like liver, pancreas and kidney function, blood sugar, blood cell counts, loss of protein into the urine, the presence of "crystals" in the urine, etc. Because most degenerative diseases progress over time, running these types of tests not only indicate when there is a problem, but often identifies values that are trending toward being problematic. So, in animals that are prediabetic we might see blood sugar levels trending upwards over time, and when a certain threshold is surpassed, we are likely to see sugar spilling over into the urine. This could take place over a period of many months or years. In this case, identifying the prediabetic allows us to consider changes that might change the trajectory of the disease and perhaps even prevent the pet from ever going on to develop actual diabetes. Ideally, we would run these tests first in young adulthood and then periodically after that until pets are considered senior, at which time the testing becomes more comprehensive.

Senior screening makes sense. Senior pets are at higher risk for

Mariska (courtesy Tyra Sherry).

many problems, including heart disease, kidney disease and many others. There is some debate, though, on when pets should be considered "senior." Is it reasonable to consider all pets senior when they hit a specific age, regardless of breed and lifespan considerations? Currently, many veterinary hospitals define all pets as senior based solely on age and that arbitrary age is usually 7 years. Now, 7 years of age is a fine average, but as a definition, senior is often a term used to describe when a pet enters the final 25 percent of its anticipated lifespan. So, 7 may be a great age for the average, but for some relatively short-lived breeds, screening should start before then, and for long-lived breeds, the senior designation might be later. The point we are making is that senior screening is important, but when a pet should be considered senior involves more deliberation than just when they reach their 7th birthday.

In addition to routine and periodic laboratory testing, there are some additional new and exciting prospects available in both human and veterinary medicine. Biomarkers (a short form for biological markers) refer to objective measurements that can predict diagnoses or outcomes. For example, there are a variety of different ways of evaluating heart functions, from listening with a stethoscope to doing an ultrasound examination of the heart (echocardiography). However, biomarkers can also be helpful in this regard, such as cardiac troponin I and B-type natriuretic peptide (BNP). These tests can help predict damage to heart muscle and can be early indicators of processes that might not be detected clinically yet. Other biomarkers might be useful in assessing prognosis or the likely outcome of disease processes. The utility of biomarkers is not limited to heart disease. There are biomarkers for specific cancers, evidence of chronic inflammation, atopic dermatitis, kidney damage and many other processes. Anticipate that they will become more commonplace in routine health care for both dogs and cats.

Do We Need to Test for Everything?

Screening should have a positive impact if we are going to do it. It is not just an academic exercise. If the results of such testing can be used to help a pet, or alter what we were planning to do, then it is worthwhile. That being said, there are some cautions when it comes to testing. The goal is not to test for testing sake, or to test even if it won't influence treatment approaches or outcomes, but to be proactive in keeping pets as healthy as possible for as long as possible and testing preemptively based on a pet's specific risk factors. Accordingly, much of this testing is conducted in a pet-specific manner of trying to preserve healthspan more than lifespan. Thus, early detection can be used with lifestyle changes or surveillance to reduce the risk of disease or to detect it early enough to treat it most effectively.

Another important feature of proactive testing is that sequential tests might indicate trends. For example, as we explored earlier, pets don't become diabetic overnight. Their blood glucose values tend to trend upwards over time until they cross a threshold when the diagnosis of diabetes is warranted. Such testing allows us to identify when the pet is trending toward becoming diabetic and then consider interventions that can be made to hopefully change the course of the disease.

Once again, there is no need to run every test in every circumstance. Testing is only indicated if there are actions that would be taken differently if testing results are known. The downside of testing is that the more tests we run, the greater the chances that, just by statistical chance, there is a greater likelihood that we'll find at least one test result outside of the typical reference interval (the so-called "normal range"). No need to panic. What we want to avoid in cases when a single laboratory value is amiss is overreacting and causing what is sometimes referred to as a "cascade of care." This is when we start running an array of other tests to try to explain an abnormal laboratory result. Stop. Breathe. If your pet has a value like this, and most do from time to time, just submit another test to see if the result is repeatable. If it can't be explained, your veterinary team may consult with the laboratory or with a veterinary specialist to see if it warrants further evaluation. However, we treat pets, not laboratory results, so it's important to keep things in perspective.

Case Example

Percy Langston is a frisky 16-week-old intact (not neutered) male Persian kitten. Deborah Langston is very protective of Percy. When the veterinarian first recommended DNA testing, Deborah was hesitant, but she decided to follow the recommendation and had the test run at 12 weeks of age.

Mrs. Langston was somewhat shocked to learn that Percy had a detectable variant for polycystic kidney disease (PKD). She had spent a lot of money for Percy, and he came with "papers." The veterinary health care team acknowledged that the result was not anticipated but that it was the reason they recommended performing such testing in all pets at risk, and Persians are definitely considered a breed at risk for this condition.

Dr. Green explained that polycystic kidney disease is an autosomal dominant hereditary disease, which means that inheriting a problem gene from either parent is enough for pets to be affected. The cysts in the kidneys tend to be present from birth and are small, but they can grow over time, so they need to be monitored. Deborah was concerned but relieved to learn that most affected cats don't have clinical problems until middle age and that the hospital would be monitoring the situation since the clinical course could be quite variable. Dr. Green provided a handout on polycystic kidney disease that provided an action plan for how the condition would be monitored with laboratory testing and ultrasound, including tests that would detect the earliest hint of kidney disease.

Deborah learned a lot about hereditary diseases. She also realized why it is so important to work with veterinary teams that are knowledgeable about such proactive care.

Case Example

Valerie Thompson presented her two-year-old Doberman Pinscher, Brutus, for routine evaluation and vaccination. Brutus had genetic testing as a puppy and was determined to be "affected" on a DNA test for dilated cardiomyopathy. Initially Valerie was quite concerned and considered relinquishing Brutus to a shelter, but the veterinary team at ABC Veterinary Hospital helped put things in perspective.

It was true that Brutus had the PDK4 (DCM1) mutation that was associated with an increased risk for dilated cardiomyopathy, but Valerie now understood that the mutation did not cause the disease (it was just associated with increased risk in a certain cohort of Doberman Pinschers), that it was not the only mutation associated with the disease, and that there were also likely other factors that could influence cardiomyopathy onset in a complex manner. In fact, she also read about some dietary factors that could possibly be associated with nongenetic forms of the disease in some animals.

The team at ABC Veterinary Hospital helped establish a sensible ongoing screening protocol with their local veterinary cardiologist, and Valerie felt quite relieved that they had identified a risk factor but now had a sensible program in place to make sure Brutus would have the care he needed.

Recommended Reading

Ackerman, L. 2020. *Proactive Pet Parenting: Anticipating Pet Health Problems Before They Happen.* Problem Free Publishing.

_____. 2019. "The Skinny on Genes—What You Should Know About Genetic Testing." *AAHA Trends* 35 (6): 39–42.

_____. 2011. *The Genetic Connection, 2nd Edition.* Lakewood, CO: AAHA Press.

"American Animal Hospital Association-American Veterinary Medical Association Preventive Health Guidelines Task Force." 2011. *Journal of the American Veterinary Medical Association* 239 (5): 625–29. https://www.aahanet.org/Library/Preventive/Healthcare.aspx.

Baker, Lauren, Peter Muir, and Susannah J. Sample. 2019. "Genome-Wide Association Studies and Genetic Testing: Understanding the Science, Success, and Future of a Rapidly Developing Field." *Journal of the American Veterinary Medical Association* 255 (10): 1126–1136. https://doi.org/10.2460/javma.255.10.1126.

Bell, Jerold, Kathleen Cavanagh, Larry Tilley, and Francis Smith. 2012. *Veterinary Medical Guide to Dog and Cat Breeds.* Teton Newmedia.

Buckley, Reuben M., Brian W. Davis, Wesley A. Brashear, Fabiana H.G. Farias, Kei Kuroki, Tina Graves, LaDeana W. Hillier, et al. 2020. "A New Domestic Cat Genome Assembly Based on Long Sequence Reads Empowers Feline Genomic Medicine and Identifies a Novel Gene for Dwarfism." Edited by Gregory S. Barsh. *PLOS Genetics* 16 (10): e1008926. https://doi.org/10.1371/journal.pgen.1008926.

Companion Animal Parasite Council. http://www.capcvet.org

Dell'Osa, D., and S. Jaensch. 2016. "Prevalence of Clinicopathological Changes in Healthy Middle-Aged Dogs and Cats Presenting to Veterinary Practices for Routine Procedures." *Australian Veterinary Journal* 94 (9): 317–323. https://doi.org/10.1111/avj.12481.

Lewis, Hugh B. 2006. "Healthy Pets Benefit from Blood Work." Banfield Data Savant. 18–20. http://www.banfield.com/getmedia/1216c698-7da1-4899-81a3-24ab549b7a8c/2_1-Healthy-Pets-benefit-from-blood-work.

Paepe, Dominique, Gaëlle Verjans, Luc Duchateau, Koen Piron, Liesbeth Ghys, and Sylvie Daminet. 2012. "Routine Health Screening." *Journal of Feline Medicine and Surgery* 15 (1): 8–19. https://doi.org/10.1177/1098612x12464628.

Prieto, J.M., P.C. Carney, M.L. Miller, M. Rishniw, J.F. Randolph, S.V. Lamb, N.J. Place, and M.E. Peterson. 2020. "Short-Term Biological Variation of Serum Thyroid Hormones Concentrations in Clinically Healthy Cats." *Domestic Animal Endocrinology* 71: 106389. https://doi.org/10.1016/j.domaniend.2019.106389.

"Promoting Preventive Care Protocols: Evidence, Enactment and Economics." 2018. American Animal Hospital Association. https://www.aaha.org/practice-resources/pet-health-resources/preventive-care/.

Shaffer, Lisa G., Anja Geretschlaeger, Christina J. Ramirez, Blake C. Ballif, and Casey Carl. 2019. "Quality Assurance Checklist and Additional Considerations for Canine Clinical Genetic Testing Laboratories: A Follow-up to the Published Standards and Guidelines." *Human Genetics* 138 (5): 501–8. doi.org/10.1007s00439–019–02013–9.

Stull, Jason W., Jessica A. Shelby, Brenda N. Bonnett, Gary Block, Steven C. Budsberg, Rachel S. Dean, Michael R. Dicks, et al. 2018. "Barriers and Next Steps to Providing a Spectrum of Effective Health Care to Companion Animals." *Journal of the American Veterinary Medical Association* 253 (11): 1386–1389. https://doi.org/10.2460/javma.253.11.1386.

Timsit, Edouard, Renaud Léguillette, Brad J. White, Robert L. Larson, and Sébastien Buczinski. 2018. "Likelihood Ratios: An Intuitive Tool for Incorporating Diagnostic Test Results into Decision-Making." *Journal of the American Veterinary Medical Association* 252 (11): 1362–1366. https://doi.org/10.2460/javma.252.11.1362.

"Why Do We Run Diagnostic Tests?" 2018. Veterinary Practice News. February 7. https://www.veterinarypracticenews.com/why-do-we-run-diagnostic-tests.

Willems, A., D. Paepe, S. Marynissen, P. Smets, I. Van de Maele, P. Picavet, L. Duchateau, and S. Daminet. 2017. "Results of Screening of Apparently Healthy Senior and Geriatric Dogs." *Journal of Veterinary Internal Medicine* 31 (1): 81–92. https://doi.org/10.1111/jvim.14587.

8

The Changing Nature
of Pet Medications

If we want to avoid problems with our pets, what we administer to them in the form of medicine is also a concern. They live in our homes, are part of our lives, and also share risks for many of our medical conditions. When it comes to maintaining *almost* perfect pets, we need to know how to intelligently use medications to benefit our pet's health as well as our own well-being.

New Types of Medications

There are many new types of medicines available now, often with very different mechanisms of effectiveness from the common drugs of yesterday. If you watch television at all, you are likely bombarded with commercials for these breakthroughs for humans, but you may not be aware that many of these types of medications are available for pets as well.

For most of the history of modern veterinary medicine, we have relied on "drugs" of various classes for the management of disease. Whether we are discussing antibiotics, parasite-control products, or anti-inflammatory drugs, our focus was on these chemical agents and how they were to be dosed in our patients. However, times have changed, and a variety of more "targeted" therapies have now become available.

While we have become quite comfortable with the concept of chemical or molecular therapies (such as antibiotics), medicine has changed appreciably with the advent of biopharmaceuticals. Biopharmaceuticals, also known as biologicals, are pharmaceutical drugs derived from biological sources. These products often behave differently than regular synthesized pharmaceuticals. Biopharmaceuticals include products like blood and blood products, immunotherapies, vaccines, hormones (such as insulin), gene therapies, stem cell therapies, and monoclonal antibodies.

Some biological-based products can be designed to target their action against a disease process or an aspect of the immune system more specifically than more traditional pharmaceuticals. This specific action may allow treatments with fewer side effects than traditional therapies. For example, biological response modifiers are substances that modify immune responses. Monoclonal antibodies are biological response modifiers tailored to focus against a specific disease target rather than a broader attack. Veterinary medicine is just starting to see an influx in therapeutic antibodies being used to treat a variety of conditions (allergies, osteoarthritis, etc.), and many more are bound to be introduced. Most of these are monoclonal antibodies developed for dogs and/or cats and target specific inflammatory mediators. In general, these antibody treatments target the problem specifically, which results in fewer side effects than traditional therapies, although they are certainly not devoid of all side effects.

Stem cell therapy involves collecting stem cells (cells capable of evolving into other cells) from patients, manipulating them, and then reintroducing them by injection into areas of disease or dysfunction. The hope is that the stem cells will undergo cell division to develop into functional cells that will result in tissue renewal. Transplanted stem cells may not survive long in their new locations, but it is still thought that their secretions or "secretome" may recruit other stem cells to the area and enhance tissue repair. Although there are few studies that actually support the beneficial effects of stem cell therapy, its clinical use for conditions, especially osteoarthritis and feline stomatitis (an inflammatory disease of the mouth), is growing. Further investigations into potential benefits would be helpful, and much research needs to be done.

Gene therapies rely on the introduction of functional genes to treat or prevent problems. While currently experimental, gene therapies have been used in a variety of veterinary settings, including correcting inborn errors such as in certain forms of retinal dystrophy. In fact, research in pets is often the basis for introducing these treatments in people. Gene therapy can be used to replace a defective gene (that is causing or will cause issues) with a normal copy of that gene. It can also be used to inactivate a defective gene that is acting improperly or to introduce a new gene to help fight or protect against disease.

As you work to keep your pet problem free, be open to learning about and considering new treatments suggested by your veterinary team. It is easy to become comfortable with what has worked for you in the past, but some of these new therapies are significantly safer than older drugs. For instance, in the past allergies in pets were treated with cortisone-like steroids to suppress inflammation. These corticosteroids did that, but they also came with a whole range of side effects, because those chemicals had effects on many different cells in the body. Today, most of the therapies used are biologicals, which are considered safer because rather than a shotgun blast to the immune system, the new medications have a very narrow effect on certain cell processes while sparing most others. That doesn't mean that biologicals have no side effects or that there are no concerns about their use, but be receptive to learning all the facts and choose the option that will be safer and most effective for your pet.

Buying Medications

These days, there are a lot of options for where we obtain medications for our pets. For those medications requiring a prescription, we either purchase them directly from a veterinary hospital or the veterinary hospital authorizes a prescription to be filled by a licensed pharmacy. Both are acceptable options but with some caveats worth knowing.

Veterinary hospitals aren't retailers, so they don't stock every product that a pet may need over its lifetime. They concentrate on keeping products on the shelf that they deem to be the best for their patients and clients, and by limiting products, the team tends to gain more familiarity and experience with them, including feedback of what pet owners like about certain products and what they don't like about others. When team members are familiar with products, they also appreciate what to expect when the medication is used, the types of side effects that might occur, and what to do when animals aren't responding as anticipated. Veterinary teams are also keenly aware of why some medications may be preferred over others, including convenient packaging, ease of dosing, pricing, and predictable outcomes.

Veterinary teams are very focused on outcomes. It's not enough that you just purchase a product; the team wants to make sure that your pet actually receives all the benefits from the medication dispensed. So, for example, it doesn't much matter if you buy a year's worth of heartworm preventive meant to be given monthly if that doesn't end up being given according to schedule (see compliance and adherence below). A product that you've purchased and that sits on a shelf in your cupboard doesn't do your pet any good, so veterinary teams will also want

Mariska and Ivan check out the view (courtesy Tyra Sherry).

to help you with reminders or whatever prompting you need to administer the medication as directed. Because veterinary hospitals often don't buy medications in bulk and they usually cater to a relatively small client base, it should not be surprising that prices might be slightly higher than at retailers that offer the same or similar products. But, if you are having problems with a medication, questions about its use, or difficulty administering it, you will likely find your veterinary hospital team to be quite responsive. By the way, if you find making your purchases online to be more convenient, many veterinary hospitals have this service available for their clients in which they partner with an online pharmacy that they trust to send medications directly to your home.

If you are looking to get medications cheaply, then large chain pharmacy retailers and online pharmacies can be an option. They buy medications in larger quantities than even the largest veterinary organizations and focus more on retail sales than providing veterinary counseling. Prescription drugs for pets are now available from a number of human pharmacies, as well as online pharmacies, and nonprescription medications, especially for flea and tick control, are now available in many retailers. Large retailers can definitely compete effectively on price but may not be able to provide advice on the use of the medications they sell. If you are having problems, they are most likely to direct you back to your veterinary team, even though you bought the medication from them.

Most people will trust the pharmacies at which they purchase their own medications, but it's another thing with Internet pharmacies. There are horror stories about online pharmacies selling products that are not approved for use or that are counterfeit and could be harmful. There are a lot of ethical, certified, and licensed online pharmacies, and you should take the time to investigate before placing any online order. Some clues that an online pharmacy might not be legitimate is if you were sent an unsolicited email, if it allows you to buy prescription medications without a lawful prescription from your veterinarian, if it is not licensed by a pharmacy board, or if its prices seem too good to be true. Everyone would like to save money on their prescriptions, but keeping your pets problem free also requires you to make smart decisions for your pet.

Veterinary Medications Versus Human Medications

When it comes to medications for our pets, it's important to realize that while we have great medicines that have been designed exclusively for use in pets, there is sometimes a need to rely on human medications that don't (yet) have a pet equivalent. Medication intended for pets is typically prepared and certified under the same conditions as human medicines, but it generally comes in doses and forms more suitably designed for dogs and cats and also has had appropriate testing for safety and effectiveness in pets for the conditions listed on the product's label. This is important because veterinary teams rely on the research done by product manufacturers to know about effective dosing, course of therapy, the metabolism on the drugs in a pet's system (which can not only be very different between humans and pets, but even between dogs and cats), and potential side effects. All this is necessary so that the veterinary team can appropriately counsel you about the proper use of the medication and everything that you should expect.

On the other hand, there are instances when we may need to rely on human medications for treatment. This is most often needed for relatively specialized medications and applications for which a veterinary drug is not available. It is important to realize that human drugs are not considered in any way to be either superior or inferior to veterinary drugs, but not all drugs available for humans have a veterinary equivalent and vice versa. In these cases, use of a human product may be considered, but pet owners need to realize that this is "extra-label drug use," something for which the manufacturer does not have an approved use. That means that if there is a problem, the drug manufacturer has no responsibility because the drug was not used as intended. By the way, sometimes people are treated with drugs intended for animals if there is no human drug equivalent, and this is also considered extra-label drug use. One other point worth mentioning is that the price of a product should not be a factor in determining drug appropriateness. Whether a human or animal drug is cheaper, it should not affect selection, and medications should only be used in the proper species according to label recommendations ... unless there are no alternatives. Avoid problems in your pet by selecting products that have been tested and found to be safe and effective for your pet's specific circumstances.

Generics and Biosimilars

Generic drugs are chemical copies of existing brand name pharmaceuticals and can be legally produced when the patent on a medication expires. Generic drugs have the same active ingredients as the original pharmaceutical (within limits) and the same dosing instructions, but they can have slightly different components (formulation, color, taste, etc.) and go through a slightly different regulatory process since manufacturers are not required to conduct clinical trials, only prove that the active ingredients are identical or substantially similar to a product that is already licensed. The advantage of generic drugs is that they are typically cheaper to purchase, so they lower the costs of health care. These days, there are also "branded generics" in both human and veterinary medicine in which companies leverage their brand identity to hopefully convince you that their generic versions might be more trustworthy. It is interesting to note that when a family member is sick (human or pet), caregivers often select brand names over generics for the care of loved ones, likely due to this trustworthiness factor. While we might know the ingredients are the same or similar, human nature often plays a role in product selection, so don't feel guilty if you make such decisions.

Compared to regular small-molecule pharmaceuticals such as antibiotics, biopharmaceuticals tend to be larger and more complex. However, just as with legend pharmaceuticals, they will have their generic equivalents, which are known as biosimilars. Unlike generic medicines, biosimilars are unlikely to be an exact copy of the innovator product and are assessed through a different regulatory pathway. In general, this pathway requires more testing—but still less than a completely new drug application. Yes, it's a bit confusing, but it's worth knowing what you are buying and what you are administering to your *almost* perfect pets.

Compliance and Adherence

Without a doubt, the most important aspect of this chapter is this topic of compliance and adherence. Whatever medications you choose for your pets, compliance and adherence are key to ensuring that those medications get administered as directed. We have access to great products, but they only work well when you use them as recommended. Sadly, people with the best of intentions often fail to give medications to their pets according to the correct schedule. There are many definitions of compliance and adherence, and if you search the terms online, you'll see that there are various and often conflicting uses of the terms. So, let's not worry about universal definitions for these terms, which we are not going to be able to achieve, and settle instead for simple versions for the purposes of this discussion. As far as *almost* perfect pets and your role as pet parents are concerned, compliance applies to your getting the product for your pet, and adherence refers to your giving it appropriately according to the directions that come with the product. For example, if you purchase a year's worth of heartworm preventive meant to be given monthly, but it remains in your pantry because you forget to give it on schedule, you might have compliance of 100 percent, since you bought the product, but

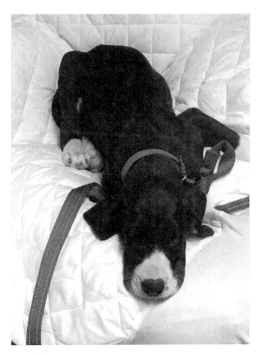

Young animals need their rest. Rifka, at three months, required about 18 hours of sleep daily. Adequate rest balanced with play are extremely important for young pets (courtesy Janice Adams).

adherence of 0 percent because you never administered it. The fact is that if your pet doesn't receive the medication on schedule, the medication provides no benefit just by virtue of being present in your home. Whatever definitions of compliance and adherence you personally prefer, the important part is that we complicate the situation when we fail to acquire a needed medication or fail to give it appropriately.

The example just provided may seem extreme, but you might be surprised at how common this problem is. Maybe you buy the heartworm medication and intend to give it monthly, but perhaps some months it gets given on schedule, some months you miss it, and some months you remember to give it, but it may be late by a few weeks. This is, unfortunately, very common and one of the main reasons why pets get heartworm even when their owners have purchased a preventive for them.

Another common example happens with antibiotics. Suppose your pet is prescribed an antibiotic meant to be given by mouth every 12 hours. Perhaps surprisingly, every 12 hours does not mean the same as twice a day when it comes to medications. Drugs are dosed based on how they are metabolized in the body, so evenly spaced doses are important for some medications. Unfortunately, that may not be convenient for whoever is doing the administration. So, while it might be most appropriate to give a twice-daily dose at 6 a.m. (06:00) and then 12 hours later at 6 p.m. (18:00), perhaps a busy pet owner might try to give two doses in a day, but sometimes the second dose is on time, sometimes it might be at midnight, and sometimes a dose gets forgotten altogether. In fact, in studies that have been done looking at the ability of pet owners to administer a medication orally every 12 hours for only 14 days, the majority could not accomplish this on schedule. Before you think these pet owners were derelict in their duties, it is sobering to appreciate that adherence is similarly miserable in human patients, even those with serious medical conditions such as heart disease, chronic obstructive pulmonary disease (COPD), and even cancer.

There are lots of reasons why compliance and adherence are so challenging, but part of the solution is to acknowledge that the struggle is real. The main impediments to compliance (buying the product) are price and postponing decision-making. If you think the recommended product is beyond your budget, you might hesitate. If you are not sure about whether you should use the medication (such as by being afraid of potential side effects), the very process of your taking time to think about it means that you are likely to put it in the back of your mind as you get busy with other things. Adherence is a different story, as you already made the commitment and bought the product. Challenges here might be that it is difficult for you to administer the medication or to remember to give the medication or your pet resists accepting the medication. Other aspects of adherence have to do with not giving it on schedule because it is not convenient or giving less than the full dose because the medication is expensive, and you are trying to stretch out the medicine that you have. A dangerous lack of adherence happens when you are given a course of therapy (such as with an antibiotic), and you discontinue it early because you think your pet is looking better; this is dangerous because it encourages the development of resistance (see below). In any case, it is all too common that pets don't get the medication that they need when they need it.

If you are having trouble with either compliance or adherence, please discuss this with your veterinary team. There is nothing worse for them than trying to piece together why there was a treatment failure, especially if we feel guilty and don't admit to the reality that we didn't give the medication as directed. If they falsely believe that the medications were given correctly, that might lead them to believe that there might be a resistant organism or that the diagnosis is in question. Do your pet a favor, and be truthful about problems you have giving a medication. We've all been there, so be upfront about it, and there may very well be alternatives.

Because compliance and adherence issues are so common, you can expect that your veterinary team will be understanding and appreciative that you let them know. In many cases, there might be products that can be administered by injection, which can eliminate the responsibility for giving medicines orally. There are also lots of tricks and training that can be used to make administering oral medications easier. It takes patience and gentle handling, but in time you can train pets to be more accepting. That might not work immediately when you have a current need, but keep training in mind for preparation for the next time. Some medications can also be "compounded" into flavors and formulations or hidden in tasty morsels that may make administration easier, and other products might be able to be administered topically. So, for example, there are heartworm medications that can be administered by injection, orally or topically ... so you do have options.

Drug Resistance

Drug resistance happens when medicines that used to be sufficient for treatment or prevention no longer work as well as they once did. It is an acquired issue in that the problem is not with the drug itself but with organisms that adapt and are no longer as susceptible. Most of us are probably familiar with microbial resistance, such as methicillin resistance (you have likely heard of something being "resistant to penicillin"), but we also see resistance in parasites to medications, including heartworm and hookworm.

You might wonder why we would include a section on drug resistance in a book about *almost* perfect pets, but drug resistance is everyone's concern. If we don't deal with it directly, many drugs will not be available when we need them.

Drug resistance occurs through several different mechanisms, but the way that we can do our part to keep them working is to ensure that we don't use products such as antibiotics unless we absolutely need them, but if we do need them, then we need to use them exactly as directed. When we skip doses or decide not to finish the prescription because our pet is looking better, we give organisms the chance to adapt. This is extremely serious because once resistance develops, microbes can confer that resistance on other microbes. Before long, we can have microbes resistant to multiple drugs, making it harder and harder to find suitable drugs that will work. Even worse, because multiple drug

Where's Mariska? Check the shower curtain (courtesy Tyra Sherry).

resistance can be spread to microbes that affect humans, we can create scenarios that adversely affect both human and pet health.

The best way to guard against the development of resistance is to use medications exactly as directed and for the entire period of time prescribed. Even if your pet is looking better, do not stop the prescription before instructed to do so. The other thing we can do to help is to fight the temptation to treat every infection with antibiotics. For example, many skin infections can be adequately treated with topical antiseptics. Antibiotics should be reserved for those cases where they are truly needed.

Nutritional Therapeutics

Nutritional treatments are popular, but many misconceptions and myths abound that need to be addressed and corrected. People supplement commercially prepared diets for some compelling reasons. The very process of commercially preparing pet foods is exacting and potentially destructive to nutrients, especially vitamins. Also, the exposure of vitamins and fatty acids to light, oxygen, wide pH changes, heat, and moisture can result in significant loss of potency. Finally, it can be argued that some animals benefit from more "optimal" nutrient sources than the average pet. All of these reasons might make it sound as if supplements are necessary, but most commercial diets provide nutrient levels meant to compensate for any loss during storage. Cases of nutritional deficiency are extremely rare in pets fed commercial diets. Still, many pet owners want to use supplements, much as we do for ourselves (with our possibly significantly less nutritionally balanced diets). In reality, more medical problems are caused by supplementation than are fixed.

Nutraceuticals represent a massive business enterprise, but they are largely untouched by regulations and often unsupported by scientific scrutiny. That doesn't mean that pets can't benefit from some nutrients or herbal remedies, but don't give anything that you haven't discussed with your veterinary team. You want to make sure whatever you are giving works with, and not against, their efforts.

Nutritional therapy is not new, it is not a "miracle cure," and it is not quackery. In fact, many of the most popular drugs used today were originally isolated from nature rather than being created "new" in a laboratory. Nutritional therapies should not necessarily replace drug therapy, but both might work better together than either one alone. And if nutritional therapies help reduce the dosages of other needed medications, they've more than done their job.

Fatty acid supplements are probably the most useful nutraceuticals in veterinary medicine. These are not literally "essential" fatty acids, because the active ingredients (eicosapentaenoic acid, docosahexaenoic acid) are not considered essential for either dogs or cats, but they have at least some mild documented anti-inflammatory effectiveness in cases of allergies and arthritis. The needed ingredients are often found in marine (fish) oils and are present in a variety of veterinary formulations.

Glycosaminoglycans (GAG) are important constituents of joint cartilage. Supplementation is typically attempted to supply glucosamine and chondroitin to help repair joint damage. These are some of the most common supplements used in pets, but there really is not much scientific evidence to support that they are doing what is intended.

There are also a variety of nutrients that have been used for therapeutic effect, even in animals for which no deficiency exists. Nutrients like zinc, vitamin A, L-carnitine and taurine have been used for therapeutic benefit in some breed-specific instances. Once again, the effects are not due to deficiencies, because diets were found to be adequate, as were blood levels of the nutrients. In these cases, it is important to note that therapeutic doses were used rather than smaller supplement doses,

Large dogs often benefit from raised food dishes. It can help prevent strain on their joints over time (courtesy Janice Adams).

so it should never be attempted without veterinary supervision. This is especially critical because at these doses, pets also need to be monitored for potential side effects.

Calcium is a nutrient that pet owners should not administer unless expressly instructed to do so by the veterinary team. It is dangerous to add calcium to the diets of most pets, especially those that are growing rapidly or are pregnant. These, however, are usually the ones given excess amounts of calcium by well-meaning pet owners. The fact is that calcium levels in the body are carefully regulated by hormones (such as calcitonin and parathormone) and vitamin D. Supplementation disturbs this normal regulation, causing many problems. Calcium supplementation has been shown to cause bone and joint disorders and to impair the absorption of zinc from the intestine. Don't do it!

Probiotics are live microbes that, when ingested in appropriate amounts, are believed to positively affect the normal intestinal microbial balance (microbiome) and to beneficially impact health. They are believed to work through a variety of mechanisms to stimulate immune defense mechanisms and quell inflammatory reactions. Most probiotics are derived from a small variety of normal intestinal microbes. It is not known precisely how these microbes cause health benefits, but there appears to be some benefit documented for at least some health issues, including chronic digestive problems and potentially even allergies. Please discuss potential use with your veterinary team first since some supplements have resulted in the overgrowth of undesirable gut microbes.

Nutritional supplementation seems like it should be safe, but it is important to realize that just because these items are not designated as "drugs" does not mean they don't have side effects. In most cases, nutritional supplements are best used as part of a well-planned strategy with your veterinary team, in which specific outcomes are intended. Giving "something" may make you feel better, but in most instances, there is little discernible benefit unless it is given as part of an overall strategy.

Cannabinoids

Cannabinoid (ingredients derived from cannabis) use has become commonplace in pets today, even if much of this is done by pet owners directly and not by veterinarians. Cannabis is legal in many locations today, and pets have been exposed to it for years, either accidentally or on purpose. In fact, toxicities are commonly reported to poison control centers. In addition to recreational and medical use of marijuana, there are a variety of products that include cannabidiol (CBD) that are derived from hemp and have low or no levels of THC (tetrahydrocannabinol), which is the main psychoactive element in marijuana. Research to date is scant, but studies have been looking at whether different subtypes of CBD and terpenes may be effective for seizure disorders and pain management. Be aware, however, that certain hemp products designed for people contain xylitol, which can be toxic to pets. While it may be an uncomfortable conversation, if you are using cannabinoid products, confide in your veterinary team. They may have some legal restrictions as to what they can advise, and there is little documentation of long-term benefits or problems, but it is always better that they are aware.

Case Example

Shaquana Johnston presented Deiondre, her two-year-old Labrador Retriever, to ABC Veterinary Hospital for a recurring skin infection. It seems that every time she took Deiondre to the park and he went swimming in the pond there, he developed a rash afterwards on his belly and inner thighs. Shaquana was hoping that she could get an antibiotic to treat the infection, preferably something that could be given only once a day since she worked long hours and giving more than that would be inconvenient, and she would be likely to miss doses.

Dr. Solomon examined Deiondre and found that he did indeed have what looked like a bacterial infection but that it was very superficial and could be addressed with topical medications. Shaquana preferred an antibiotic, but Dr. Solomon eventually convinced her that she was actually better off with a topical therapy, since antibiotics would not be able to "cure" this, and she ran the risk of relying on antibiotics that would become less and less effective (and potentially more and more expensive as stronger products became necessary) over time.

Dr. Solomon dispensed a topical antiseptic to use on the rash and scheduled a reevaluation in two weeks to make sure everything cleared up as anticipated. During that time, he asked that Shaquana not let Deiondre swim in the pond, to confirm that was the actual cause of the problem. If it were, the veterinary team would devise a plan to control the rash, hopefully without antibiotics, and still make it possible for Deiondre to enjoy his swimming opportunity. Shaquana still thought that an antibiotic would be more convenient, at least in the short term, but she did understand why it was important to avoid antibiotic resistance and could appreciate that in the long run it was definitely in Deiondre's best interest.

Recommended Reading

Ackerman, L. 2019. "Ready to Partner with an Online Pharmacy?" *AAHA Trends* 35 (1): 49–53.

_____. 2009. "What's the Future of the Veterinary Pharmacy?" *Veterinary Forum* 26 (12): 2–17.

Amato, Nicole S. 2019. "Mesenchymal Stem Cell Therapy." Clinician's Brief. June. https://www.cliniciansbrief.com/article/mesenchymal-stem-cell-therapy.

Bauer, John E. 2006. "Facilitative and Functional Fats in Diets of Cats and Dogs." *Journal of the American Veterinary Medical Association* 229 (5): 680–684. https://doi.org/10.2460/javma.229.5.680.

Benyacoub, J., S.N. Sauter, and R. Knorr. 2007. "Probiotics as Tools to Improve Health: Perspectives for Pets." *Supplement to Compendium of Continuing Education for the Practicing Veterinarian* 29 (2A): 11–19.

Cunha, Andreia. 2017. "Genomic Technologies—From Tools to Therapies." *Genome Medicine* 9 (1): 71. https://doi.org/10.1186/s13073-017-0462-9

Freeman, Lisa M., Sarah K. Abood, Andrea J. Fascetti, Linda M. Fleeman, Kathryn E. Michel, Dorothy P. Laflamme, Cassandra Bauer, Brona L.E. Kemp, Janine R. Van Doren, and Kristina N. Willoughby. 2006. "Disease Prevalence Among Dogs and Cats in the United States and Australia and Proportions of Dogs and Cats That Receive Therapeutic Diets or Dietary Supplements." *Journal of the American Veterinary Medical Association* 229 (4): 531–534. https://doi.org/10.2460/javma.229.4.531.

Frey, Erin, and Megan Jacob. 2020. "Development of a Method for Creating Antibiograms for Use in Companion Animal Private Practices." *Journal of the American Veterinary Medical Association* 257 (9): 950–960. https://doi.org/10.2460/javma.257.9.950.

Gamble, Lauri-Jo, Jordyn M. Boesch, Christopher W. Frye, Wayne S. Schwark, Sabine Mann, Lisa Wolfe, Holly Brown, Erin S. Berthelsen, and Joseph J. Wakshlag. 2018. "Pharmacokinetics, Safety, and Clinical Efficacy of Cannabidiol Treatment in Osteoarthritic Dogs." *Frontiers in Veterinary Science* 5: 165. https://doi.org/10.3389/fvets.2018.00165.

"How to Buy Medicines Safely from an Internet Pharmacy." n.d. *U.S. Food & Drug Administration.* U.S. Food & Drug Administration. https://www.fda.gov/consumer-updates/how-buy-medicines-safely-online-pharmacy.

Khoo, C., J. Cunnick, K. Friesen, et al. 2005. "The Role of Supplementary Dietary Antioxidants on Immune Response in Puppies." *Veterinary Therapeutics* 6 (1): 43–56.

LeBlanc, C.J., J.E. Bauer, G. Hosgood, and G.E. Maudlin. 2005. "Effect of Dietary Fish Oil and Vitamin E Supplementation on Hematologic and Serum Biochemical Analytes and Oxidative Status in Young Dogs." *Veterinary Therapeutics* 6 (4): 325–340.

Mealey, Katrina L. 2019. *Pharmacotherapeutics for Veterinary Dispensing.* Hoboken, NJ: Wiley.

Packaged Facts: Pet Medications in the U.S. 2019. 6th ed. https://www.packagedfacts.com/Pet-Medications-Edition-12543601.

Zicker, Steven C., Karen J. Wedekind, and Dennis E. Jewell. 2006. "Antioxidants in Veterinary Nutrition." *Veterinary Clinics of North America: Small Animal Practice* 36 (6): 1183–1198. https://doi.org/10.1016/j.cvsm.2006.08.002.

9

Nutritional Considerations

Many people are very concerned about what they feed their family members. Naturally, they are concerned about feeding pets healthy and nutritious foods, too. There are many pet food options, and the selection can feel overwhelming. How do you choose with so much choice? You may, at one time or another, question your veterinarian, breeder, groomer, trainer, or a salesperson at a pet supply store about which food may be best for your pet. But don't be surprised if there is no consensus, because while it is not difficult to select a diet that would be appropriate for your *almost* perfect pet, it is not unusual that everyone will have an opinion about what might be best and what you should avoid.

The good news is that if you are purchasing a pet food that has been certified to be balanced for your pet's life stage based on feeding trials (not just nutrient profile), then you have a lot of selection. The bad news, however, is that you have a lot of selection ... and it can be difficult to choose. Still, that's not really such a bad problem to have.

Basic Pet Nutrition

We'll get to a discussion of pet foods soon, but if you want to avoid problems, it's worth first considering the role of food in the life of our pets. Most pets are food motivated, and there is an innate desire for us to feed them and for them to be fed by us; this can either be a positive force or a negative one. If we use food to signal our role as leader or as a reward to entice desirable behaviors, good for us! However, if we reward begging, or give food whenever pestered to do so, then we are setting some dangerous precedents that we will likely later regret.

Just as parents are head of a household, pet parents must include furry family members in the household, too. As the leader, you are responsible for setting rules around food and behavior. Do not abdicate this responsibility. Every happy household needs a loving parent figure to create consistent rules and expectations. Pets thrive with consistency and limits. To help pets get accustomed to the rules, feed them from the same location and at the same time each day. While it is not necessary that pets always eat when you do, it can be comforting to them when you feed them twice a day, even if they can actually go longer between meals. However, from the start, do not feed them from the table, or this will quickly become an expectation. If they know that they only get fed from their feeding station at specified times, they will quickly come to accept this. By the way, while some may espouse a leader of the pack philosophy that states that pets should only be fed after the leader, there is little to no rationale for doing so. Just as with feeding children, it doesn't really matter if they eat with us, before us, or after us; as long as they understand the rules of the household and they appreciate that they are going to be fed, flexibility will be well tolerated. Pets don't need mealtime to share what they have done during their day with other family members, so feeding needn't be a social outlet and can be done on our schedule. Time would be better spent training pets when and how they should expect to be fed and to not disturb other family members while they are eating their meals.

Similarly, snack time can be difficult if you don't appropriately coach your pets. If you are on the couch eating pizza, nachos, or anything else that your pet might otherwise be happy to share, avoid the temptation to give up your parental status that entitles you to eat what you want when you want without being harassed. While it may seem kind to share, you are creating a pet that will expect this behavior, feel entitled, and whine and beg each time you settle in to eat. While this may initially seem cute, it can quickly become both annoying and unhealthy

Leira relaxing (courtesy Antoinette Falzone).

for your beloved companion. If you want to give your pets snacks, wait for times when you are not being pestered, and then offer them healthy snacks such as carrots, popcorn, and broccoli crowns. Consider a vegan marshmallow if you are feeling particularly decadent. If you choose to give them snacks at times they are not expecting them, and when you are not eating yourself, you are much more likely to have rule-abiding *almost* perfect pets.

You are likely going to feed several different foods over the lifetime of your pet. Most decisions will be based on life stage. So, if you adopt a puppy or kitten, you will at first feed diets approved and tested for this stage of rapid growth. Just as with babies, the formulations are typically quite different than foods meant for adults, and so you will eventually transition to an adult food after this initial stage. The length of this first dietary stage depends on your pet and when it is presumed to have finished its main growth period. Large and giant breed dogs tend to have bone growth that extends over a longer time period, so they may be on growth diets longer, perhaps until 15–16 months of age. In this case of large or giant breeds, you should also check the product label to make sure that it meets the requirements for this particular group. You are probably familiar with the concept of growth charts as they apply to children, and there are growth standards created by the World Health Organization (WHO) and the Centers for Disease Control (CDC). As you might imagine, this is more complicated for dogs and cats, but some progress has been made. There are currently a series of evidence-based growth charts based on body weight that have been developed for some size categories in dogs ... so that's a start (see Recommended Reading). Keeping young pets growing at the correct pace not only helps assure proper growth but can lessen the risk of adult obesity as well as a variety of developmental orthopedic diseases, including hip dysplasia. This shouldn't be a surprise. As you've seen from other sections of this book, you may need a particular dietary strategy for your specific pet depending on its risk for certain conditions. So, if you have a pet prone to orthopedic conditions such as hip dysplasia or prone to obesity (we even have a DNA test for the risk of that in some breeds), it will be important to keep your pet lean and avoid rapid growth spurts during this critical period. Food management is extremely important because weight, diet and growth rate play an important role in whether or not heritable conditions like hip dysplasia actually become a problem, much as they do in many human conditions.

After pets are fully grown, they typically go on adult diets and stay on these for most of their lives. Unless a pet is competing in some activity, is intended for breeding, has a medical condition, or is serving some special purpose, these diets are meant to be balanced and sufficient for maintenance purposes. When animals are considered "senior," and this is variable between pets, they may be switched to diets formulated for this life stage. Senior diets often contain ingredients that are more digestible and appropriate for older pets, but many pets can remain on adult diets indefinitely if they remain healthy. In fact, when it comes to diets, the terms "senior" and "geriatric" don't refer to defined characteristics of a food but are used mainly for marketing concepts that may or may not be relevant for your specific pet.

Throughout your pet's healthspan, don't just add some food into your companion's bowl. Measure the serving size either in a cup with gradations or by weight on a scale. Keeping pets from becoming overweight or obese is incredibly important in keeping them healthy. Controlling amounts fed and making necessary adjustments is much easier if you have a specific amount of food fed with each meal.

With the basics covered, we can now venture into the sometimes controversial topic of actual pet foods.

Commercial Pet Foods

Not all pet owners share the same view of nutrition and that is why so many different pet foods are on the market. Some people just want a simple food that will meet their pet's nutritional requirements at an economical price. Some want to feed raw foods because they believe this is closer to what animals would eat in the wild. Others buy into the "premium pet food" market because they're convinced that their pets deserve the best and that these foods are the best because they're more expensive. Would these individuals be surprised to learn that the terms "premium" and "gourmet" are not regulated and therefore can be used with any product? While wanting the best for your beloved companion, it is easy to be misled. You have to know the facts!

You might think that choosing a commercial pet food could be one of the toughest decisions you need to make for your pet. However, it needn't be. It's really a matter of matching your preference for storage (canned, dry, semi-moist, frozen, etc.) with your pet's life stage (growth, adult, senior, etc.), level of activity, and a brand from a manufacturer you are inclined to trust (knowing that most brands have had a recall at some point in time). Over time you'll likely experiment and find that your pet prefers some formulations over others or that you are happier with the firmness of the poop produced on one diet over another. Relax about whether or not you picked the quintessentially best diet, and be satisfied that if the diet is balanced (on the basis of feeding trials), your pet can actually have a little variety in what it is being fed. You don't want to change diets too abruptly, or you are liable to cause some digestive upset, but there is no problem mixing and matching appropriate diets based on availability, price, or just the day of the week. If you are switching between diets, though, it is best to mix the end of one food with the beginning of the next to ease the transition over a few days and avoid digestive upset.

You can invest a bit of time and gain some expertise in reading pet food labels if you'd like, but you'll quickly learn that it can be difficult to determine the quality of a pet food just by reading the label. There are many gimmicks that manufacturers use to support their marketing claims, so it is easy to be fooled. There are too many pet food marketing tricks to cover here, but if you are prepared to do the research, you'll quickly learn how confusing it is to rely on label information alone.

Another marketing trap when it comes to pet foods regards protein content, often with the mistaken belief that more protein is better for pets or that somehow you can judge the quality of a pet food by its protein content. The fact is that most pet food labels only report *crude protein*, and even that is just an estimate based on the calculated amount of nitrogen in the diet. In fact, adulterants such as melamine (which is nitrogen rich) can fraudulently lead to estimates of high protein in a diet, so don't overinterpret crude protein levels as something desirable. Pets do not have dietary requirements for protein—they have requirements for specific essential amino acids, and if they have those, they have everything they need to make needed proteins. If they don't have those, it really doesn't matter how much crude protein is in the diet. The fact is that once the dietary requirement for amino acids is met, excess protein just provides more calories to the pet, can contribute to obesity, or can tax the kidneys as excess protein is excreted into the urine. So, don't focus on crude protein; most nutritionists will evaluate diets based on feeding trials as well as their amino acid concentrations and ignore crude protein as primarily a marketing tactic.

While protein definitely garners the most attention when reading pet food labels, it is not alone. Pets don't have any specific nutritional requirements for carbohydrates, but they are generally there as fillers, a source of fiber, and a cheaper form of energy (calories). There is not really a rationale for it, but some pet food purchasers may shun carbohydrates in favor of higher protein diets, and grain-free diets were trending for a while. Clearly carbohydrates are not the enemy, but theories abound about what should and should not be in pet food formulations. Similar to proteins, fats aren't a nutritional requirement, but there are essential fatty acids that are required in the diet (alpha-linolenic acid and cis-linoleic acid in the dog, while cats also have a requirement for arachidonic acid). Saturated fats may be tasty for pets, but there is no nutritional requirement for them. Pet foods usually have a full contingent of vitamins and minerals to meet the known daily requirements established by regulatory bodies. The biggest risk for deficiencies in this regard is from improper storage of the pet food (before or after sale) or other ingredients in the ration that might interfere with the absorption of vital nutrients. It can be confusing, especially if you are prone to believing "hype," whether it is generated by marketers or influencers.

If you need an opinion, ask your veterinary team, but if you are going to make a selection yourself, consider foods manufactured by a company you are prepared to trust. These companies have the most to lose by distributing inferior products because they have a reputation to protect. Fad diets and manufacturers will come and go, but the pet food companies that intend to be around will be the ones most concerned with adequate nutrition.

Once you've selected a commercial diet, be aware that the feeding directions on the label might not be appropriate for your specific pet. Consider the label directions to be a starting point, but be prepared to

Did someone say treats? (courtesy Liz Love).

adjust the amount fed according to body condition and weight. Just as in humans, we care much more about maintaining lean body mass than we do the total amount fed. This is all about remaining problem free, so pay attention to whether your pet enjoys the diet, whether it upsets their digestive system (vomiting, diarrhea, constipation, flatulence, etc.) and whether they look good, feel good and can maintain their optimal weight while on the diet.

If you are like most pet owners, once you have selected a commercial diet, you want to know what else you can feed your loved one. We could say that you shouldn't feed anything else because you are already providing a balanced diet, but that would not be realistic because we know you are going to feed other things anyway. Most people want to share little extras with their pets. We might as well acknowledge that up front and then go about suggesting what could be reasonable to supplement.

The general rule is that whatever you give should not constitute more than 10 percent of the total amount being fed, or you run the risk of unbalancing the balanced diet you just selected. So, if you are preparing a family meal and you want to give your pet some lean cuts of meat, poultry or fish (cooked) or some broccoli, cauliflower, carrots or celery or some sweet potatoes, rice or quinoa, it shouldn't be a problem. That being said, there are some things that you should definitely keep away from your pet, including onions, garlic, chocolate, raisins, grapes, macadamia nuts, raw bread dough, caffeinated products, and xylitol (a low-carbohydrate sweetener). Further, if you have a cat, don't feed it dog food—serious nutritional deficiencies could result. If you want to supplement from family meals, focus on healthy choices. Before you consider feeding anything, realize that it could possibly be toxic, and do an online search. You just might save your pet's life.

We love to feed our pets treats, and there is certainly no shortage of these available. The one caution when selecting products is that many treats tend to be quite high in calories. Manufacturers make these tasty for a reason, and that reason is that when your pets love their treats, you are more likely to buy them. So, regardless of how enthusiastic your pet is, be careful of how many you are feeding in a day, or you may end up dealing with a weight issue. That being said, if you are interested in training your pet to do some cool stuff, or if you need to keep them preoccupied so they won't mind other stuff you are trying to do to them, those tasty treats tend to be good motivators.

Remember that when you add things to the diet that it likely means that your pet won't eat as much of its regular food (which is the one that is balanced), or if it eats everything, it might become overweight (see overnutrition below). This is often compounded if you add fats or oils to the diet (such as bacon drippings or vegetable oil), and biscuit snacks are often very rich in calories. After you've spent all that time searching for a balanced diet, avoid the temptation to feed "human food" and snacks in quantities that will compromise the planned nutrition.

At some time in your pet's life, your veterinary team may uncover a disease process that warrants changing your pet's regular diet to a therapeutic diet that will help with managing the condition. These diets can help with heart and kidney disease, urinary tract "stones," joint disorders, allergies, cognitive decline (dementia) and many other issues. While these diets serve a very important role in the management of a variety of health conditions, it is important to remember that they are intended to be used under the direction of a licensed veterinarian as part of an integrated health management program, not as stand-alone therapies. For example, if your pet has heart disease, your veterinary team may recommend a low-salt therapeutic diet, but that is likely only part of the program needed to manage the condition. Check with your veterinary team before contemplating adding anything else to these diets, or you may undo the therapeutic good they are attempting to accomplish.

If you are feeding a commercial diet, eventually you will hear or read something that suggests that food preservatives in these diets are bad. Whether these are chemical (butylated hydroxyanisole, butylated hydroxytoluene, ethoxyquin) or natural (tocopherol, ascorbate) preservatives, we need to consider why they are present in pet foods and whether we think there is a fair trade-off. Preservatives are present (mostly in dry foods) because we want to buy several weeks' worth of food and be able to store it in our homes without it going rancid and without taking up space in the refrigerator. We also want to be able to open and then reseal a bag without the food going bad. Whether it is our food or our pet's food, preservatives are required if we want to have perishable ingredients remain stable and edible without refrigeration. On the other hand, most canned foods do not require preservatives because they are vacuum sealed and meant to be consumed immediately or within a few days if then refrigerated. If you want to avoid preservatives, you may opt for canned food or food that can be stored in a freezer or refrigerator. If we want economical foods that can be stored for extended periods without refrigeration, take some solace that preservatives used in our foods and those for our pets are generally recognized as safe (GRAS) even if they may not sound wholesome. Whether you are eating snack food or feeding your pet, there is no need to feel guilty; preservatives have just become part of our busy lifestyles, and it would be hard to get by without them.

For some reason, the food world is prone to fads, and this can affect the choices people make for their pets. For example, grain-free diets were trendy, at least until there was some question that surfaced about whether they could be associated in some way with some cases of non-genetic heart disease (cardiomyopathy). The cause is likely complex and not solely due to the actions of rogue lentils and peas, but one benefit of feeding standard diets is that they are being fed to millions and millions of pets, often over many generations, and so health trends tend to be easier to recognize. Whether there is any real link between grain-free diets and cardiomyopathy is anecdotal at the moment, and any dietary association is likely to be more complex with certain dietary aspects (ingredient sourcing, processing, formulation, digestion, etc.) impacting underlying genetic and medical situations.

Homemade Diets

Most people's lives are too busy for them to even consider regularly preparing fresh cooked meals for their pets, and that's a good thing, because it is exceptionally difficult to balance those meals nutritionally.

Although a homemade diet can be prepared with wholesome ingredients that don't contain preservatives, additives, or colorings, you run a greater risk of improperly nourishing your pet and potentially causing problems. Whenever a diet is prepared at home, there is a danger that the ingredients will not be balanced properly. If you are committed to making homemade meals for your pet, it is important to be aware of risks and research the requirements for a balanced diet for your specific pet before you start cooking.

As our pet companions have become extensions of our own image, some pet owners think about matching their pet's diet to reflect their own preferences and beliefs. So, if someone is a vegetarian or vegan, for example, they may have objections to keeping meat products in the home, including commercial pet foods, which are very likely to include such ingredients. The same may be true for those who are on other special diets themselves and sincerely (but generally mistakenly) believe these dietary choices might also benefit their pets. This includes ketogenic, paleo, vegan, zone, Dukan, South Beach and other diets, diets conforming to certain religious restrictions, and anything else where we want to impose our food choices on our pets. This is a book about sharing important social bonds with our pets, but keep in mind that dogs and cats have different physiology, nutritional requirements and metabolism than us, so this can be extremely complicated and risky for our beloved companions. In some cases, it may be impossible to meet the nutritional needs of a pet with a restrictive diet. For instance, cats are considered obligate carnivores, meaning they must consume meat, and it can be unhealthy to try to maintain them on vegetarian or vegan diets. The sentiment may be pure, but consider things carefully before imposing choices on species for which we often do not have sufficient information that they can be managed safely.

There are other aspects of creating homemade diets that are worth mentioning. It's not unusual that pet owners choose homemade food preparation so that they can use organic ingredients in the meal preparation for their pets. This is laudable, as the goal is to reduce the amounts of potential carcinogens present in the food supply in order to promote long-term health. Going organic is a great concept, but it is very difficult to create completely organic meals while providing a balanced diet. More likely, if you are committed to this concept and prepared to invest your energy in homemade meals, you may still need to accept some nonorganic ingredients to meet all your pet's nutritional needs. It also has not (yet) been shown that feeding pets organic diets increases their lifespan or decreases their risk for cancer, which are two main reasons for considering it.

Nubs curling up (courtesy Katrina O'Gahan).

More and more pet owners are now becoming locavores (sourcing foods locally), which tends to reduce our carbon footprint, support local economies, provide opportunities to get fresher ingredients, reduce storage needs, and is a more sustainable practice. There is no downside at all to this, but it is still very difficult to construct an entire balanced pet diet based only on locally sourced ingredients.

One final consideration is genetically modified organisms (GMO) in the food supply. The DNA in these crops is typically altered to increase nutrients, make them more resistant to parasites, herbicides and weeds, and in some cases to confer virus resistance to the plants. In some countries, including the United States, the majority of common crops (including soybeans, rice and corn) are genetically engineered. Whether you are for or against GMOs and whether they should be fed to people and pets, regulations may differ on a country-by-country basis, and it may not be required for manufacturers to indicate whether a product contains GMOs, so it can be difficult to know which foods contain them.

If you are still committed to preparing balanced homemade diets for pets, consult a veterinary nutritionist to help ensure that you minimize the risk that your recipes could cause harm. In almost all cases, special supplements need to also be formulated because it is important that specific nutrients be provided in the right amounts and in the right ratios and that is difficult to do because the nutrient profiles can vary widely in fresh prepared foods. That's why even nutritionists will often recommend that you not feed homemade diets for more than two months in a row and then alternate with commercial diets to ensure some balance in the rotation. In time, most owners modify recipes either for convenience or to adjust to their pet's taste preferences, effectively unbalancing most rations in a process sometimes referred to as "recipe drift."

Raw Food Diets

Raw food diets are periodically popular, although there is little evidence that they are healthier and much evidence that they pose health care risks to dogs, cats and human family members. Proponents of raw food diets claim that these are more natural diets for dogs and cats (at least ancestral varieties of these species), that regular processing of commercial diets destroys the natural nutrients found in those foods, and that raw diets make pets healthier.

This is an emotionally charged issue, and it is not possible to influence either true believers or nonbelievers, so we'll look at why there is such controversy around the topic. It's possible that there are some health benefits with raw food diets, but there are not really scientific studies to support such theories. The main reason why health care professionals are wary of raw food diets is that there are risks for family members handling raw meats and serving dishes, because they may be contaminated with dangerous microbes, including *Salmonella, E. coli, Campylobacter, Yersinia enterocolitica,* and even tuberculosis organisms in some countries.

To reduce health risks in people, the United States Food and Drug Administration (FDA) recommends that makers of raw pet foods use human-grade meat and poultry, that the product be frozen until used, and that labels contain guidelines for safe handling, including warnings that raw meats be kept separate from other foods and that consumers wash hands, utensils and surfaces after handling meat. It is also recommended that households using raw food diets for their pets prepare those diets on surfaces and in spaces separate from those used to prepare food for the humans in the household. To be on the safe side, it is probably best that those who are pregnant not handle such raw food ingredients.

Keep in mind that foodborne illness is a problem even in the foods we buy for ourselves, and it is not limited to meats, fish and poultry. It is almost impossible to screen all foods entering the country for all potential contaminants. There have been instances of green onions carrying hepatitis A virus, bagged spinach contaminated with *E. coli* and lettuce contaminated with *Listeria.* We don't mean to single out prepared raw pet food diets, but most raw foods come with some health risks.

Pets are fairly resistant to the effects of these contaminants, so they don't often get food poisoning; most of the concern is actually for human family members. Studies have shown that while pets tend to be more resistant to these foodborne microbes than people, once fed, the microbes may continue to reside in the digestive tract and then contaminate the home environment, posing yet another risk to other animals and people. Microbes can be transmitted to household members through close contact with pets that are shedding the organisms. People that are immunosuppressed, have HIV/AIDS, have had organ transplants, are on chemotherapy are or on other medications that impair the immune response are at greatest risk of infection, but all family members are at some risk, depending on their level of hygiene and the closeness of their contact with the pet shedding those microbes.

If there were a very well-defined benefit from feeding such diets, it would be much easier to weigh that benefit against the risks and make an intelligent decision for such a selection. One day there may be such a study done that proves or disproves the claims of raw food enthusiasts, but for now it is simply a matter of faith. This is a book about raising *almost* perfect pets, and if people in the home get sick—that would not be considered perfect.

Sustainability

There is marked interest in not only providing safe and healthy products for pets but also for reducing waste and preserving the environment. This also involves appropriate sourcing of materials and ingredients, changing pet industry employee practices, and rethinking packaging. It is also important to reconsider our perceptions of what should be in pet foods. As pet parents, we naturally prefer to think of our pets eating "human-grade" meals, but that not only puts extra pressure on an already-stretched global food system, but it doesn't even reflect what would be the natural preferences of dogs and cats. In fact, the wild cousins of dogs and cats would first gorge on the nutrient-rich internal organs of their kills, with the meat being a secondary consideration. Animal products and byproducts may not look particularly wholesome on a pet food label, but regarding sustainability, they can be very nutritious, and they represent the parts of animals that people often don't eat and that otherwise could end up as waste.

Sustainability is a moving target as consumers slowly shift to an eco-friendlier future. The pet industry has taken note, so pet owners need to do their own research and not just rely on clever product marketing.

Overnutrition

It's a sad fact that the number one nutritional disorder in pets today is overnutrition, often manifested as our pets being overweight or obese. In fact, overnutrition is more common than all nutritional deficiencies combined.

Everyone knows the dangers of obesity in people but don't always apply the same logic to pets. Food is often considered a token of love and is an important way that we bond with our pets, but overnutrition is killing them. Obese pets suffer from many of the same issues as humans. Obese pets don't live as long as pets of normal weight. They suffer more from heart problems, they fatigue easily, there is more pressure on bones and joints, and they are at increased risk of developing diabetes. Obese pets also have a decreased resistance to infection and are more prone to anesthetic complications during surgery. On the other hand, restriction of food intake to maintain a normal weight and body condition is associated with increased lifespan and can help delay the onset of signs of chronic diseases (arthritis, diabetes, etc.).

Genetic factors likely have some role in the development of obesity, and there are several breeds that are more prone to obesity than others. In fact, we even have a genetic test that can help predict a predilection to obesity in some breeds. Apart from genetics though (and not to minimize the role of genetics in obesity predisposition), the most significant causes of obesity are excessive calorie intake and inadequate physical activity. The household pet that is rarely exercised, confined to the home, and fed a high-quality diet (which is typically high in protein, fat and calories) is the most prone to obesity.

The pet food industry has come a long way in making diets that are tasty and calorie-dense so that obesity is readily achieved. It is easy to be swayed by advertising and believe that your pet deserves the best, which often means a high-protein diet. What could be healthier than a diet loaded with protein? Well, the fact is that unless your pet is a high-performing athlete, excess protein is either converted to fat or excreted in the urine. And diets high in meat protein are also high in meat fat, often saturated fats. These diets

Some toys are also food dispensers but require engagement and strategy. They can help the puppy problem solve at the same time as getting a meal or snack. They also can alleviate boredom (courtesy Janice Adams).

are therefore loaded with calories! This problem is often compounded by inappropriate feeding practices, such as providing access to food throughout the day, rather than just at mealtimes, and then adding snacks to the equation.

If your pet has a weight issue, work with your veterinary team to address the problem. However, as we often mention in this book, the best path is actually to prevent obesity from occurring in the first place. This often involves being mindful of the role that food plays in the bond with our pets, employing appropriate feeding strategies, and not getting into situations where you feel guilty withholding food when your pet looks at you with those soulful eyes. Yes, this can be done without harming that bond at all. It just requires commitment and mindfulness. Truly, your companion's love does not depend on high-calorie foods.

Case Example

Justin works as a driver for a ride-sharing app and is hoping to increase his financial prospects by adopting a pet that he can also breed for extra money. He locates a nearby amateur Great Dane breeder and purchases a fawn-colored pup which he names Viserion.

Since Justin has high hopes for Viserion's breeding possibilities, he decides to spare no expense and to feed Viserion home-cooked meals of beef and rice. He anticipated that Viserion would likely be growing quickly so also thought to add a calcium supplement to help build strong bones. Justin was proud that Viserion seemed to be happy and enthusiastic at mealtime.

By 6 months of age, Viserion didn't seem to be as tall as other Great Danes, at least as much as he could tell from online resources, so he decided to double up on the calcium supplement.

At 9 months of age, while playing at a dog park, Viserion appeared to trip and hurt his leg. Justin brought him to ABC Veterinary Hospital, and they took radiographs (x-rays) and diagnosed that Viserion had suffered a spontaneous fracture and that his bones were not as mineralized as they should be. When Justin told them that was unlikely because he had been giving Viserion calcium supplements, he learned something unsettling—calcium supplements are actually some of the worst things to give a rapidly growing breed because they interfere with the body's own ability to regulate bone minerals.

Justin also learned, to his dismay, that the diet he was feeding of beef and rice was not balanced and had resulted in a condition known as nutritional hyperparathyroidism. The veterinary team thought that

Viserion was likely to recover for the most part with appropriate nutritional correction but that his short stature and skeletal abnormalities would likely make him a poor candidate for breeding. Fortunately, that didn't make him any less lovable.

Recommended Reading

Ackerman, Lowell J. 1999. *Canine Nutrition: What Every Owner, Breeder, and Trainer Should Know.* Loveland, CO: Alpine Publications.

Chen, Tom T., Deep K. Khosa, Scott A. McEwen, Sarah K. Abood, and Jennifer E. McWhirter. 2020. "Readability and Content of Online Pet Obesity Information." *Journal of the American Veterinary Medical Association* 257 (11): 1171–1180. https://doi.org/10.2460/javma.2020.257.11.1171.

Dodd, C.E., S.C. Zicker, D.E. Jewell, et al. 2003. "Can a Fortified Food Affect the Behavioral Manifestations of Age-Related Cognitive Decline in Dogs?" *Veterinary Medicine* 98: 396–408.

Elliott, Denise A. 2006. "Nutritional Management of Chronic Renal Disease in Dogs and Cats." *Veterinary Clinics of North America: Small Animal Practice* 36 (6): 1377–1384. https://doi.org/10.1016/j.cvsm.2006.08.011.

German, Alexander J. 2006. "The Growing Problem of Obesity in Dogs and Cats." *The Journal of Nutrition* 136 (7): 1940–1946. https://doi.org/10.1093/jn/136.7.1940s.

Gwaltney-Brant, S., J.K. Holding, C.W. Donaldson, et al. 2001. "Differing Opinions of Raw Food Diet Research … Renal Failure Associated with Ingestion of Grapes or Raisins in Dogs." *Journal of the American Veterinary Medical Association* 218 (10): 1555–1556. https://doi.org/10.2460/javma.2001.218.1553.

Joffe, D.J., and D.P. Schlessinger. 2002. "Preliminary Assessment of the Risk of Salmonella Infection in Dogs Fed Raw Chicken Diets." *Canadian Veterinary Journal* 43: 441–442.

Kealy, Richard D., Dennis F. Lawler, Joan M. Ballam, Sandra L. Mantz, Darryl N. Biery, Elizabeth H. Greeley, George Lust, Mariangela Segre, Gail K. Smith, and Howard D. Stowe. 2002. "Effects of Diet Restriction on Life Span and Age-Related Changes in Dogs." *Journal of the American Veterinary Medical Association* 220 (9): 1315–1320. https://doi.org/10.2460/javma.2002.220.1315.

Laflamme, Dottie P. 2006. "Understanding and Managing Obesity in Dogs and Cats." *The Veterinary Clinics of North America. Small Animal Practice* 36 (6): 1283–1295, vii. https://doi.org/10.1016/j.cvsm.2006.08.005.

Means, Charlotte. 2003. "Bread Dough Toxicosis in Dogs." *Journal of Veterinary Emergency and Critical Care* 13 (1): 39–41. https://doi.org/10.1046/j.1435-6935.2003.00068.x.

Michel, Kathryn E. 2006. "Unconventional Diets for Dogs and Cats." *Veterinary Clinics of North America: Small Animal Practice* 36 (6): 1269–1281. https://doi.org/10.1016/j.cvsm.2006.08.003.

Morley, Paul S., Rachel A. Strohmeyer, Jeanetta D. Tankson, Doreene R. Hyatt, David A. Dargatz, and Paula J. Fedorka-Cray. 2006. "Evaluation of the Association Between Feeding Raw Meat and Salmonella Enterica Infections at a Greyhound Breeding Facility." *Journal of the American Veterinary Medical Association* 228 (10): 1524–1532. https://doi.org/10.2460/javma.228.10.1524.

Roudebush, P., S.C. Zicker, and C.W. Cotton. 2005. "Nutritional Management of Brain Aging in Dogs." *Journal of the American Veterinary Association* 227 (5): 722–728.

Salt, Carina, Penelope J. Morris, Richard F. Butterwick, Elizabeth M. Lund, Tim J. Cole, and Alexander J. German. 2020. "Comparison of Growth Patterns in Healthy Dogs and Dogs in Abnormal Body Condition Using Growth Standards." Edited by Juan J. Loor. *PLOS ONE* 15 (9): e0238521. https://doi.org/10.1371/journal.pone.0238521.

"The Savvy Cat Owner's Guide to Nutrition on the Internet." n.d. World Small Animal Veterinary Association. https://wsava.org/wp-content/uploads/2020/01/The-Savvy-Cat-Owner-s-Guide-to-Nutrition-on-the-Internet.pdf.

"The Savvy Dog Owner's Guide to Nutrition on the Internet." n.d. World Small Animal Veterinary Association. https://wsava.org/wp-content/uploads/2020/01/The-Savvy-Dog-Owner-s-Guide-to-Nutrition-on-the-Internet.pdf.

Strohmeyer, Rachel A., Paul S. Morley, Doreene R. Hyatt, David A. Dargatz, A. Valeria Scorza, and Michael R. Lappin. 2006. "Evaluation of Bacterial and Protozoal Contamination of Commercially Available Raw Meat Diets for Dogs." *Journal of the American Veterinary Medical Association* 228 (4): 537–542. https://doi.org/10.2460/javma.228.4.537.

Yaissle, Jill E., Cheryl Holloway, and C.A. Tony Buffington. 2004. "Evaluation of Owner Education as a Component of Obesity Treatment Programs for Dogs." *Journal of the American Veterinary Medical Association* 224 (12): 1932–1935. https://doi.org/10.2460/javma.2004.224.1932.

Mindfulness
and Pet Care

Promoting Positive Pet
Mental Health

It might seem strange to have a chapter on pet mental health in a book on *almost* perfect pets, but the fact is that paying attention to a pet's mental health is one of the best ways of ensuring that pets remain problem free. While we may not want to admit it, when we look at populations of animals in our shelters, there are more pets relinquished for behavioral reasons than for all medical conditions combined. So, a pet that has "accidents" in the house, chews on our favorite possessions, causes damage in the home, or disturbs the neighbors is at very real risk of losing cherished family pet status and may be facing a very uncertain future.

Mindfulness

Mindfulness is a process in which we bring ourselves to live in the moment while still acknowledging other forces, thoughts, sensations and feelings. Mindfulness is more than just a form of meditation. It is a way to help reduce stress, anxiety and even depression and is thought to provide both physical and mental health benefits.

The good news is that pets often demonstrate their own versions of mindfulness techniques and can lead the way to our own enlightenment. Pets are very much "in the moment" when they interact with us. They are singular in their focus to maximize their enjoyment of the time they spend with us. When they are totally engaged with us, whether it is a walk in the park, a belly rub on the couch, or a casual head scratch during work-at-home breaks, we never get the impression that they would rather be somewhere else or doing something else. They are completely committed to us, and there is definitely something that can be learned from this.

What's required to make a difference in the life of a pet as well as your own? Take a few minutes each day, put your phone down, step away from your computer, and just interact with your pet in a very direct way. You don't have to do an activity, and it certainly doesn't need to involve food, but just make a very real connection, be present, and appreciate the role you play in your pet's life and the role they play in yours. If you're like most people, you'll find the interaction as meaningful as meditation or prayer and experience the calm that comes from spending some quiet time with a creature who lives entirely in the moment and is happy for just a small morsel of your time.

Pets don't ask for much, and it is well worthwhile that for at least short periods of time that we put aside all the other things that are going on in our lives and for those few moments be entirely engaged with our pets. Taking that time can do a lot to reduce stress and anxiety (in our pets as well as us) and restore a sense of calm. It is time well spent.

Stress and Anxiety in Pets

You might wonder why pets would have stress and anxiety in their lives. After all, they don't have to go to work, they don't have to worry about paying the mortgage or rent, and they don't have to be concerned as to where their next meal is coming from. Still, the mental health of our pets is often a reflection of sharing our lives, competing for our attention, and dealing with anxiety in periods when they are not with us.

Dogs and cats are genetically programmed to live within a group structure, and so they are used to rules and fully anticipate respecting the group leader—that would be you! So, for pets, they are actually most content when there are clear boundaries and someone who can gently guide them to behaving properly. When that doesn't happen, pets are likely to act out—not because they want to misbehave but because they are stressed about what should be happening.

In some cases, pet mental health issues can also evolve into physical manifestation of stress and anxiety even if the association seems difficult to discern. For example, an inflammatory bladder condition in cats, known as feline idiopathic cystitis (and similar to bladder pain syndrome/interstitial cystitis in humans), seems to worsen in the face of internal or external stressors. Who would have thought a pet's bladder disease could be caused by anxiety and stress?

Nubs ponders life (courtesy Katrina O'Gahan).

When it comes to stress in pets, it is important to work with genetic tendencies and not against them. Many problems result when we adopt a pet that has been bred for a specific purpose but then try to raise them in a completely different setting. So, for example, when we take a working breed, such as a Siberian husky, and try to impose a sedentary lifestyle, we may see some rebellious behaviors such as digging and even running at large if given an escape path. Border collies were raised to herd, and if you don't keep them busy, you may find them trying to herd family members if given the opportunity, such as by nipping at their heels. As you can imagine, this can be disturbing, but it is just an innate behavior that has been built into the breed, and if you don't give it an outlet, it could become a problem. On the other hand, sometimes problems you might anticipate never come to be. So, if you adopt a retired racing Greyhound, you might think that you need to provide a lot of exercise time, yet be surprised to learn that your new pet is actually quite content to be a couch potato. Just know what you are adopting, so you can avoid problems whenever possible.

There are, of course, a lot of different causes of stress in the life of a pet. There also seems to be a genetic component to some stress-related behaviors which seem to have breed predispositions. Certain pets may have noise sensitivity and be fearful during thunderstorms, others may have separation anxiety and dread being away from us when we go out, others may be aggressive when stressed (such as when someone attempts to take away a favorite toy or a food bowl), and others can display compulsive behaviors when stressed (such as pacing, or even plucking out their own fur). Finally, pets can be stressed when we appear upset with them, especially when they don't comprehend why. We might like to believe that they know when they've done wrong, or even suggest that they are acting guilty because they know they have done wrong, but often this is not the case.

Reward and Punishment

This should be an easy topic to cover since behavioral training should involve rewards only and never punishment. Yes, you heard right—there is really never a need for punishment of a furry family member. It only serves to damage the human-animal bond and does little if anything to correct problem behaviors. You may or may not believe the same is true for children, but when it comes to animals, where we can't fully explain ourselves and what is expected, there really is no place for punishment. No, if your pet has an "accident" in the house, it doesn't achieve anything positive to stick your pet's nose in it, and no, it also doesn't achieve any benefit to hit them with a rolled-up newspaper (if you can actually find a real newspaper these days). These are practices from a bygone era, and it makes much more sense to leverage the fact that your pet idolizes you than to confuse them with actions that harm the bond between the two of you.

When you see pets doing extraordinary things, such as guiding people with disabilities, being a social companion, competing in an activity, or sniffing out contraband at the airport, you can be pretty certain that all of that was accomplished with reward-based training. Pets behave at this high level because they love what they do and who they are doing it with, not to avoid punishment. If you only learn one lesson from this chapter, let it be to approach any potential problem from the perspective of using rewards to change the behaviors, and leave punishment in the dustbin of history.

When it comes to behavior modification, realize that it will always be easier to prevent bad behaviors by encouraging appropriate ones rather than to change behaviors once they have become engrained. We can teach pets to walk nicely on a lead with a head halter, we can teach sit-stay commands with rewards and request that behavior when we see a pet is about to misbehave (if you have trained correctly, it isn't possible to do a sit-stay and misbehave at the same time), and we can use a variety of techniques to "desensitize" to stressful stimuli (loud noises, other pets approaching, etc.).

When you are training your pet, it is fine to use food items if your pet is food motivated. However, if you want your pet to be able to do things without the need for an immediate food reward, you might pair requests with something like clicker training. In this case, you condition your pet that when it hears the clicker, that it has performed the desired behavior and will later receive a treat. The clicker is handy because you can immediately "mark" the desired behavior with a click, so your pet understands what behavior is being rewarded, even if there is a slight lag between performing the behavior and receiving the reward.

Animals quickly learn to pair cause and effect regarding their behaviors. So, for example, your pet will quickly learn that it is walk time when you pick up its lead. The reason punishment doesn't work is that this type of operant conditioning can ingrain negative reactions as well. If your pet only goes into the car when it is going to have a bad experience, it will quickly pair the car with the bad experience, so we need to be very careful to only pair desirable behaviors with appropriate cues or to vary the experience so negative conditioning doesn't occur (for example, visit the veterinary hospital with your pet just to get a treat and a pleasant greeting from the staff, not just for vaccinations or procedures).

As we have discussed in other chapters, prevention is the best medicine. If we give pets appropriate options for behaviors, and we reward desirable behaviors, then pets will work to seek those rewards. They won't always understand what got rewarded, but they will in time, and adding punishment to the mix only confuses things further. If you have the opportunity, participate in a training class with your pet. This not only gives you the possibility of learning how to train your pet but also is a great bonding experience. As an extra bonus, there will likely be other pets and people at those training events, and this provides opportunities for appropriate socialization exercises.

By the way, when we are striving for positive reinforcement and we are looking for a primary "reinforcer," it can be food, but it doesn't have to be. Positive reinforcers can be whatever your pet finds desirable and motivating and that can also include your personal attention, access to a favorite toy or doing an activity your pet finds enjoyable. To be effective, rewards need to closely follow the positive behavior so it is clear what is being rewarded, or the behavior needs to be appropriately "marked" (such as with clicker training) so the pet knows it has done what was expected and has earned a reward that it will later receive. Rewards also need to not be given for inappropriate behaviors (jumping up, barking, nipping, etc.), or those will get unintentionally encouraged.

Shaping is a behavior modification technique based on "successive approximation" in which pets can be trained to do relatively complex tasks by progressing in a stepwise fashion. For example, you might initially train a pet to sit and stay, but shaping can be used to encourage a "stay" for a progressively longer period of time. Initially you might start with rewards for just the sit command, and once that behavior is firmly entrenched, you can give the sit command and then give a "stay" command and initially reward for a stay that lasts at least a few seconds. When it appears your pet has learned this, give the commands but don't reward until the stay lasts for ten seconds and then 15 seconds, etc., as you back away. You can then give a "come" command, so your pet will run to you for its reward. In this way, you can use shaping to train almost any complex behavior, and your pet will understand what you are asking and be happy to oblige (as long as it is a sufficiently motivating reward initially).

Toilet Training

When it comes to *almost* perfect pets and training, one of the most important aspects on which to focus is toilet training, also known as housetraining or housebreaking. It may sound simplistic, but when pets have "accidents" in the house, it can greatly impact their longevity ... in very real ways.

When puppies are nursing, their mother cleans up after them, but by about 3 weeks of age they start eliminating away from the nesting area on their own. They initially develop preferences for where they like to eliminate by 5 weeks of age, and this becomes even more specific by 9 weeks of age, when they are attracted to certain locations by the odor of urine and feces. By the time puppies are adopted, usually around 8–10 weeks of age, it is already possible to reinforce their innate desire to keep their den clean by training them to eliminate in an area we have designated. This is accomplished with rewards and shaping, and punishment plays no role in toilet training and will just confuse the puppy and work against the normal bonding that is taking place at this time (see socialization).

Set puppies up for success by making sure they are fed on a schedule, given plenty of opportunities to eliminate in the right area, and then praised profusely when they have performed as requested. Ignore "accidents" at this stage, as pets are still learning what is being asked of them. Similarly, this is the worst time to leave them alone and confined because they are going to need to go, and you will have missed opportunities to allow them to demonstrate the appropriate behavior. Similarly, pets that are kept in cages and learn to eliminate in the cage will take longer to train to go elsewhere because habits have already been allowed to get ingrained.

Housetraining can be simple if you have the time and patience to reinforce appropriate behaviors. Start by designating a desirable spot for your pet to eliminate, give every opportunity for it to do so, and praise lavishly for a job well done. Be patient, because it typically takes 4–6 months for some puppies to become fully housetrained and for some even longer. Once again, puppies have an innate drive to keep their dens clean, so let this work for you rather than against you. Feed puppies on the same schedule each day and also have an established schedule for taking them on toilet breaks. Initially take puppies out each half hour during the day to increase the chance that they will go in the desired location and give you the opportunity to praise them. Expect that they will need to go 15–30 minutes after they eat and also following play, naps, exercise and after they have been released from any confinement (cages, crates, etc.). Until a puppy has been using its designated area and not had any "accidents" in the house for at least four weeks, it needs to be under constant supervision or confined. That being said, confinement does not imply punishment, and if you leave a puppy confined for longer than they can reasonably hold it, the entire housetraining process will be delayed. Don't expect the impossible. During the day, puppies only have a few hours of control, so give them every opportunity to eliminate according to your preferences and not in the home. By 3–4 months, with training, most puppies can make it through the night without having to go out, but they should be given the opportunity as soon as they wake up. By the way, never take good housetraining for granted, and realize that it can be lost without ongoing reinforcement.

The situation in cats is slightly different, although house soiling is still a major cause of relinquishment. Most cats will be trained to use a litter box, in which there is an innate drive to dig first, eliminate and then cover it up. That's the simple part. What sometimes complicates the situation is that cats may have strong preferences for the type of litter, the location of the litter box, and how often it should be cleaned, all of which can result in inappropriate toileting. The situation can be even more complicated if there are multiple cats in the household, and it is uncertain who has stopped using the litter box. One other related situation is that some cats "spray," in which they back up to a surface (usually a vertical surface) and direct a stream of urine, often as a sign of stress or anxiety. So, training is not very difficult at all for cats, but it is still important to pay attention and deal with issues before they become longstanding bad behaviors.

Socialization and Habituation

The socialization period is a critical time in the life of puppies and kittens and sets the stage for how well they will bond with humans and other species. If they don't develop these relationships during this period, they may never be capable of being *almost* perfect pets. The primary "sensitive" period for puppies is from about 2–12 weeks of age, while for kittens it is about 2–7 weeks of age. During this time, they have essentially no "stranger danger," naturally make attachments to all kinds of people and animals, and will then continue to develop social relationships throughout their lives. Of course, pets can regress if socialization is not continued, but early introduction to all types of people (men, women, children, people of different ethnicities, types of clothing, uniforms, etc.) improves the chances that they will be receptive to most others in their social circles. Animals that go on to become very social pets get their start with extensive contact during these early socialization periods. To make sure that pets can relate to their own species as well as humans, they

The breeder had obviously handled this two-month-old Great Dane puppy considerably. The puppy was very comfortable in her arms. This type of early socialization is critical (courtesy Janice Adams).

should remain with their littermates until at least 7 weeks of age but have regular exposure to humans. On the other hand, feral animals that have not had exposure to humans during this sensitive period may never be able to form close relationships with the humans who adopt them.

Everyone is busy these days, but a great way to encourage socialization to a variety of humans and animals is at social gatherings, often referred to as doggy daycare or kitty kindergarten. Puppies and kittens have the opportunity to socialize, and this also gives us the opportunity to see how they behave with other animals. One thing to keep in mind in such social encounters is that our pets should have started their vaccination series to make sure they are protected from infectious diseases, and there should also be a parasite-control plan in effect. If doggy daycare or kitty kindergarten is not an option for you, all is not lost. If you can take your pet to work or any other social setting, even for short periods, you provide opportunities for your pet to be exposed to other people. Even better, if those people can approach your pet, give simple commands that your pet has learned, and then reward them with a tasty treat, pets will quickly learn to accept others into their social network. By the way, if part of the reason you adopted a pet was for a form of protection, you needn't worry that socialization will interfere with this. Pets that will guard do so because they perceive danger to us or because they have been trained to respond to certain commands; we still need all pets to be well socialized.

Habituation is similar to socialization but usually applies to locations and circumstances rather than people and often extends beyond the critical sensitive period. Part of habituation involves toilet training, where we expect pets to become habituated to the location we have provided for them to urinate and defecate. This could be a section in the outdoors, a pad or other specific surface or a litter tray. Habituation also allows for pets to get accustomed to wearing a harness or collar or going for a walk on a leash or not being terrified getting into an elevator or driving in a car or getting a bath or being carried in a handbag. The earlier we get pets used to situations, the more accepting they are and the less stress they experience. Be patient and understand that we may need to break some requests into smaller steps for the pet to master, but it is amazing what can be accomplished with reward-based training.

Almost Perfect Meets Fear Free®

Whether you are raising pets or children (or both), part of parenting involves tasks that offspring might not find enjoyable. Neither children nor pets enjoy brushing their teeth, visits to the doctor, or people poking and prodding at them for reasons they don't understand or appreciate. Still, part of parenting is seeing those tasks through, even though there might be resistance. There is an entire chapter on parenting, but this is just one example and one approach.

Veterinary hospitals, shelters, boarding facilities and groomers tend to be populated by those who love animals, but it should be no surprise that pets might resist the experience. Pet owners may even tell stories about how their pet knows where it's going as soon as they turn a certain corner and when panic starts to set in. We can explain to ourselves that pets just don't understand that it's in their best interest (the same way we rationalize when children don't want to eat their vegetables, go to bed at a reasonable time, or put away their smart devices), but it would still be nice to reduce the fear, stress and anxiety that pets face in those circumstances.

The situation can be particularly difficult in veterinary hospitals, where a pet's first visits may involve examinations and a series of vaccinations. The Fear Free® movement was initiated to look for ways to make visits to veterinary hospitals less stressful and to limit the amount of fear that pets experience. Sometimes it involves spending a little bit more time for pets to become accustomed to the new sights, sounds and smells and to take a more considerate approach to the interactions. With a combination of a gentle approach, customizing care to the individual pet, and using calming sensory options (including appeasing pheromones) or medications, the situation can be made much less stressful for pets. Keep in mind that this might take a few minutes more than a strictly clinical approach, but it can make a world of difference when pets are not afraid to visit the veterinary hospital. It doesn't need to be an ordeal. Of course, the same strategies can be applied anywhere pet care is provided and have become a very popular approach for all concerned.

Environmental Enrichment

In days of yore, when family units were much different, there was often a person at home for most of the day, and so most pets at that time were not alone for long. That changed in an era of latchkey children (and pets), and today it is the rule rather than the exception that many pets spend their days alone in the home. Since pets are very social creatures, this has resulted in loneliness, which could evolve into anxiety and stress. When that happens, pets can act out and do damage, but it can also adversely affect their mental health.

Pets do best when they have a regular routine and when they have things in their environment that can keep them engaged during times of social isolation (like when you are away). This may require some creativity, but there are actually lots of ways of keeping pets occupied when you can't be there.

Some pets are happy enough if there is a television, stereo, sound system or radio on, and there are a variety of video and audio resources for keeping pets occupied. It's even possible to videoconference with them during the day or use devices to track their activities in the home (such as a webcam or "nanny" cam) and to be able to speak to them remotely. For pets that are very food motivated, there are a variety of toys with hidden food compartments which require some work for the pet to achieve a treat and thereby keep them engaged for longer periods of time. Food dispensers can be programmed to release small amounts of food at predetermined or random intervals. There are also a variety of toys, some even with wildlife scents, that can encourage predatory play and keep pets engaged. If safe to do so, an access door can allow pets outdoors, as long as this is a safe option.

Cats often do a better job of entertaining themselves than dogs (or

Torry enjoys her climbing tree (courtesy Sage O'Gahan).

Rifka at three months of age. Young animals need environmental stimulation (courtesy Janice Adams).

children), but things like scratching posts and multilevel perches can give them solace during periods without family attention, especially in multi-cat homes where they may prefer their own space.

One of the best ways of providing environmental enrichment for both dogs and cats is to arrange for someone to come in some time during the day to let them have a toilet break, provide some social time, and make sure they are safe and happy. If available, it might also be possible for pets to participate in social groups (daycare), where they have access to other people and pets. You are limited only by your imagination.

Animal Welfare

If you are reading this book, you very likely consider your pet to be part of the family and are a dutiful pet parent. Nonetheless, it is worth briefly discussing animal welfare issues because they are pervasive in society and not conducive to raising an *almost* perfect pet.

In the animal welfare field, it has been acknowledged that all animals should be entitled to five freedoms:

- freedom from hunger and thirst;
- freedom from discomfort;
- freedom from pain, injury or disease;
- freedom to express normal behaviors; and
- freedom from fear and distress.

If you are raising an *almost* perfect pet, you are likely providing much more than just this basic level of care. Still, other pets may not be as lucky, so it's good to remember this from time to time, be mindful of your pet, and fully appreciate that they are part of your life. Even if they have never experienced a lack of any of the five freedoms themselves, you should feel confident that they appreciate who you are and the role you play in their lives.

Case Example

Yu Yan is a university student who learned that the apartment building in which she was living allowed pets, and because she didn't have much experience with pets and because she was often on campus, she thought a cat would be a good choice. As it so happens, when she was doing laundry in the building, she saw a note on the bulletin board that someone was moving and looking for a new home for their cat, a male tabby named Maestro. Yu Yan was immediately smitten with Maestro and adopted him on the spot. She was glad that it was summer break, so her schedule would allow her plenty of time to bond with Maestro.

After a week of a somewhat stressful adjustment to his new accommodation, Maestro seemed to settle in nicely, and Yu Yan was very happy with her new roommate. However, a few months later, after Yu Yan had returned to classes, she noticed that Maestro was defecating in his litter box, but often there were wet spots on the carpet that she was sure were urine. She did some research online and found that some cats will stop using the litter if it is not in a desirable location or sometimes if they don't like the composition of the litter substrate, so she changed those, but the problem persisted.

Yu Yan was getting frustrated with Maestro but brought him to ABC Veterinary Hospital, where the veterinary team determined it was feline idiopathic cystitis (FIC), which can result in painful urination because of inflammation in the lower urinary tract. Most cases aren't caused by bacteria, so antibiotics were not warranted, but the veterinary team discussed some stressors that might be associated with the sudden presentation and that they would provide a diet that would increase water intake to make the urine more dilute, provide a pheromone diffuser that should have a calming effect, and if Maestro didn't quickly improve, they would dispense some pain medicine. They also discussed some potential environmental changes, including adding some additional litter boxes in different locations to give Maestro more choices, providing more water bowls to encourage fluid intake, changing the litter more frequently, maintaining a regular mealtime, getting a perch and some toys to provide environmental enrichment, and scheduling more time for gentle one-on-one contact.

After a week or so, Yu Yan reported that Maestro was feeling much better, and she also came to the realization that Maestro must have been in some pain with the FIC because he seemed to have much more energy now and be in much better spirits.

Recommended Reading

Defauw, Pieter A.M., Isabel Van de Maele, Luc Duchateau, Ingeborgh E. Polis, Jimmy H. Saunders, and Sylvie Daminet. 2011. "Risk Factors and Clinical Presentation of Cats with Feline Idiopathic Cystitis." *Journal of Feline Medicine and Surgery* 13 (12): 967–975. https://doi.org/10.1016/j.jfms.2011.08.001.

Fear Free Pets. https://www.fearfreepets.com.

Landsberg, Gary, Wayne Hunthausen, and Lowell Ackerman. 2013. *Behavior Problems of the Dog & Cat*. 3rd ed. Edinburgh: Elsevier.

Moody, Carly M., Cate E. Dewey, and Lee Niel. 2020. "Cross-Sectional Survey of Cat Handling Practices in Veterinary Clinics throughout Canada and the United States." *Journal of the American Veterinary Medical Association* 256 (9): 1020–1033. https://doi.org/10.2460/javma.256.9.1020.

Patronek, G.J., L.T. Glickman, and A.M. Beck. 1996a. "Risk Factors for Relinquishment of Cats to an Animal Shelter." *Journal of the American Veterinary Medical Association* 209: 572–581.

_____, _____, and _____. 1996b. "Risk Factors for Relinquishment of Dogs to an Animal Shelter." *Journal of the American Veterinary Medical Association* 209: 572–581.

Salonen, Milla, Sini Sulkama, Salla Mikkola, Jenni Puurunen, Emma Hakanen, Katriina Tiira, César Araujo, and Hannes Lohi. 2020. "Prevalence, Comorbidity, and Breed Differences in Canine Anxiety in 13,700 Finnish Pet Dogs." *Scientific Reports* 10 (1). https://doi.org/10.1038/s41598-020-59837-z.

Seksel, Kersti. 2008. "Preventing Behavior Problems in Puppies and Kittens." *Veterinary Clinics of North America: Small Animal Practice* 38 (5): 971–982. https://doi.org/10.1016/j.cvsm.2008.04.003.

Stanley, A. n.d. "How Pets Can Help You Meditate and Be More Mindful." https://www.shape.com/lifestyle/mind-and-body/how-your-pets-can-help-you-meditate.

Strand, Elizabeth B. 2006. "Enhanced Communication by Developing a Non-Anxious Presence: A Key Attribute for the Successful Veterinarian." *Journal of Veterinary Medical Education* 33 (1): 65–70. https://doi.org/10.3138/jvme.33.1.65.

Williams, Lauretta. 2019. "How Pets Can Sharpen Your Mindfulness Skills." Animal Wellness Magazine. September 18. https://animalwellnessmagazine.com/pets-mindfulness/.

11

Pet Parenting

Now that we've had a chance to cover some basics about health care and behavior, it is time to tackle a potentially more difficult subject—actual parenting. We discussed very early in the book that pet parenting can mean very different things to different individuals, so nothing has changed in this regard. Whether you think of your pet as a furry child or whether it is just a welcome companion in your household, approaches to parenting can very much determine whether you are bound for an *almost* perfect relationship ... or not.

Whether you are parenting a child or a pet, it's never as easy as it looks on television ... or social media. Still, although some pets are easier to parent than others, all benefit from a consistent, considerate, and loving approach. That doesn't mean you need to allow your pets to control your household, but it also doesn't need to include ruling the roost like a dictator so you are feared by your pets.

To be successful in pet parenting, it helps to keep a few things in mind. Like other types of parenting, just about everyone will have an opinion on what you are doing (right or wrong), whether they will tell you directly or whether they prefer to share with others when you are not around. Given that as a fact of life, it's worthwhile to remind yourself often that you will establish expectations for your pet's behavior, and you will actively coach your pets toward those expectations, and it really doesn't matter if others agree. As the pet parent, it is ultimately your responsibility to build the relationship you want with your pet, and you don't have to do so by consensus. It helps if you set these expectations from the start, because otherwise you will mistakenly believe that others know the secrets to parenting, but those details were never shared with you. The truth is that everyone struggles at one point or another with parenting, and it's often impossible to know the exact best response to every novel situation that could happen, but if you proceed in good faith, and you promptly turn to your veterinary team when you encounter issues, you will likely successfully weather most problems and prevent them from becoming recurrent and overly stressful.

It is also worthwhile to remember that most pets, if properly socialized, inherently understand that we control all resources that interest them (food, attention, access to activities, etc.) and are motivated to do what is necessary to "earn" those resources. It is thus critically important to realize that most misbehaviors are associated with us unintentionally

Aspen on a walk (courtesy Nancy Schlussel).

creating the wrong incentives. So, if your pet displays an unruly behavior such as jumping up on you, and you throw a treat to distract it so it gets off you, you have inadvertently reinforced that bad behavior. Before long, the pet will learn to jump up on you and then retreat to await its reward. Unfortunately, we often anthropomorphize the situation and attribute ulterior motives to the pet's behavior, but it's usually much simpler than that—pets often repeat behaviors that they feel are being rewarded, whether we understand why or not. Pets don't really understand our language apart from some basic commands that we teach them, they don't try to analyze us or try to understand what the intention is behind our actions, and they don't comprehend when we yell at them for something that happened hours ago. They just don't have the capacity for that type of thought.

The reason to review all this is that pets are capable of bonding strongly to us, but when parenting them, it is best to realize that we can't have a discussion with them and tell them how we would like them to behave. We need to use their inherent motivators to coach them to behave in acceptable ways, and the more clear-cut the path, the easier it is for pets to accommodate. If you try to reason with your pet, it may make you feel like more of a nurturing parent, but it is unlikely going to change your pet's behavior. If you try to punish your pet whenever it makes a mistake, it may make you feel like more of a strict parent, but it is also unlikely to change your pet's behavior, although it may make them more fearful of you. We can often convince ourselves that pets know they did something wrong because they look guilty when we return home, find things amiss and confront them. However, don't be so sure that guilt is the displayed emotion. Pets have very expressive faces, but many body postures and facial expressions that we attribute to guilt are more often associated with fear. Are you really so certain your pet feels a complex emotion like guilt, which requires reflection on a deed, or could it just be that it is responding to the emotions it detects in you as a response to that deed. Your pet wants to please you, so help it do so by using established techniques to parent effectively. If you need help, there are books, videos, classes and so much more to help. Ask your veterinary team for appropriate resources.

The reason why parenting is so critical to the problem-free paradigm is that the bond between parent and pet is sometimes more fragile than most of us would like to admit. Every year millions of pets are relinquished, not so much because they had some devastating disease that the family couldn't afford to treat, but because the pet displayed some behavior that could not be tolerated. That's right. Whether it is a pet that destroys your possessions, has "accidents" on the carpets,

Dogs that are left alone often do well when they have access to a window into the world. Boredom can lead to undesirable behaviors (courtesy Janice Adams).

is unruly, or is aggressive to others, that pet can lose its "cherished companion" status and be relinquished or abandoned. We like to think that perhaps the pet would be a better match for another family, but in too many cases, misbehavior can earn them a death sentence. That's why with a problem-free philosophy, it is so important to parent effectively.

Parenting Styles

Parenting pets is different than parenting children, in fundamental ways. The classic parenting styles recognized for children are: authoritarian; authoritative; permissive (or indulgent); and uninvolved. We certainly see all of these styles used in pets, but do pets truly behave like children, and are our actions consistent with actual parenting?

Authoritarian (or disciplinarian) parenting uses strict discipline, and punishment is often common. This is most commonly seen with regimented training and limited flexibility. We do see this as a preferred approach with those adherents to pack leadership, "alpha" personalities, and asserting dominance. This is often based on the assumption that our pets (especially dogs) respond in a hierarchal relationship that was once attributed to wild wolves. Proponents may suggest that pets should earn everything they get (akin to working for a living), and this includes feeding, attention and even entertainment resources (e.g., toys). It's the pet version of "tough love." There is no doubt that people have successfully trained dogs with this style, but it is likely based on a flawed premise. Modern research in wolf behavior no longer purports that alpha wolves control through aggression and imposing their will on others. Studies suggest that they care for pack members, in times of scarcity they may allow the young to eat first, and they often survey the pack from the rear rather than always taking a lead position. When offspring mature, they often do not challenge the wolf leader for dominance. They often find a mate and start a family of their own without conflict. Pets can be trained with an authoritarian style, but if the rationale is that such training mimics wild wolf behaviors (which pets have been separated from for thousands of years), then this model does not seem to be very evidence based.

Permissive or indulgent parenting tends to let children do mostly what they want, typically with limited guidance or direction. The parents appear to be warm and nurturing but tend to set few expectations for their children, and there is little or no correction when the children misbehave. This is also a common parenting style with pets, and while some pets inherently have little tendency to get themselves into trouble, it can lead to pets being unruly, destructive, aggressive and developing other undesirable behaviors (such as urinating or defecating in inappropriate locations). Some pet parents might even think that it is cute when their pet is naughty, but this type of parenting is not really conducive to training and coaching appropriate behaviors.

Uninvolved parenting is seen when children have limited guidance from their parents. It can occur either because parents make a conscious effort in that direction, or they are unavailable for other reasons (e.g., work, activities), or they are just not interested in parenting. The same happens in pets, especially when pets are adopted for the wrong reasons (a child promises they will take care of a pet but don't, and the parent doesn't step in as the responsible party) or when pets are relegated to the yard or garage or other station where they have limited owner interaction. Think long and hard before bringing a pet into this type of situation. Sometimes children occur as an unintended consequence, but pets should only be adopted when the family intends to actively parent the pet.

Authoritative parenting, not to be confused with authoritarian parenting discussed above, is nurturing, fully establishes expectations and goals, and communication is appropriate for the level of understanding of the child. This style is believed to be the most beneficial to child development and to pet development as well. Unlike children, pets can't articulate if they have questions about what is expected of them, so shaping of behavior must be done in a logical manner so pets understand commands and have the opportunity to respond to them correctly. This fits in best with the concept of *almost* perfect parenting in which we have realistic expectations, we prevent problems from happening in the first place, and we identify issues as early as possible and correct them expeditiously. If you have successfully parented children, just assume your pet is a furry child that you have adopted and that it does not speak the same language as you. There is no doubt that you would patiently guide them through the learning process and not overreact when they make mistakes. Be that pet parent!

So, when we are speaking of pet parenting, it is obvious that there are a variety of parenting styles and all are not equally recommended. However, what seems clear is that if you chose a pet to have a close family relationship with another living being, think carefully about what your hopes are for that relationship. Most experts agree that any pet training should be based on rewards and not punishment. That doesn't mean that we don't set rules, but punishment can impact the human-animal bond, and we often incorrectly judge that pets know that they did something wrong even though that is often not the case. Like all parents, we are going to make parenting mistakes. Like all parents, we are sometimes going to experience parental guilt. There are wonderful resources available on training and parenting, and it is important to intervene early before inappropriate behaviors become ingrained. It is sometimes extremely difficult in these hectic times, but if possible, practice "slow parenting" in which you take the time to become mindful of your pet and the relationship you share and what would be involved in nurturing and even improving that relationship.

Social Creatures: Dogs

Since we can't expect complete verbal comprehension from our pets, it makes sense to facilitate communication by taking advantage of their own social expectations.

Dogs are social creatures, and while it has been thousands of years since they behaved like wolves, they require regular social interactions with their own species and others, including us. Dogs were not really designed to lead a solitary existence for long spans of time. Even if you believe that dogs, like ancestral wolves, would hunt or scavenge for their food in the wild, today's typical pet dog is no longer that animal. Over successive generations, they have come to depend on us to meet their needs, and just as we, as a species, have evolved to be consumers rather than hunters, neither dogs nor ourselves are typically suited to function in the wild without our comforts. After all, in the early days of COVID-19, panic ensued when toilet paper was in short supply. Dogs have come to expect that food appears in their bowl through our actions as providers, and most of us can sympathize that the pets with which we share our lives are not really suited to fending for themselves in harsh and unforgiving environments. They may lead a pampered existence, like our children, but we really don't want to envision them as wild animals struggling to survive. That's not really why we adopt them and act as their protectors and benefactors.

Not only have dogs evolved long ago away from their ancestral needs to hunt and scrounge for food, but when we expect them to thrive as house pets, we want them to live by an entirely different set of rules than their evolutionary ancestors. Rather than mating, nesting, hunting in packs and forging relationships with only members of their own species, we have isolated them in our home environment and still expect them to cope with challenges they never would have faced in the wild. Dogs still crave exploration and living in an environment that they find complex and challenging, and this was covered in the mindfulness chapter as a need for environmental "enrichment" to keep them engaged and stimulated. After all, we may have rescued them from the wild, but they are still extremely social creatures, and while they are fully prepared to accept us as their family members, like all living creatures they still need to be mentally engaged in their environment, especially during times when we are not there to be with them.

If dogs don't have the opportunity to engage in positive playful and exploratory behaviors, we should not be surprised when they develop so-called displacement behaviors and act out, often due to frustration and anxiety. It cannot be stressed enough that the majority of objectionable behaviors occur when pets don't have acceptable and positive outlets for their energies. In this way, they are very much like our children, but we can't effectively reason with them as to why their needs can't be immediately met.

Similarly, when we attempt to exert dominance over pet dogs in the

Many pets like to carry objects in their mouths, but for animals that tend to chew items they carry, make sure those items can't splinter or break (courtesy Lou Ann Armstrong).

household to try to show our alpha leadership role, we may be able to force a dog to capitulate, but we shouldn't fool ourselves that this is the way that dogs would typically react with one another. Dogs have evolved to avoid physical confrontation and communicate instead through their body posturing, facial expressions, vocalizations and pheromones (chemical factors that trigger predictable social responses). That's why confrontational approaches and punishment have reactions that vary based on the individual animal and the perceived threat level and can have unfortunate consequences. There is also little or no evidence to support our need to be the alpha leader to have well-behaved pets. Pack theory would suggest that as the dominant leader we should always eat first, but since we control when pets get fed, whether they eat before us or after us, is totally at our discretion—we are always in control. Dogs always appreciate being fed, and we can certainly use food rewards for appropriate behaviors, but we already establish the rules for when and how pets get fed (e.g., sit command, then OK to give permission for pet to eat, etc.). Dogs observe us closely, and they learn to assess what works and what doesn't; most are not trying to be in charge of the household. Positive training, consistency and rule structure lead to better obedience, fewer behavioral problems and less aggression in animals, so avoid problems by embracing positive reinforcement and a rewards-based system. Confrontation and punishment may make for entertaining reality television but greatly increase the chance of untoward effects. Instead of trying to achieve dominance, focus on developing a positive relationship with your pet, consistently reward desirable behaviors, and give your pet every opportunity to display those desirable behaviors.

Dogs are very social animals and quickly establish relationships with other dogs, humans, and potentially other species. While they can bark and make other sounds, they communicate with us primarily through facial expressions, body postures, and outright body contact. As mentioned earlier, there might be a temptation to think that when dogs join our family they are just considering us part of their "pack," but that's not really what is happening. The relationship that we create with dogs is much different than what they would experience in a pack. Dogs actually learn to interpret our facial expressions, our words and our actions, and if properly socialized, they tend to be highly committed to pleasing us. Most problems result when they fail to understand what we are attempting to communicate, when there are family inconsistencies in response to certain behaviors, or when punishments lead to conflict, anxiety, or uncertainty as to what is being requested of them. Dogs very much want to do the right thing that will achieve for them the desired reward, whether that is a morsel of food or a loving embrace. It's important to use that motivation to create a pet that is the envy of all, rather than to let the situation devolve into unruly behavior that can quickly become habit. If you are not sure what you might be doing wrong, contact your veterinary team or a behaviorist to get things back on the right path while the relationship can still be redeemed. It is your response, your words and your postures and facial expressions that inform the pet as to what they should expect, so it is critical not to give inappropriate signals.

Social Creatures: Cats

Cats are not small dogs, and their behavioral and social interactions must be considered differently from those of dogs. Information on socialization has been provided in the chapter on mindfulness, and predatory types of play behavior are often noticed in kittens by about 3 months of age. In fact, even kittens that are weaned early can still become competent hunters, so predatory behavior must be considered to be highly ingrained in the species. It is even evident in play that most cats stalk silently and then pounce on their prey. Unlike their larger wild cousins, domestic cats don't really have the stamina to chase their prey for long periods.

While dogs have largely evolved to depend on us entirely for their needs, cats can be self-sufficient if given the opportunity. In fact, there are often three very distinct ways that domestic cats exist. They can be owned and entirely part of our households, they can be semi-owned and have variable access to the outdoors where their needs can be partially met, or they can be "feral" and live in the wild. Also, unlike dogs, once properly socialized cats can potentially move between these situations, living part of their lives in the household and part in the wild. In fact, some may be considered "neighborhood" or "community" cats in which they don't even have one consistent owner but visit several households for occasional food and social interaction. While this itinerant lifestyle may work for some cats and interested cat lovers in the community, there are very real considerations for keeping domesticated cats solely within a home environment. Cats that wander outdoors are more likely to sustain traumatic injuries (fights, bites, fan belt injuries, being hit by car, etc.) but are also more likely to pick up infections and parasites, some of which may be transmitted to unwary family members. Because of this, and for other public health reasons, it is typically considered healthier for all family members when pet cats are maintained entirely indoors other than supervised excursions outdoors, such as on a leash.

There has been a lot of misinformation about the social nature of cats, and at one point they were incorrectly considered asocial (not social) and not in need of relationships. We now know that individual cats are quite variable in their need for social systems, with some cats preferring a solitary existence, while others will live in large colonies or as happy participants in households with or without other pets.

To be happy within a family setting, cats should have outlets for predation and chase, social interactions, scratching, climbing, and comfortable places to perch. While some families may allow their pet cat outdoors to achieve some of its needed environmental enrichment, this can also be achieved, and achieved more safely, through accommodations made to the household (e.g., perches, scratching posts, prey toys, outdoor walks with a halter, etc.).

It is important to remember that cats are natural hunters, and they need suitable surfaces for claw maintenance, which also provides an opportunity for normal territory-marking behavior. Again, this is a normal behavior, so if cats are not given an appropriate alternative, they are likely to scratch furniture and potentially do significant damage. We can prevent these problems from happening if we provide an appropriate outlet for these behaviors as we do for helping ensure other

Barnabas and Bonnie relax (courtesy Katrina O'Gahan).

problem-free options. Most cats can be taught to use a scratching post, and it is worthwhile to have several available in the household in different locations that might be preferred by the cat. There are even pheromones available (mimicking feline interdigital semiochemical) that can attract cats to use the scratching posts provided. Trimming the claws or applying soft caps to them can also lessen the potential for damage to the household. It's worth mentioning here that in the past, surgical options were commonly used to remove the claws entirely so cats couldn't do damage. In most countries, veterinarians no longer will perform this type of declawing surgery, which actually amputates the individual toe bones to which the claws are attached. That type of surgical approach is a rather extreme way of dealing with an issue that could be anticipated and managed without altering the cat's normal conformation.

Cats don't require as much social interaction as dogs, and they may even be selected as pets specifically for this reason, but that doesn't mean they don't enjoy play, cuddling, and spending time with family. Cats prefer hunting games in which they can chase and pounce on simulated prey, but things don't need to be elaborate, and cats can even be satisfied chasing a light on the floor, such as provided by a laser pointer. They can also be happy with playing in cardboard boxes, climbing toys, and other things they can bat around with their paws. Stuffing food or catnip into a toy may also encourage play and chase. Many cats also enjoy an indoor garden box with catnip, grass or catmint on which they can roll around and occasionally nibble.

While we are on the topic of catnip and catmint, they are both plants that are members of the mint family that can induce euphoria and even hallucinogenic reactions in some cats. The active ingredient is nepetalactone, and it exerts an effect in perhaps 50–70 percent of cats. That feature, of responding to catnip, is believed to be an inherited trait, and cats that will respond usually have evidence of this by about 8 weeks of age. For cats that enjoy the effect, it can be used prudently as a reward motivator, but it is important not to overdo things because catnip intoxication has been reported. Similarly, if a cat doesn't have the genetic response to catnip, fight the temptation to increase the dosage just so that they will react the way some other cats do. It doesn't work that way.

It is no surprise to cat lovers that cats differ greatly in personality and temperament and their need for social interaction. To a certain extent, their sociability reflects genetics, the amount and quality of handling and exposure during the socialization period, as well as individual variability. Some cats are independent and satisfied with only occasional contact with humans and other cats, while others maintain social relationships with humans and other pets that can span a lifetime.

It's important to know that cats don't maintain a rigid social hierarchy, and so it can be difficult to predict which ones are going to be most receptive to living with other pets or changes in family dynamics.

This, however, should not be construed as cats not being social, just that they have very definite preferences when it comes to their place within social groups. Once again, most cat lovers are well aware of these social dynamics and may even like that cats may sometimes be aloof. While assertive and confident cats may actively solicit attention and play, others are just as happy to be regarded as shy or timid and seek a more solitary existence—or at least attention on their terms.

Succeeding Together

Having that successful relationship with your pet is more than just coexisting. New pet owners are sometimes surprised by the intensity of the relationship that can develop between different species, and this is a testament not only to genetics but to domestication, evolution, and training. *Almost* perfect pets don't happen by accident. They are most often the product of very deliberate selection and then putting in the time needed to coach a pet to become a valued family member. Fortunately, pets are as amenable to the interactions as we are and are prepared to bond with us as intensely as we bond to them.

There are a lot of things that happen in our world that can be stressful for pets, but it is also worth knowing that there are options for relieving stress even when we are not around. As alluded to throughout the book, pheromones are chemical substances that can affect behavior in others. They include appeasing pheromones, alarm pheromones, food trail pheromones, sex pheromones, and many others that affect behavior or physiology. They are particularly interesting because of their importance in animal behavior and that relatively little is known about their impact in humans. While pheromones are known as chemicals that are excreted or secreted by animals as a means of communication with members of their own species, the term semiochemicals is sometimes used to describe the larger family of chemical mixtures that can have effects within a species or even between species. For example, appeasing pheromones are produced by new mothers shortly after giving birth, and they play a role in the attraction and attachment of newborns to the mother.

Pheromones are particularly interesting because the effect is not due to a smell exactly but rather to a chemical substance that is processed in a special gland in the nose known as the vomeronasal organ. The pheromones bind to specific receptor proteins that then stimulate structures in the brain that either alter the pet's emotional state or lead to the release of hormones that tend to have a specific effect. In real life, cats rub their faces on things in the environment and deposit feline facial pheromone to mark boundaries, and this also provides them with emotional stability, perhaps by helping them determine objects that they have claimed as their own. Synthetic forms of this pheromone are available commercially and can be used to help control stress and anxiety and the unwanted behaviors that might be associated with these emotions (e.g., urine marking, loss of appetite, reduced desire to play, etc.). It can also be used to reduce stress when traveling or changing social dynamics within the home (new love interest, new pet, moving, etc.). Synthetically derived appeasing hormones can provide a relaxing effect for both young and adult animals and can be used to allay apprehension and to have a calming effect. There are actually several different pheromones that affect cat behavior, and several are available commercially to help prevent or address behavior problems.

Of course, dogs have pheromones too, although the effects to date have been more muted than in cats. Dog-appeasing pheromone can be used to help prevent and control anxiety and stress, although it typically must be used in conjunction with behavior modification techniques. The dog pheromone may be helpful in stressful situations, such as dealing with separation anxiety, house soiling, vocalization and even exaggerated and fearful responses to sounds (such as thunderstorms, fireworks, etc.). Pheromones are not a cure-all, but they are worth considering for animals that are prone to stress. This isn't voodoo, and there are very real applications for stress reduction.

By the way, humans are also believed to produce pheromones, but most attention is actually given to a variety of hormones that are responsible for the unique natural scents of individuals (such as androstadienol and androstenol), often found in sweat. We often know to whom we are most attracted based on smell, so we shouldn't be surprised that biology plays a role in humans as well. People do have a vomeronasal organ, like most animals, but it is vestigial and largely nonfunctional. However, there are many different animal species for which pheromones provide important chemical communication.

Case Example

Tiny Whitman is a precocious male Yorkshire Terrier puppy belonging to Stan and Britney Whitman. Stan actually would have preferred a larger dog, and he always had retrievers and shepherds growing up, but Britney had seen Tiny at the mall, had immediately fallen in love with him, and brought him home that day.

One of Stan's jobs was to walk Tiny first thing in the morning while Britney got ready for work. Britney had bought a jewel-studded collar for Tiny and decided to tag along on this first outing as she had cats growing up and never needed to take a pet for a walk. She was looking forward to learning from Stan, who had much more dog experience.

As they walked down the street, Tiny was excited and lunging ahead on the lead, but whenever Stan gave the leash a tug as a "correction," Tiny would make a honking sound, and his tongue appeared to turn purple and hang out of his mouth. Britney was upset with Stan and said that he was hurting Tiny, who was just a little dog. Stan assured her that he had seen enough dog-training shows on television and that it was important to make sure Tiny knew who the pack leader was and that as the "alpha" it was important that Tiny learn to respect the leader. After a few more episodes of Tiny lunging ahead and then getting corrected, Britney broke into tears, swept Tiny up in her arms, and then they walked back to the house in silence. They had Tiny's post-purchase veterinary exam scheduled for the next day so decided that they would bring this up then and let the veterinarian determine who was right.

Dr. Feldman gave Tiny a thorough examination, and everything seemed fine except for a small umbilical hernia that would be repaired at the time of neutering surgery. Britney guardedly brought up the issue of Tiny pulling on the lead and then making a strange honking sound like he was hurt, and Dr. Feldman nodded in appreciation of the situation. Apparently, it is not uncommon for Yorkies to suffer from hypoplastic trachea in which there is a congenital narrowing of the cartilage rings in the windpipe. Since Tiny wasn't demonstrating any other issues typically associated with the condition (such as breathing difficulties at times other than walk time), she thought that if they could address the walk issue and Tiny didn't have any other problems, that they might not need to do further assessment at the moment.

Dr. Feldman heard the rest of the walk story and commented that the concept of "alpha" was interesting but not really supported by current animal behavior studies but that most importantly, Tiny, as a Yorkshire Terrier, was not very closely related to wolves in the wild, so there were other solutions worth considering. She recommended the use of a halter, which would not put any pressure on the neck but still provide a lot of body control. She also introduced the couple to Natalie, a veterinary technician who frequently taught obedience classes at the hospital. Natalie showed them how to use the halter and how to use reward-based motivation to get Tiny to walk nicely on a lead. In fact, Tiny was doing much better after just a few minutes of coaching. Stan and Britney learned that they didn't need to dominate Tiny for Tiny to follow their commands, and both were happy that they had plans going forward and even signed up for an obedience class that was going to be started the next week.

Recommended Reading

Becker, Marty. 2018. *From Fearful to Fear Free*. Deerfield Beach, FL: Health Communications, Inc.

Cozzi, Alessandro, Céline Lafont Lecuelle, Philippe Monneret, Florence Articlaux, Laurent Bougrat, Manuel Mengoli, and Patrick Pageat. 2013. "Induction of Scratching Behaviour in Cats: Efficacy of Synthetic Feline Interdigital Semiochemical." *Journal of Feline Medicine and Surgery* 15 (10): 872–878. https://doi.org/10.1177/1098612x13479114.

Dewar, Gwen. 2018. "Parenting Styles: An Evidence-Based Guide." Parentingscience.com. Parenting Science. February 28. https://www.parentingscience.com/parenting-styles.html.

Elzerman, Ashley L., Theresa L DePorter, Alexandra Beck, and Jean-François Collin. 2019. "Conflict and Affiliative Behavior Frequency Between Cats in Multi-Cat Households: A Survey-Based Study." *Journal of Feline Medicine and Surgery*, October, 1098612X1987798. https://doi.org/10.1177/1098612x19877988.

Herron, Meghan E., Debra Horwitz, Carlo Siracusa, Steve Dale, and American College Of Veterinary Behaviorists. 2020. *Decoding Your Cat: The Ultimate Experts Explain Common Cat Behaviors and Reveal How to Prevent or Change Unwanted Ones*. Boston: Houghton Mifflin Harcourt.

Horwitz, Debra, John Ciribassi, Steve Dale, and American College of Veterinary Behaviorists. 2015. *Decoding Your Dog: Explaining Common Dog Behaviors and How to Prevent or Change Unwanted Ones*. Boston: Mariner Books, Houghton Mifflin Harcourt.

Landsberg, Gary, Wayne Hunthausen, and Lowell Ackerman. 2013. *Behavior of the Dog & Cat*. 3rd ed. Edinburgh: Elsevier.

"Position Statement on the Use of Dominance Theory in Behavior Modification of Animals." n.d. American Veterinary Society of Animal Behavior. https://avsab.org/wp-content/uploads/2019/01/Dominance_Position_Statement-download.pdf.

12

Pet Health Care Affordability

When we are discussing *almost* perfect pets, it is tempting to gloss over the costs of pet ownership and concentrate on the love and companionship we get from our pets. However, this is a mistake. Pets come with very real costs, and if we don't come to terms with them, eventually there could be a reckoning that can grind that *almost* perfect philosophy to a halt.

There is no avoiding the reality that pet care can be expensive and pet owners are responsible for that expense. In addition, there are not many social safety nets to help with these costs. Pets are often considered a luxury item rather than a necessity, so there is little or no government assistance to help pet owners care for their pets. As veterinary care becomes more advanced, more diagnostic and care options are available to improve outcomes and quality of life. Unfortunately, these improved treatments come with costs. There is a risk that more and more people may not be able to afford the level of care available. This is somewhat perilous, because while we want all the medical advances that we can access, the gap between those who can afford such care and those that cannot increases. As that gap expands, we become faced with a potential "affordability crisis" for our pets.

For those who are wealthy, pet care is unlikely to be a major concern because it is a bargain compared to human health care, but for most of the rest of us, money that goes into pet care means that there isn't money available for other things we may want or need. Most people can budget well for the things they know (basic veterinary care, pet food, grooming, etc.), but the situation can quickly unravel when unanticipated expenses creep into the picture (visit to an emergency clinic, pet develops a chronic medical problem, expensive medications needed, etc.). The average consumer today has less than 10 percent of their salary available for all discretionary expenses and often little cash reserves, so

Toys don't need to be elaborate to be engaging (courtesy Lou Ann Armstrong).

when pets experience issues, it can be difficult to quickly access funds to meet the need. To maintain *almost* perfect status in such instances, it is important to plan for the inevitable.

When we start thinking about what it costs to maintain a pet, we often do so with blinders on. Sure, there's food, and yes, we need to think about flea and tick control, and of course there are those periodic visits to the veterinarian. When we start listing things in earnest, there's a good chance that we'll pick up additional items, such as the treats and toys we buy with regularity, the cost of pet sitters and activities, and perhaps even grooming expenses. That's great, but we're still not close to a lifetime total. To get a real sense of anticipated expenses, it is helpful to consider planned expenses by category as a starting point in looking at costs. There are one-time costs, ongoing monthly costs, annual costs, and periodic costs, and that's just a start (see Figure 11.1). Once we have our initial veterinary visits and create an anticipated "maintenance schedule," we'll likely be able to add additional items to screen our pets based on the risk factors that have been determined, and those will need to be performed at specific ages. The costs of care in Figure 11.1 include the costs of routine care. Prevention and early detection are key components of problem-free care and need to be customized for each pet. Prevention is both better for a pet's health and less costly than treatment.

Unfortunately, not all costs can be anticipated. Unforeseen and unanticipated costs are inevitable. We don't want to think about our pets needing a visit to an emergency clinic or developing a chronic medical problem (e.g., allergies, arthritis, kidney disease), but emergencies and medical conditions do happen, and they can be costly. Emergency care, diagnostic testing, ongoing monitoring, chronic medication expenses, and specialist care (yes, veterinary medicine has most of the same types of specialists as human medicine) all have very real costs. When we calculate all these expenses over the likely lifespan of our pets, the final number can be sobering. It can also be downright frightening if you fail to plan accordingly.

One of the reasons that it is so important to be proactive regarding the financial aspects of pet care is that when something happens (and the likelihood is that something will happen over the course of your pet's life), your response will need to be urgent. Rarely is there time to start saving for a needed procedure or emergency or referral. As we mentioned in the chapter on veterinary care, pets admitted to a veterinary hospital will require a substantial upfront payment based on likely expenses and that will be due at the time of admission. To complicate matters further, when your pet is in need, you are likely to be emotional and functioning in crisis mode, and your decision-making abilities may be compromised. So, to the best of your ability—plan ahead. When situations catch you by surprise, you are rarely at your best. When you have to make choices between the care of your pet and meeting your other financial obligations, there are likely to be no easy answers.

One important aspect of the *almost* perfect pet philosophy is to try to anticipate your expenses as much as possible in advance so you can plan for them. Nobody likes surprises when it comes to expenses, so budgeting based on what you know and can guesstimate can increase your preparedness when it comes to pet care costs.

No matter how well you construct a budget, you are likely going to find that you have underestimated your costs, and the wild card will typically be health care costs. As you follow the advice in this book

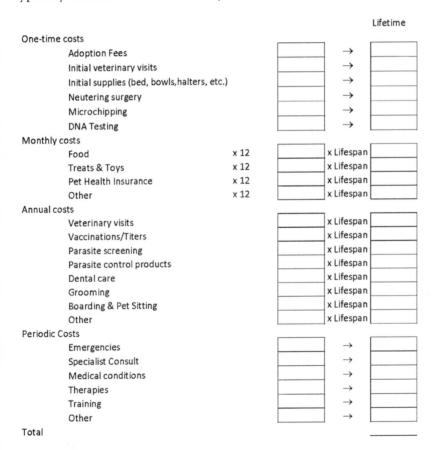

Figure 11.1. Rough template for determining lifelong costs for pet ownership. For monthly and annual costs, you will need to multiply costs by the approximate typical lifespan for your type of pet.

regarding your *almost* perfect pet, you will remember that the cornerstone of the health care strategy is to prevent problems whenever you can, embrace early-detection approaches to get ahead of any problems, and then treat appropriately and with facilitated compliance and adherence. While that may front-load some expenses in terms of surveillance, it is the best way of optimizing care over a pet's healthspan. If you have completed the budget exercise—congratulations!—you now have a much better idea of lifelong costs. If you didn't complete the exercise, take a guess at what you think those lifelong costs might be, and the actual number is likely to be five to ten times higher!

Pet Health Insurance

Pet health insurance is not available in every country, but in the countries where it is an option, it is often the best way of planning for unanticipated expenses. There are a lot of misconceptions about pet health insurance, so let's explore why this is often a good solution for *almost* perfect pets.

Pet health insurance is a budgeting tool rather than a money-saving plan. It is based upon the concept of paying a set monthly sum to purchase protection that helps make future costs more predictable and affordable in emergencies and chronic care situations. Pet health insurance critics sometimes calculate the lifelong cost of care for an animal and conclude that pet owners could do as well by not buying insurance and instead putting the money that would have been spent on premiums over a lifetime into a savings account to use exclusively for pet care. This is fine in principle, but the point is that almost nobody keeps a dedicated savings account for their pet and makes regular deposits month after month and year after year. In addition, it would take years to save enough money to cover potential veterinary expenses, especially given that it is not possible to predict when those funds will be needed. Imagine starting a savings account on the day you adopt a pet and realizing two months later, when faced with an emergency, that you have saved nowhere near enough for the expenses you are about to face. Sooner or later, most pets are going to develop medical problems that require ongoing medical care and monitoring (e.g., arthritis), need a referral to a specialist, or have a mishap that requires a visit to an emergency clinic. However, as far as planning goes, it is not possible to know when the need will arise, so you should be prepared from the very start. For most people, having a pet health insurance policy is the best way to deal with those likelihoods. Pet health insurance plays the role of taking the cost of pet health care out of available discretionary funds and turns it into a budgeted, affordable expense. Without such insurance, it can be very expensive to provide the type of care that most pet owners would prefer and to have the money available exactly when it is needed.

It might seem counterintuitive, but people don't buy insurance to save money—they purchase insurance for the peace of mind that comes with knowing that if the unexpected happens, they will have the

Leira (courtesy Antoinette Falzone).

resources available to do what needs to be done. The same is true for pet health insurance. Its main role is to "flatten the curve" of pet care expenditures so that they can be treated as anticipated costs and not unanticipated costs. Rather than a sudden spike in health care costs when they can't really be predicted, insurance allows us to spread those costs on a monthly basis and not have to deal with financial surprises.

If you are distrustful of health insurance in general, you may be pleased to learn that pet health insurance is not actually health insurance—it is property & casualty insurance for your pet. Unlike many human health care plans, it typically does not have in-network and out-of-network providers. For the most part, it doesn't even involve dealing with insurance agents, and most pet health insurance policies can be directly purchased online. Once your pet is insured and the policy in effect, you can visit the veterinarian or the specialty or emergency clinic of your choice; you pay the veterinary hospital for the services they provide, and then you submit the claim to the insurer for reimbursement (less any deductibles or co-pays). In some cases, the claims can be initiated by the veterinary hospitals themselves on your behalf.

All insurance policies define what is covered in the policy and also what is excluded from coverage. The most common exclusion is for preexisting conditions, problems that have been identified in the pet prior to the insurance policy taking effect. For example, if a pet has arthritis prior to being covered by insurance, it should be anticipated that the ongoing care of arthritis will be excluded from policy coverage. This is one of the reasons why it is so important that pets have insurance coverage early in life, when nothing is considered preexisting and the pet appears completely healthy. Pet health insurance can be a good option for pets of any age, but it has the most utility when it can be started when there are no preexisting conditions, and everything is covered.

Some pet health insurance policies extend the concept of exclusion to conditions known or believed to have a heritable component. So, if a certain breed is known to be "predisposed" to certain ailments, coverage of those conditions may be excluded in some policies. The best way to safeguard against this is to enroll in policies that clearly state that genetic or inherited problems are covered by the policy (if they are not preexisting). It should be expected that such policies are likely to be slightly more expensive, but they are often well worth it, since it can be disappointing to have insurance only to learn that conditions that pose considerable risk for your particular pet might not be covered. Similarly, some policies can appear cheaper if they do not offer chronic care coverage. So, for example, if a pet develops diabetes mellitus during the policy term, it will be covered, but when the term renews, the diabetes could now be considered "preexisting" and excluded from further coverage. Everyone wants to save money on insurance, but such short-term savings are rarely worth it. Do your research, ask questions, and select policies that will provide ongoing care for chronic conditions as well as coverage for hereditary conditions (see Figure 11.2).

If you have pet health insurance, you may wonder how much you will get reimbursed and that is typically a function of the type of policy you purchased. Deductibles refer to amounts that are "deducted" from the insurance reimbursement. Some policies have deductibles that apply per incident, while others might have an annual deductible so that once that amount is reached, further deductibles will not apply for the remainder of the term. Deductibles are meant to keep premiums affordable by ensuring that pet owners have some stake in the process. Co-pays reflect the relative proportion of the covered amount to be paid for by the insurance company and the pet owner. For example, while there are a variety of possible co-pays, depending on what you might like the premium to be, a typical co-pay may be that the insurance company will reimburse 90 percent of the covered amount after the deductible, while the pet owner will be responsible for 10 percent. If you are prepared for higher co-pays, you will likely see slightly lower premiums, but you will be paying for a higher percentage of your pet's care.

We've mentioned this several times throughout the book, but if you are considering buying pet health insurance for your pet, please do so as early as possible (typically when pets are about 8 weeks of age) before any conditions occur that might be considered preexisting. Waiting until an incident has already occurred can be costly.

Many people first learn about pet health insurance during initial puppy and kitten visits. There may be insurance brochures provided in puppy and kitten kits, and members of the veterinary team may mention them specifically, but this tends to be a very busy (and often expensive) time for new pet owners, and their focus may not be on insurance, which many people find to be confusing ... and boring. Also, since veterinary hospitals don't sell insurance (true insurance can only be sold by insurance professionals), this may be a relatively passive information exchange. Ask the veterinary team for specific recommendations if at all possible, or be prepared to do your own research with comparison tools such as those seen in Figure 11.2. It can seem daunting to compare policies that will likely seem confusing, and this can result in "analysis paralysis," but persevere and hopefully put a policy in effect by the time your pet is 8 weeks of age and before anything happens that could be perceived as a preexisting problem that will then forever be excluded from coverage. By the way, while it is true that actual insurance can only be

Coverage	Sample	Plan A	Plan B	Plan C
Accidents & illness	✔			
Emergency & specialty visits	✔			
Genetic and "predisposed" conditions	✔			
Ongoing care for chronic conditions	✔			
Clinical visits & diagnostic tests (not including wellness care)	✔			
Pre-clinical screening	✔			
Telehealth (Virtual Care)	✔			
Prescription medications	✔			
Surgeries & hospitalization	✔			
Rehabilitative, Acupuncture, & Chiropractic Care				
Vaccinations, parasite control, and routine wellness exams	**Optional add-on**			
Annual Limit	**Unlimited**			
Exclusions	None			
Deductible	Annual			
Co-pay	10%			
Price				

Figure 11.2. Example of a chart for comparing different insurance policies

sold by insurance professionals, at present the vast majority of all pet health insurance policies are sold direct to the public on the Internet. Even if you contact the insurance professional with which you already have insurance policies, they may or may not have access to pet health insurance products for you and may or may not be familiar with how these products work.

Finally, it is important to distinguish between insurance plans and discount plans. Discount plans may sound like insurance, but they are not. They are buying groups that sell discounted services and then rely on a network of veterinarians to provide those discounts in exchange for being promoted within the network. They may save you some money at an individual veterinary hospital for specified services, but they often can't be used at other specialists and emergency clinics; they tend to have significant limitations and do not provide the long-term safeguards of insurance. It's just important that you have a realistic understanding of what you are purchasing.

Payment and Wellness Plans

We discussed that pet health insurance can be a great way to deal with unanticipated expenses, but what about all those anticipated expenses, like veterinary visits, vaccinations, and routine testing? Here, you have several options. First, you can plan and save for these anticipated and generally predictable costs. After all, we know when these expenses will be due, so we should be able to plan for them. Alternately, with some insurance companies, it is possible to get pet health insurance policies or add-ons that will cover this type of routine wellness

A sleeping Barnabas (courtesy Katrina O'Gahan).

care. Veterinary hospitals may provide another great option, often offering comprehensive packages that include this type of care, spreading annual costs over periodic (often monthly) payments.

Such payment plans, which might also be referred to as wellness plans or concierge plans, include any services to which you and your veterinary hospital agree. They are entirely customizable. Typically, payment plans cover services over a 12-month period, but that, too, is customizable.

The most common payment plans are for "wellness" visits and might include the number of well-pet visits during the plan period (from one to unlimited), vaccinations, parasite testing, certain diagnostics (e.g., heartworm testing, DNA screening, vaccine titers, etc.), identification (e.g., microchipping), and other services. Virtual care (telehealth) visits may also be included. Payment plans needn't be limited to wellness visits, however. They can encompass treatment plans (e.g., planned visits, diagnostics and medications for a specific problem over a specific time period).

The important distinction between these plans and insurance is that payment plans are limited to a specified "bundle" of services contracted, and they also do not include visits to other veterinary hospitals, including emergency facilities and specialists. So, a payment plan may work fine to cover some of your known veterinary expenses, but they are not designed to assume any risk for any other medical problems a pet might develop. It's important to understand this, because if you purchase a payment plan that includes wellness visits and vaccines, you should not expect that if your pet develops a medical problem that this will also be covered.

Payment plans may come in tiers (such as good-better-best, bronze-silver-gold, etc.) that allow you to select a level of care you prefer at a monthly cost you can afford, but each plan still provides coverage for only a defined basket of services specific to that tier. One important aspect in this regard is that if you pay for services—use them. It does not do any good if you purchase an array of services but then neglect to benefit from them.

Depending on the plan and how it is organized and administered, there may be a fee to enact the plan, either as a fixed amount or as a percentage of the plan total. Payment is typically collected on a recurring basis by credit card or bank transfer, and some veterinary hospitals may use a financial services company as an intermediary to make sure everything runs smoothly.

Other Options

In addition to paying for veterinary services as needed, or using pet health insurance or payment plans, there are circumstances in which pet owners may need other options to pay for services. Most veterinary hospitals are small businesses and unable to extend credit, but there are a variety of companies that are prepared to provide what is known as third-party financing for those who are credit worthy. They typically offer private-label credit cards that can only be used at veterinary clinics. You might be aware of these because they are also used for financing different human health care needs (such as dentistry, chiropractic and vision care).

Veterinary-specific credit cards can be used at different locations but only for veterinary expenses and only at providers that are part of the company's network. These credit cards typically provide a revolving line of credit that can be used to pay for veterinary services within the company's network of enrolled providers. Most provide no-interest loans if the debt is paid in full within the established payback period and fixed monthly payments at established interest rates for longer periods.

In most instances, credit approval is quick for those with a good credit rating and can be accomplished online, by app, or by telephone in real time. Once the application has been approved, the cardholder can use the card for purchases at veterinary clinics up to the approved limit.

Rifka, at five months of age, still appreciates many of the same toys she played with as a younger pup (courtesy Janice Adams).

The approval rate for such cards may be higher than for typical credit cards, but creditworthiness is the major determinant.

Other options for third-party financing include loans and payment plans. There is often considerable flux within the industry, with companies entering and exiting the marketplace and names changing with corporate mergers and acquisitions. Do your homework to make sure you understand the terms of your agreement so there are no surprises.

Our discussion would not be complete without at least a brief mention of crowdfunding platforms where you can appeal to others for funding. Expect this marketplace to continue evolving, and it is necessary to verify the integrity of such lending platforms. There are also a variety of charitable organizations that either provide services for those in need or otherwise have assistance funds available, but these organizations are often stretched to capacity to meet the needs of their stakeholders. Similarly, there are some not-for-profit veterinary hospitals available, often in large urban areas, and some may limit their services to truly indigent clients. There is little doubt that many pet owners would like to avail themselves of discounted veterinary services, but such services are in short supply and may require "means testing" to verify that services provided are going to those who are the most needy.

Incremental Care

Despite all the options available for financing veterinary care, sometimes pet owners just find themselves in a position where they do not have the money to provide the level of care that they would otherwise prefer. It happens, and it is heartbreaking because there is an animal involved that needs care and often a pet owner who feels guilty for not being able to meet their parental obligations. This is also difficult on veterinary teams who, as members of a caring profession, would want to do everything in their power to help but realize that it can't always happen. In some cases, pets are even put to sleep in what is sometimes known as "economic euthanasia," when pet owners cannot see a path forward in dealing with the financial consequences of a medical situation.

Veterinary teams often deal with these situations and come up with options for all types of budgets in what is sometimes referred to as a "spectrum of care." So, if a pet owner can only afford a certain amount of incremental care for their pet, the team will try to devise the best plan they can that still conforms to an acceptable standard of care and meets ethical considerations. It might not achieve a "gold standard" of care but acknowledges it is the best option given needed compromise. Unfortunately, it is also recognized that sometimes there are no low-cost options available. Sometimes we just need to make the best decisions we can with what we have available to us.

While you cannot always prevent sad scenarios in which finances affect care decisions, being proactive and planning can greatly reduce the likelihood of these situations. Prevention and early detection are critical in this regard. Unfortunately, in both human and animal health care, some individuals are reluctant to pay for preventive care and early detection in the mistaken belief that such decisions will save them money. Instead, it makes it more likely that conditions will be more advanced at the point of diagnosis, requiring more costly and heroic treatments and likely poorer health outcomes. Being proactive and planning ahead is always the best option. As we have discussed throughout the book, if we focus on health management rather than disease management, we are likely to have better outcomes. It is true, though, that there are costs associated with the investment in keeping pets healthy.

Till Death Do Us Part

It might be a bit of a morbid topic in a book about *almost* perfect pets, but if we do plan to care for our pets for their entire lives, we have to come to terms with the fact that they might outlive us or our ability to care for them. This is not only the case for long-lived animals or older pet owners. Anyone can find themselves in a situation (accident, infirmity, debilitating illness, natural disaster, terrorist event, etc.) when they are unable to properly care for their pets and need assistance in this regard, either while still alive or following death. Without planning, our pets may not receive the continued care we would have wanted, and these pets may end up relinquished to a shelter or even euthanized.

Even if there are individuals willing to care for our pets when we are no longer able, if there is not a will or trust that mentions the pet and our intentions for its care, then there may be legal quandaries over who is allowed to take the animal and how to deal with pet-related expenses. Wills and trusts are methods for individuals to make their wishes known regarding their pets. However, pets cannot directly be left property, including money, following their owner's death, so a human intermediary is required.

A will can transfer assets following a death, but it cannot dictate ongoing supervision. A trust, on the other hand, can outline the continued care of pets, name new caregivers, provide funding for pet care, and empower the trustee, who has a legal duty of carrying out the wishes of the person who created the trust. Accordingly, most attorneys recommend trusts for pets rather than just including a pet in a will. Low-cost alternatives to wills and trusts can be prepared documents or actual pet protection agreements, although they might not be fully enforceable.

Pet owners can include their pets as provisions in their wills, but wills can take weeks or months to be executed, might have to go through probate, and can be contested by others. When pets are transferred in a will, they are conveyed as any other type of property, and the person who created the will can specify what they hope for in terms of pet care and even provide support in the form of monetary assets for this purpose, but the beneficiary is under no obligation to act as the document recommends. Also, a will only goes into effect when we die, which may not be helpful if we remain alive but unable to provide adequate care and would just benefit from some assistance in caring for our pets.

Trusts provide for the care of a pet in the event of either disability or death. The pet owner does not even need to be incapacitated for the trust to take effect, as long as they are deemed unable to manage their pet's care. Since the laws about trusts differ so much between jurisdictions, you should have a trust drafted by an attorney with experience in this area of law and for a given location. Trust funds are not subject to probate, the terms of the trust are not part of the public record, and there are no funding delays once the trust has been triggered by a specified situation.

The instructions in a pet trust can be very specific, so you can feel confident that the trust is likely enforceable by law and that your wishes regarding your pets will be respected. Such instructions might include the frequency of veterinary visits, favorite foods to be fed, grooming requirements, and even the mode of burial or cremation after the pet's death. The pet's anticipated standard of living should be well documented within the trust.

Don't be secretive with friends and family members about your intentions for your pets. Discuss such arrangements with anticipated caregivers to ensure that such individuals are willing and prepared for the task proposed. Without this agreement, it will likely be left up to the trustee (the person who has access to the funds from the trust) to find an appropriate individual or organization to provide such services. Because both trustees and caregivers are susceptible to the same fates as the rest of us, thought should be given also to successor trustees and caregivers who would be next in line should first choices no longer be able to provide the services requested. Secondary beneficiaries are also named in the event that assets remain in the trust after the beneficiary pets have died.

Nobody wants to think about their own mortality, but if you do not have a plan, consider what will likely happen to your pets in the case of your death or disability. Not having any plan can create a hardship not only for any pets involved but also for those that are ultimately going to be left with making decisions related to those pets.

Whenever money is involved, fraud can also exist, so care should be taken to ensure that the pet can be accurately identified. Suitable permanent forms of identification include microchipping and archived DNA samples from which identification can be confirmed.

There are significant differences between jurisdictions in pet trust laws, including how long they can remain in effect, how much can be left for a pet beneficiary, and how enforceable a pet trust might be, so trusts should only be created after consultation with an experienced estate attorney with expertise in the likely place of residence of the pet and caregiver.

Case Example

Strudel, a four-year-old Miniature Schnauzer, had been continuously insured since puppyhood without any insurance claims. In fact, Strudel's owner had considered discontinuing the insurance because it hadn't been used, but she continued it on the advice of her veterinarian. A few months later, Strudel was admitted to ABC Veterinary Hospital with acute abdominal pain that was later confirmed to be pancreatitis (inflammation of the pancreas, a very serious condition). Strudel was hospitalized for three days, maintained on intravenous therapy and then finally released. The hospital bill was considerable, more than the total insurance premiums paid to date. Strudel's owner, Mrs. Steinberg, put the charge on her credit card and promptly submitted the bill to her pet health insurance company. Within a few weeks, she received her reimbursement, in which the majority of the bill was covered after the deductible and co-pay. Mrs. Steinberg was relieved that the insurance allowed her to manage the emergency costs in what otherwise might have been an expense she would not have been able to afford.

Recommended Reading

Ackerman, L. 2020a. Pets Trusts & Wills in *Five-Minute Veterinary Practice Management Consult*. 3rd ed.

_____. 2020b. Third-Party Financing in *Five-Minute Veterinary Practice Management Consult*. 3rd ed. Wiley.

_____. 2019. "Why Pet Health Insurance Is Important for the Profession." *EC Veterinary Science* ECO.02: 06–07.

American Bar Association. 2013. *The American Bar Association Guide to Wills & Estates: Everything You Need to Know About Wills, Estates, Trusts, and Taxes.* 4th ed. New York, NY: Random House Reference.

"AVMA Guidelines on Pet Health Insurance for Pet Owners." n.d. American Veterinary Medical Association (AVMA). https://naphia.org/find-pet-insurance/avma-guidelines-on-pet-health-insurance-for-pet-owners/.

Brockman, Beverly K., Valerie A. Taylor, and Christopher M. Brockman. 2008. "The Price of Unconditional Love: Consumer Decision Making for High-Dollar Veterinary Care." *Journal of Business Research* 61 (5): 397–405. https://doi.org/10.1016/j.jbusres.2006.09.033.

Carlson, Deven, Simon Haeder, Hank Jenkins-Smith, Joseph Ripberger, Carol Silva, and David Weimer. 2019. "Monetizing Bowser: A Contingent Valuation of the Statistical Value of Dog Life." *Journal of Benefit-Cost Analysis* 11 (1): 131–49. https://doi.org/10.1017/bca.2019.33.

Coe, Jason B., Cindy L. Adams, and Brenda N. Bonnett. 2007. "A Focus Group Study of Veterinarians' and Pet Owners' Perceptions of the Monetary Aspects of Veterinary Care." *Journal of the American Veterinary Medical Association* 231 (10): 1510–1518. https://doi.org/10.2460/javma.231.10.1510.

_____. 2009. "Prevalence and Nature of Cost Discussions During Clinical Appointments in Companion Animal Practice." *Journal of the American Veterinary Medical Association* 234 (11): 1418–1424. https://doi.org/10.2460/javma.234.11.1418.

Congalton, David, and Charlotte Alexander. 2002. *When Your Pet Outlives You: Protecting Animal Companions after You Die.* Troutdale, OR: Newsage Press.

Dekker, Joanne. 2016. *Planning for Pets: Trusts, Leash Laws and More.* Briarcliff Manor, NY: Parker Press.

Guzman, Z. n.d. "Owning a Pet Can Cost You $42,000, or 7 Times as Much as You Expect." *Consumer News and Business Channel (CNBC).* https://www.cnbc.com/2017/04/27/how-much-does-it-cost-to-own-a-dog-7-times-more-than-you-expect.html.

Hirschfeld, Rachel. 2007. "Ensure Your Pet's Future: Estate Planning for Owners and Their Animal Companions." https://www.animallaw.info/sites/default/files/arus9marqeldersadvisor155.pdf.

_____. 2010. *Petriarch: The Complete Guide to Financial and Legal Planning for a Pet's Continued Care.* New York: American Institute of Certified Public Accountants.

Kass, Robert E., and Elizabeth A. Carrie. 2011. *Who Will Care When You're Not There?: Estate Planning for Pet Owners.* DetroitI: Carob Tree Press.

Kinnison, Tierney. 2016. "When Veterinary Teams Are Faced with Clients Who Can't Afford to Pay." *Veterinary Record* 179 (23): 594–595. https://doi.org/10.1136/vr.i6436.

Kipperman, Barry S., Philip H. Kass, and Mark Rishniw. 2017. "Factors That Influence SmallAnimal Veterinarians' Opinions and Actions Regarding Cost of Care and Effects of Economic Limitations on Patient Care and Outcome and Professional Career Satisfaction and Burnout." *Journal of the American Veterinary Medical Association* 250 (7): 785–794. https://doi.org/10.2460/javma.250.7.785.

Kondrup, S.V., K. P. Anhøj, C. Rødsgaard-Rosenbeck, T. B. Lund, M. H. Nissen, and P. Sandøe. 2016. "Veterinarian's Dilemma: A Study of How Danish Small Animal Practitioners Handle Financially Limited Clients." *Veterinary Record* 179 (23): 596–96. https://doi.org/10.1136/vr.103725.

Lue, Todd W., Debbie P. Pantenburg, and Phillip M. Crawford. 2008. "Impact of the Owner-Pet and Client-Veterinarian Bond on the Care That Pets Receive." *Journal of the American Veterinary Medical Association* 232 (4): 531–540. https://doi.org/10.2460/javma.232.4.531.

"Monthly Payment Preventive Healthcare Plans." n.d. Partners for Healthy Pets. https://www.partnersforhealthypets.org/preventive_pet_healthcare.aspx.

"Pet Insurance Buyer's Guide." n.d. https://www.naphia.org/find-pet-insurance/insurance-buying-guide/.

"Pet Trust Primer." n.d. American Society for the Prevention of Cruelty to Animals. https://www.aspca.org/pet-care/pet-planning/pet-trust-primer..

"State of the Industry Report." 2019. North American Pet Health Insurance Association (NAPHIA). https://www.naphia.org.

Stull, Jason W., Jessica A. Shelby, Brenda N. Bonnett, Gary Block, Steven C. Budsberg, Rachel S. Dean, Michael R. Dicks, et al. 2018. "Barriers and next Steps to Providing a Spectrum of Effective Health Care to Companion Animals." *Journal of the American Veterinary Medical Association* 253 (11): 1386–1389. https://doi.org/10.2460/javma.253.11.1386.

Index